Making Sense
of Shakespeare

Making Sense of Shakespeare

Charles H. Frey

Madison • Teaneck
Fairleigh Dickinson University Press
London: Associated University Presses

Associated University Presses
440 Forsgate Drive
Cranbury, NJ 08512

Associated University Presses
16 Barter Street
London WC1A 2AH, England

Associated University Presses
P.O. Box 338, Port Credit
Mississauga, Ontario
Canada L5G 4L8

The paper used in this publication meets the requirements of the american National Standard for Permanence of Paper for Printed Library Materials Z39.48-1984.

Library of Congress Cataloging-in-Publication Data

Frey, Charles H.
    Making sense of Shakespeare / Charles H. Frey.
        p.   cm.
    Includes bibliographical references (p.   ) and index.
    ISBN 0-8386-3831-7 (alk. paper)
    1. Shakespeare, William, 1564–1616—Criticism and interpretation.
2. Shakespeare, William, 1564–1616—Study and teaching.   3. Reader-response criticism.   I. Title.
PR2976.F664   1999
822.3′—dc21   99-30591
                                                                         CIP

PRINTED IN THE UNITED STATES OF AMERICA

For C. M. H.

She speaks, and 'tis such sense
That my sense breeds with it.

(Measure for Measure, 2.2.147–48)

Methinks in thee some blessed spirit doth speak
His powerful sound within an organ weak;
And what impossibility would slay
In common sense, sense saves another way.

(All's Well That Ends Well, 2.1.177–80)

Contents

Preface

THROUGH THIS BOOK, I ADDRESS "YOU" AS READER OF SHAKESPEARE and other imaginative writers. As you read such writers, I urge you to honor the engagement of your senses in your sense-making.

To make sense of a text (or a day), you and I organize disparate parts—sounds, images, textures, tones, and feelings—into coherent wholes—sensations, perceptions, words, concepts, moods. In the course of such organizing, we share a tendency, I believe, to select from sensory experience so as to construct models of understanding. These models lack the vivid concreteness and particularity that arise when appearances are attended to carefully. We may attend selectively, of course, to concrete as well as abstract data, still, in much of life, the tendency to abstract concepts from concrete experience enhances progress through the day. Simply to heed its signal, I needn't notice that the stoplight is dirty, dented, or swaying in the wind. In other parts of life, however, undue abstraction may hinder our purposes.

In the study of imaginative literature (and indeed all art), a tendency to construct selective interpretations may interfere with appreciation. "Shall I compare thee to a summer's day?" (*Sonnet* 18.1) can signal more to a reader than the abstract message: "you are lovely." Considering how a cherished person might compare to a summer's day—reaching into memories of summer days and pondering attributes that might link a lover or a friend to light, fragrance, warmth, happy sounds, relaxed postures, or movements through the tender air—may initiate an unaccustomed journey into complex, nonvisual, sometimes disturbing, sensory registers. Visual imagination, in particular, may resist yielding to or adding on nonvisual empathies, preferring to "see" the "darling buds of May" shake at some distance rather than to focus on sensations of bodily movement, the kinesthetic feel, of shaking in "rough winds." Trained as we are, moreover, to read for "content," as for the abstract message of words, we may find

9

the invitation of imaginative writing to move away from the abstract toward the concrete, away from the general to the particular, away from structure toward texture, away from "reality" toward "appearance," away from interpretation toward experience, a challenging invitation to accept. Much of the challenge lies in facing indeterminacies of time, change, loss, and, death as well as heretofore-unknown pleasure and beauty.

In classrooms and in critical writings, Shakespeare (with other imaginative writers) has suffered, I argue, from our collective tendency to form abstract thoughts and judgments before our senses have had a chance to work and play. Still, "the poet is engaged in saving imagination from abstractness" or at least in blending the abstract and concrete.[1] This book seeks to help correct the balance of abstract and concrete (in experience of Shakespeare) by arguing for and exemplifying "sense-reading" that engages our senses more fully than does other reading.

I assume some familiarity with Shakespeare, but I think that students and general readers working freshly with Shakespeare will grasp my argument and methods. To enhance that grasp, I propose first to give you some prefatory background for the theories and practices explored in this book. My text is designed to address an audience of students, teachers, critics, and general readers. I believe in Shakespeare for everyone and in a teaching that brings teachers, critics, students, and general readers together on at least some common ground. I would like to write, therefore, without condescension or arcaneness, so that readers of varied experience and persuasion may still engage what they share of Shakespeare. In some respects, we stand together before a Shakespeare that is ever strange, ever new.

Ever since Plato charged that poetry feeds the passions and Aristotle responded that poetry purges or purifies them, Western minds have pondered how emotion meets meaning in literature.

Aristotelian "defenses" of emotion in poetry often follow Sir Philip Sidney's *Apology for Poetry* (1595) in actually subordinating artistic emotion to moral wisdom. Sidney says poets give their readers "heart-ravishing knowledge," a "delightful teaching."[2] He believes poetry provides knowledge about emotion; we receive "a more familiar insight into anger than finding in the schoolmen his genus and difference" (165) as poetry helps us to "see through" (166) virtues, vices, and passions.

So to subordinate feeling to insight in poetry has remained a common theme of critics and teachers. In verbal arts, they often tend to search, as suggested, for abstract ideas as opposed to concrete sensations and somatically realized feelings. Even in visual and musical arts, where affect most obviously evades transcription into words, we find a historically overrationalized, hence limited, understanding of relations between emotion and meaning. Thus, in his important study, *Emotion and Meaning in Music*, Leonard B. Meyer approvingly depicts an aesthetic empathy that carries no emotion with it: "even an empathetic response to the materials delineating mood or sentiment does not require a resultant affective experience. We may sympathize with the mood of another individual without having an emotional experience ourselves."[3] And aestheticians such as Suzanne Langer, building on nineteenth-century aesthetics of Schlegel, Kant, and Schopenhauer, go to great lengths to distinguish a mentalized aesthetic affect from bodily feeling. In hands of many postmodernists (who deny stable connections between sense experience and perceived meanings), aesthetic response becomes further disembodied.[4]

In literary criticism and teaching, an illogical divorce between empathetic recognition of affect in another and affectless experience in oneself was the dissolute hallmark of the old New Criticism with its famous distrust of the "affective fallacy": the allegedly fallacious belief that, in accounts of the significance of literature, readers' emotional responses are as relevant as supposedly objective properties of the art work.[5] The divorce has continued not only in criticisms based upon knowledge or its impossibility (such as rationalist, skeptic, or deconstructive approaches) and upon social energy or power (such as New Historicist, cultural materialist, or feminist approaches) but also in most reader-response criticism concerned as it has been with identifying communities of linguistic competence (Stanley Fish) or personal identity themes (Norman Holland) or other discourse-based learning. While the psychobiology of aesthetic experience has been investigated, at least tentatively, by some scholars of ritual (such as Victor Turner, Eugene d'Aquili, and Richard Schechner), visual arts (D. E. Berlyne), and cultural anthropology (Ellen Dissanayake), it is difficult to overestimate "how far the body, the reader's sensorium, has traditionally been kept from the field of literary concern."[6]

It is true that early critics of Shakespeare such as Dryden,

Pope, and Johnson, were impressed with Shakespeare's power to make audiences and readers laugh and cry or to feel the emotions of his characters. Such emotions, for these early critics as well as for their nineteenth-century counterparts—Edward Dowden, A. C. Bradley, and others—were widely subordinated, however, to character analysis and to moral teachings of the Bard.[7]

Twentieth-century Shakespeareans have explored an expanding horizon of critical approaches, but sensuous responses of readers and audiences remain neglected. G. Wilson Knight provides spatial, whole-play interpretations aiming at Shakespeare's vision. Pioneers in the close study of imagery such as Caroline Spurgeon, Wolfgang Clemen, and Edward Armstrong expose the range of Shakespeare's metaphors, their patternings in plays, and their contributions to an understanding of Shakespeare's development:[8] they do not discuss readers' somatic responses through changes in muscle tension, posture, heartbeat, skin resistance, breathing patterns, facial expressions, or reported internal, organic sensations. Even those (such as Harley Granville-Barker, E. E. Stoll, Alfred Harbage, Bernard Beckerman, C. L. Barber, John Holloway, Michael Goldman, and Stephen Booth)[9] who study Shakespeare's plays as playhouse experiences, attending partly to audience reactions, tend to generalize and abstract concrete experiences into insights, ideas, attitudes, and moral values among audiences. Though such scholars sometimes mingle cognition and emotion, they offer few means to study physical and emotional responses of audiences or readers.

While it is undeniable that sensation, perception, emotion, and cognition inextricably mingle in two-way circuits (so that, for example, neural activity in the brain and elsewhere helps select and hypothesize patterns of sensation and perception from a welter of often-ambiguous data in external or internal environments), it is also undeniable that abstract intelligence, conceptualizing cognition, often closes itself off from sustained engagement with shifting immediacies of visceral arousal that condition emotional experience. Hence bodily concomitants of aesthetic emotions tend to suffer effacement in accounts of aesthetic experience, including the interpretation and criticism of Shakespeare's art.

There have been flickers of interest among a few recent Shakespearean critics in "emotions which words cannot express," in "nonverbal, extratextual features of the play that emerge only in performance," in sensing "what it feels like" to perform the action of characters, and in how Shakespeare's texts "invade us and invite us to make . . . a sympathetic act of closure with them-selves."[10] Views of emotion implicit in such criticism generally fail to place the mind in the body, however, and so emotional re-sponse remains etherealized: "Shakespeare knew Sidney's work well, and in his comedies he so mixes laughter, pain, and wonder as to bring his spectators to a Sidneyan rapture."[11] Even when emotive response *is* seen partly in physical terms, the body's role tends to be generalized into vague assertions of muscular, kines-thetic mimicry of actors by audiences.[12] Or else "the aural, visual, and kinetic dimensions of stage production" are equated with all "the sensory dimensions" of "what an audience hears, sees, and experiences."[13]

We need the vocabulary and confidence to take us from kinetic observation of actorial grace to kinesthetic experience of our own mimicries or oppositions. What is the contribution of a viewer's or reader's *own* experience to the registering of artistic emotion? A learned critic of performance has observed:

> Convention also governs the interpretation of emotion through appo-site signs: rage is associated with red or pale faces and with threaten-ing gestures, cowardice is linked to trembling. These expressive signs act through a kind of artistic shorthand. Red faces and the appear-ance of trembling are only the outward and most obvious signs of inner emotion, but in a painting or poem they signal a more complex state of mind, to be imagined through the viewer's or reader's own experience.[14]

It is the precise process of our "own" experiential imagining (con-crete and sensuous as well as abstract and mental) that perform-ance critics tend to ignore and that I want to explore. Obvious signs of inner emotion may signal complex states of body, imag-ined through the viewer's or reader's own bodily experience. To challenge critical equation of "inner" emotion with a "state of mind" is to challenge, furthermore, academic preferences for cog-nitive views of emotion, and that challenge will be taken up throughout this book.

Though teaching and study of Shakespeare through student performance, as well as reading via performance, provide further means to invoke clearly somatic responses, those activities pro-vide no necessary reflection upon such responses. It is safe to speculate that precious few teachers, students, or general readers have received much encouragement to care for just how they breathe, move, and feel their way through Shakespeare. Despite the paradoxical increase of contemporary interest in thematics and in social constructions of "the body," actual bodily experience in engaging Shakespeare (and other literature) remains scandalously neglected. Reasons for such neglect are not hard to find in the history of Western attitudes toward the body, the general celebration of abstraction in "higher" education, and the difficulty of applying verbal terms to nonverbal states and behaviors.

Contemporary teachers and critics too often assume that reader-response criticism provides appropriate study of both feelings and thoughts in responses of readers to literature such as Shakespeare's writings. Insofar as the work of reader-responses proponents (such as Louise Rosenblatt, Walter Slatoff, Wolfgang Iser, Hans Robert Jauss, Norman Holland, Stanley Fish, Alan Purves, and David Bleich)[15] treats readers' feelings, however, those feelings are devoid of genuine bodily connection. Such advocates of reader-response approaches concern themselves with the construction of mental meanings and show almost no interest whatsoever in the embodied nature of readers' emotions (except perhaps residually in metaphors of filling gaps, walking paths, and so on).

Shakespeare inhabits the center of the Anglo-American, if not world, canon of literature partly because, in his relentlessly materializing imagination and his paralinguistic energy, he most successfully resists the emptyings out of discursive criticism in its tendency to convert embodied emotion to heady meaning. Shakespeare continually makes physical and emotional sense of rational or mental sense. When, for example, near the ending of *King Lear*, the aged King enters with his daughter, Cordelia, dead and in his arms, we know that we see a sorry sight. Shakespeare could in theory have ended his play at this moment, leaving us to hold in mind the gender-reversed pietà he has devised. Instead, Shakespeare gives to Lear a speech of remarkable anger, despair, and hope:

> Howl, howl, howl! O, you are men of stones!
> Had I your tongues and eyes, I'd use them so
> That heaven's vault should crack. She's gone forever.
> I know when one is dead and when one lives;   265

She's dead as earth. Lend me a looking glass;
If that her breath will mist or stain the stone,
Why, then she lives.

                                    (5.3.262–68)

Now, as a reader, I may choose to note, say, three ideas in the
speech: 1) the bystanders too tamely register the horror of what
they see; 2) Cordelia, Lear knows, is definitely dead; 3) Lear wills
himself to hope, nonetheless, that she lives. The speech, however,
sonically enacts fierce rage and grief. Unless I choose to perform
and embody its sounds, I lose much of its affective force. If I reduce "howl," for instance, to merely an imperative—Lear tells
the bystanders to wail—I am likely to speed up the sound and
forego its lung-emptying sonority. Though a word with some ono-
matopoetic resonance, bearing "echoic origins" (*Oxford English
Dictionary*), the word "howl" does not constitute an interjection
or expletive in common dictionary parlance. Shakespeare has creatively decided to employ the noun/verb "howl" as an interjection, an exclamation or ejaculation expressing, not denoting,
emotion. When emotion is not simply identified or labeled but expressed, it commonly evokes responsive emotion. Emotion begets
emotion. Emotion echoes emotion. Think of a baby crying or a
wolf howling. For adequate comprehension and response, Lear's
"Howl! Howl! Howl!" thus *demands* a responsive feeling and not
just an abstract label.

True, the very events of *King Lear* appear to deny what I have
just argued. Lear believes he confronts "men of stone," persons
who adamantly refuse to use their tongues to howl as circum-
stance pleads. Earlier, Gloucester assured Regan that she had no
power to deny empathy to the storm-driven Lear, not even if
wolves had "howled" at her gate (3.7.66). Regan proves Gloucester so thoroughly wrong that Lear's later "Howl!" could seem to
echo hollowly. What could prevent it from doing so?

Despite the vast pessimism of *King Lear* as to whether persons
such as Goneril, Regan, and Edmund, and perhaps persons generally, can be induced to share and care for the feelings of other
persons, Shakespeare employs throughout the play the counter-
argument of his soundplay, meter, and imagery. Such features
work precisely to concretize and to enhance the communication
of perceptions, thoughts, and feelings. Thus the repetitions of

"howl" serve little abstract or conceptual purpose; they are intended to induce feeling. So is the expletive "O" that follows
them. The groan of "O" also enters, of course, into enunciation
of "stones" in "you are men of stones!" "Men of stones," in turn,
because it occupies and echoes in the same end-line position as
"stain the stone" below, sonically calls up the willful stopping of
breath and search for breath that the passage is all about. Not to
physically hear or say the connection is to miss how the verse
works, just as not to hear the pause between the last "howl!" and
the "O" is to miss the point of the expressive gap, the missing
accent in the nine-syllable, off-pentameter line:

Howl, howl,| howl! [silent accent]| O, you| are men| of stones!|

(I assume the omission of the fourth, normally stressed fourth
syllable is not "fatal to our sense of the beat" but provides instead "an almost audible, perhaps kinesthetic beat."[16])

To howl is to use all one's breath in the expression of deep emotion. In the passage and later, Lear searches desperately for Cordelia's breath, reducing the full-throated aspiration of "howl" to
the cutoff hisses of "If that her breath will mist or stain the
stone," and even remembering that "her voice was ever soft, /
Gentle, and low" (5.3.277–78). All this contrasts with painful
irony against the first scene of the play in which Lear continually
advised Cordelia: "Speak," "Speak again," and "Mend your
speech" (1.1.86, 90, 94). Then Cordelia could say only, "Nothing." The nothing she says at the end of the play proves a much
deeper nothing. Lear dies, still seeking her breath: "Do you see
this? Look on her, look, her lips, / Look there, look there!" No
longer asking for filial flattery or even for appropriate gratitude,
Lear dies valuing to the utmost his daughter's merest breath. Not
as an idea but as an experience that includes bodily feeling, the
text works to change a reader's or audience member's awareness
of and reverence for the literal breath of life.

It can hardly be doubted that Shakespeare employed the titanic
resources of his artistic genius to induce audience and reader empathy for the desperate and dying Lear. When I recognize that
those resources include deploying living sounds to echo within audiences the somatically imagined feelings of stage characters such
as Lear, then I recognize as well my duty to attend carefully to
such sounds. Though I've said almost nothing here about effects

in the passage produced by Shakespeare's metrical art, repeated phrases, consonance and assonance, predominating monosyllables, pronominal contrasts, and the like, I hope I have said enough to suggest how close care for bodily feelings of "howl" or any feelingful phrases can lead to fruitful study of relations between our responses and Shakespeare's speech. That care and that study are significant parts of what I call making sense of Shakespeare.

For some years, I have been writing and lecturing on relations of emotion and meaning in Shakespeare and in literature more generally. In 1978, in "Interpreting *The Winter's Tale*," I reviewed the then-pertinent literature and argued for criticism responsive to "temporal-affective" dimensions of Shakespearean drama.[17] In 1979, in "*The Tempest* and the New World," I outlined interchanges between historicist, political readings of the play and more freely imagined, romance-inspired readings.[18] These and other essays pointing toward what might be called functional or process-oriented criticism were collected in my *Experiencing Shakespeare* (1988) wherein I suggest that not only do bodies inform culture and that minds work in bodies but also that study of Shakespeare necessitates corporal study.[19] I have continued to refine this argument through honors courses in Emotion and Meaning in Literature and The Relevance of Mind/Body Theory and Therapy to Literary Study, through graduate courses on teaching Shakespeare through performance and on Shakespeare and the Reader's Body, in lectures on bodily responses to Shakespeare among readers and spectators, and in recent book chapters, "Embodying the Play," "Goals and Limits in Student Performance of Shakespeare," "The Bias of Nature," and "Making Sense of Shakespeare: A Reader-Based Response."[20] The current study emanates from those activities, and it attempts to gather previously scattered insights and methods in a coherent form.

I acknowledge with heartiest thanks the helpful contributions made to this study by my students over the years and by many interested friends, all of whose names would be too numerous to list here. I do thank especially David Bevington (who has commented on several drafts), Marie Borroff, John Griffith, Malcolm Griffith, Will Hamlin, Catherine Haynes, Don Hedrick, Maynard Mack, Tom Pautler, and Jody Tate, for their suggestions concerning prior versions. This little book amounts to the collective effort of more persons than it has pages, and my gratitude extends to everyone who seeks to understand art for all sakes.

Note on Shakespeare's Text

Except where otherwise indicated in my text, I quote and cite Shakespeare from *The Complete Works of Shakespeare*, 4th ed., edited by David Bevington (New York: HarperCollins, 1992).

Introduction:
Abstract and Concrete Senses
in Shakespeare

Shakespeare Can Help Bring Us to Our Senses, and Vice Versa

Shakespeare's art shares with other art a capacity to help bring us to our senses: awake, aware, alive—shining before death. Shakespeare drives ideas through time, abstractions through concretions, language through gesture, content through form, mind through body, spirit through sense. As one reads or sees Shakespeare, one's mental sense touches one's bodily sense because Shakespeare's images and rhythms dance ever-sensuous appeals.

Having begun with adulation, let me concede that readers who doubt the universality of Shakespeare and who also deplore regressive social structures accepted (and critiqued) in Shakespeare's works may fear such praise of Shakespeare (even if it praises him only by means of an unlikely "biological aesthetic"). Would I resist demoting to noncanonical status this dead, white, male, European, Christian, wealthy author (as imperialized by centuries of often elitist cultural production in theaters and schools)? You will soon see that my answer assumes a posture both embracing and embarrassing such a question. Through my focus upon the "solidarity of sensuality" in Shakespeare's art, I hope to help ember away hot, angry minds fanned to overdestructive flames by divisive social inequalities.[1] I want to rekindle energies to confront alienating cultural constructions yet also to confirm "psychobiological substrates of empathy."[2] I seek to do so by exploring interdependencies of mental and bodily sense in Shakespeare's worlds and in readers' behaviors. Grounding mental in bodily sense, reattaching abstractions to concrete moments, promises to reveal a core of shared experiences within characters

21

and within readers. A glance at the epigraphs to this book may illustrate.

In the first epigraph, puritanical Angelo asserts that the sense of Isabella's plea for her brother's life stimulates the sense of his sexual passion. One may say that Isabella "makes sense" in two ostensibly dissimilar ways here brought into radical conjunction. Though Angelo claims that her mental sense controls his non-mental sense, a careful reader may doubt that Isabella's mental sense, her abstract ideas, alone cause Angelo's physical sense (specifically his systems of sexual bodily arousal) to "breed." Isabella's ideas, her pleas for mercy, have been couched seductively. Not only has she described herself to Angelo as a "suitor" (2.2.30) pleading for vice (32–34), suggested his heart be "touched" (56) as hers is touched, asked Angelo to imagine how he "would have slipped" sexually (70), longed for Angelo's "potency" (72), and asked Angelo to "Go to your bosom; / Knock there, and ask your heart what it doth know / That's like my brother's fault" (341–43), but also the very sound of her voice and look of her face enforce the sexual appeal of her "modesty" (176). Angelo says: "I desire to hear her speak again / And feast upon her eyes" (185–86). No doubt other sensuous appeals in Isabella, beyond voice and eyes, encourage Angelo's response, and yet his conviction (that her "modesty" and her rational "sense" in speech awake his physical senses) deserves respect.

In the overall economy of *Measure for Measure*, as generally played, Isabella's early, novitiate zeal for "a more strict restraint" within the nunnery (1.4.4) proves excessive. She finds that her greater desire leads her to come forth from the nunnery, plead excuses for her brother's vice, negotiate a bed trick, play act to trap Angelo, join the world on its worldly terms, and then, traditionally, wed the Duke. In this view, her "modesty" contradicts the pure idea that naive, abstractive Angelo makes of it. Isabella proves no shrinking violet, no fearful ascetic or anxious separatist (such as, say, Emilia in *The Two Noble Kinsmen*). Her modesty more nearly resembles the "modesty of nature" Hamlet recommends (3.2.19) for bringing words rightly into action, the "temperance" (3.2.7) that mediates between soul and passion. Isabella's "modesty" resembles the "modesty" of the play Hamlet praises (2.2.440) as not only sweet and fine but also wholesome and handsome. Angelo thinks at first to make poles of Isabella's spiritual purity and his own sullying lust, to defile higher sense by lower sense. In the central comic image of the bed trick, however, we behold Angelo's commitment to degrading sensuality eventually converted into marriage rites; what he thinks is dirty sex, his sex, turns out to enact productive sex, his and her sex, marriageable lust, two senses in one. The bed trick, art, suggests a way of bringing Isabella's "sense" together with Angelo's "sense" and, by sleight-of-hand, a way of creating from the meeting a productive social form.

Some persons will object, again, to Shakespeare fashioning such comedy (perhaps also some of his tragedy, history, and romance) out of what seems like masculine, degraded sense rescued by feminine, higher sense. Shakespeare combines (in men and in women both), however, functions of rational and sensual sense. Thus, interpreters of the first epigraph often interpret Angelo's own "sense" as mind or spirit though it is much more inclusive. Interpreters of the other epigraph often interpret the French King's second reference to "sense" as meaning "faith." Both faith and physical sense inhere, however, in the King's term, given the context of old man privately rejuvenated by young maid, the talk of prostituting the cure (2.1.123, 173), a bawdy scene between the Countess and Lavatch while Helena cures the King behind scenes, hints in the following scene that her cure was lusty (2.3.26, 41), and the King himself insisting that Helena's "beautiful hand" repealed his banished physical "sense" (48).

Shakespeare's men often struggle to rejoin sundered higher and lower senses, while his women often teach the way. Both Isabella and Helena, like many other Shakespearean heroines, bear burdens of saint/devil, Madonna/whore polarizations, but they overcome those burdens, accommodating spiritual and bodily senses. In Shakespeare, "feminine" and "masculine" (like rational and sensuous) associations of "sense" polarize, shift poles, blur, and blend in often wholesome ways.

As Shakespeare shows an interdependence of mental and bodily senses, so he shows cultural tendencies to assign separate gender roles to each kind of sense. At the same time, Shakespeare shows the folly of such separation as he makes mental sense and physical sense intricately blend in his Vienna. Attuned to this problem, an alert reader may pay careful regard to Shakespeare's uses of "sense," to his characters' notions of their sense-relations, to ways that mental and physical senses differ and blend in whole works, and to the reader's own sensuous responses to each moment of dialogue and action. Such a reader I think of as a "sense-reader."

A sense-reader will employ a heightened awareness, mindfulness, or self-referencing to note the arousal suggested by words and images (such as "touched," "slipped," "potency"). The same sensitivity (in awareness, mindfulness, and the like) allows the reader to note and respond with intensified feeling and thought to Isabella's progress from meekly subjunctive, optative pleading ("should," "would," "might") to aggressively imperative command ("Go to your bosom; knock there"). Such sensitivity responds in similar fashion to Isabella's *lengthening* speeches as she wrests control of the dialogue from Angelo. Sense-reading responds similarly to her shifting emphasis from plaintive "I" to accusatory "you." It responds to her relentless insistence upon Angelo's own sensual weakness and upon his resemblances to sexually erring Claudio. It responds, moreover, to Isabella's increasingly oratorical deployments of assonance and consonance, exclamations, repeated words, emotion-inducing superlatives and extremes ("never," "every," "nothing," "most ignorant," "all"), shortened and lengthened lines, reversed emphasis in the first two syllables of many lines (trochaic first "feet"), extended imagery, aphoristic assurance, use of mind-baffling paradox, cosmic metaphors, Sybil-like conveyance of divine attitudes and moods, all attributes of intensified poetic—emotional and discursive—power:

> Could great men thunder   115
> As Jove himself does, Jove would never be quiet,
> For every pelting, petty officer
> Would use his heaven for thunder,
> Nothing but thunder! Merciful Heaven,
> Thou rather with thy sharp and sulfurous bolt   120
> Splits the unwedgeable and gnarled oak
> Than the soft myrtle; but man, proud man,
> Dressed in a little brief authority,
> Most ignorant of what he's most assured,
> His glassy essence, like an angry ape   125
> Plays such fantastic tricks before high heaven
> As makes the angels weep; who, with our spleens,
> Would all themselves laugh mortal.
>
> (2.2.115–28)

By asking *how* the speech is spoken, *why* one responds as one does, and *how* such response may engage one's senses, a sense-reader changes the *what*, the message, of the speech. Such reading is, once more, what I call "sense-reading," a careful regard for somato-psychic dimensions of imaginative reading (including affective responses to form and content and emotive/cognitive arrays within and without the reader—to be discussed further) that underlie abstract sense-making and magnetically resummon conceptual abstractions back into concrete moments of reading. Shakespeare thus quite literally may bring a sense-reader to her or his senses.

SENSE-READING SHAKESPEARE RESTS ON VALUING THE CONCRETENESS OF ART EXPERIENCE

To make appropriate sense of Shakespeare, then, one needs to accommodate more than Isabella and Helena's sense to Angelo and the French King's sense. One needs to accommodate the sense of Shakespeare's ideas to the sense of one's immediate, experiential engagement with text or performance. Educational settings and our society in general, I assert, tend to privilege art over nature, mind over body, spirit over sense, and man over woman (as if such polarities might stay fixed either in analogy to each pair or in alignment of each term of the polarity). Sense-reading can help us freely question meanings and relations of these categories to each other.

Let us explore further the gendering of sense in Shakespeare and explore consequences. As the epigraphs reveal, "sense" in Shakespeare's thinking (as in our own) invokes tensions of gender as well as of ambiguity between abstract and concrete senses. On the one hand, "sense" may equal "man's" reason, as when Luciana rebukes her sister Adriana in *The Comedy of Errors* (2.1.20–24), saying men "Endued with intellectual sense and souls . . . Are masters to their females." On the other hand, this pretension of men to a mastery of rational sense receives endless mocking in Shakespeare, just as men's mistrust of women's lower "sense" receives rebuke in the overall action and dialogue of many plays.

Shakespeare thus pushes abstract sense toward a wholesome relation with concrete sense. In such tragedies as *Hamlet, King*

Lear, Othello, and *Antony and Cleopatra,* diatribes of male protagonists against women's sense and sensuality, while partly vin-
dicated in behaviors of light women, confront chastening
counterexamples such as Ophelia, Cordelia, Desdemona, and possibly the dying Cleopatra. Similar counterpoints inhabit the histories. In the comedies and romances, heroines often teach men
not to assume an ungovernable, low sensuality in and with
women. Everywhere, feminine powers of providential exorcism
emerge as with the Abbess in *Comedy of Errors* or the merry
wives of Windsor in the Herne ceremony chastising Falstaff's assumption of their lustfulness. Portia in *The Merchant of Venice*
teaches Bassanio meanings of a faithful wedding ring; church-
yard rites in *Much Ado* pay penance for Claudio's accusation of
Hero's "savage sensuality" (4.1.60); Hymeneal rites presided
over by Rosalind in *As You Like It* garner up the religious magic
of conversion to likeness; the epiphanic spirit fostered by Viola in
Twelfth Night leads wise men's sons to lovers' meetings; the nun
and pilgrim heroines of *Measure for Measure* and *All's Well* exor-
cise lustful mis-takings of Angelo and Bertram; in *Pericles,* chastening songs of Marina wake Pericles from his distemperature
and then her mother, Thaisa, restores herself as priestess to him;
Imogen in *Cymbeline* undergoes a pilgrim journey that parallels
her husband's release from jealousy; in *The Winter's Tale* Hermione and Paulina awaken the faith of Leontes through an art-
spirit ceremony; goddesses Juno and Ceres bless the chaste love
of Miranda and Ferdinand in *The Tempest* as the male magician
Prospero yields up his power; and the love goddess Venus tri-
umphs over Mars to close *The Two Noble Kinsmen.* In Shakespeare, "feminine" sense, though rarely de-eroticized in the
extreme, accommodates and chastens "masculine" sense.

If "some blessed spirit doth speak" within Helena's weak
"organ," that spirit proves the same providential force that helps
women restore men, often in Shakespeare, to relatively wholesome accommodations between abstract, mental sense and concrete, physical sense. A dramatic example of such creative
"making sense" occurs at the close of *The Winter's Tale* when
king Leontes witnesses his statuelike wife, Hermione (whose
name suggests a "herm," or pillar), begin to move to music, then
descend, and take his hand. "Oh, she's warm!" says the king. Of
course such instructive "women" are also boy actors, and it all
first took place in "male" imagining, an imagining that may well

oversanctify "female" rescue and restoration. Still, when living in such climates as ours of abstractly thematic teaching and theory-ridden criticism, one may glean from such dramatic moments a suggestive analogy: as Leontes actually feels the life of the statue, palpable to sense, so the student of Shakespeare may find in Shakespeare's art the same sensible and affecting surprise: "Oh, it's warm!" It "touches" human feeling, and, even when it "coldly" seems to rebuke one's empathy, or demand disengagement and abstraction, it promotes awareness of the sensuous, perceiving ground of experience.

Such happy concretizing of Shakespeare and other art requires first an unusually concentrated attention upon concrete dimensions of reading or listening experience. Angelo's sense, for example, "breeds" in response to Isabella's sense. In place of "breeds," Shakespeare could have used a term such as "teems," but "breeds" invokes reproductive organs relevant to Angelo's aroused condition. "Breeds" also may suggest that Angelo feels something of a gender reversal in himself; his sense breeds or gives birth, in feminine fashion, as if impregnated by powers of Isabella's "tongue." In the same way, the French King in *All's Well That Ends Well*, instead of describing Helena's female speech as "A powerful sound within a voice so weak," says "His powerful sound within an organ weak." He invokes not only the physicality of Helena's "organ" but also the gender-conflating process of the allegedly male God's ("His") power coming through the maid's "sense" to the King who now seems to incorporate male and female. The King reads Helena as powerfully double-gendered in her "senses." When readers of Shakespeare's text, in turn, ruminate upon concrete, sense-related meanings of Shakespeare's terms and also upon their gender-associations, then readers move closer to living, sensual energies that pervade Shakespeare's writing.

Another example of finding living sense in Shakespeare by attending to concreteness in language and production as well as to gender-implications arising therefrom, may be found in the Bard's world-famous lines: "O Romeo, Romeo, wherefore art thou Romeo?" Generations of students, readers, and playgoers have heard here the voice of a lover, Juliet, calling plaintively to her love and calling, in effect, "Where are you, Romeo?" Shakespeare editors have tried for equal generations to correct this ubiquitous reading. Editorial glosses such as that of the popular

New Folger Library edition inform readers that "wherefore" means "why," as the rest of the passage seems to attest:[3]

> O Romeo, Romeo, wherefore art thou Romeo?
> Deny thy father and refuse thy name!
> Or, if thou wilt not, be but sworn my love,   35
> And I'll no longer be a Capulet.
>
> *Romeo.* [*aside*]
> Shall I hear more, or shall I speak at this?
>
> *Juliet.*
> 'Tis but thy name that is my enemy;
> Thou art thyself, though not a Montague.
> What's Montague? It is nor hand, nor foot,   40
> Nor arm, nor face, nor any other part
> Belonging to a man. O, be some other name!
> What's in a name? That which we call a rose
> By any other word would smell as sweet;
> So Romeo would, were he not Romeo called,   45
> Retain that dear perfection which he owes
> Without that title. Romeo, doff thy name,
> And for thy name, which is no part of thee,
> Take all myself.
>
>   (2.2.33–49)

Juliet would identify what she loves as separate from markers of name and family that, she thinks, are conventional, arbitrary, unnecessary. To her, moreover, "Why are you Romeo?" equals "Why are you Montague?" She uses his first name, Romeo, but says "Deny thy father and refuse thy name," as if Romeo's given name were his family name (unless we are to think of old Montague as another "Romeo," which seems doubtful). To Juliet, given name and patronymic identify her lover equally, yet, in truth, he became her "enemy" only as a Montague. There may be other men in Verona or elsewhere named Romeo, and none need be her enemy. As reader or listener, therefore, when Juliet asks, "Wherefore art thou Romeo?," one may hear her asking not only "Why did you have to be my official 'enemy'?" but also "Why are you this name-sound, Romeo?" "How does it connect to you?" "Where does it place you in relation to me?"

One might excuse the millions of persons who have taken "wherefore" to be an extended form of "where" rather than a word meaning "why," because many of them probably have heard merely the isolated line and known vaguely that Juliet was calling from her "balcony" (a balcony absent from early texts and added only by stage and editorial tradition). There are, however, such forms as "whereforth," "wherefro," and "wherefrom" that do have geographical rather than causative meanings, and, further, Juliet seems to love, rather than hate, the name Romeo as she intones with apparent longing: "O Romeo, Romeo."

The very sounds within the name "R-*o-m-e*-o" echo through the play as sounds of heartfelt emotion:

> O me, what fray was here . . . (1.1.173)
> O me, o me, my child . . . (4.5.19)
> O me, this sight . . . (5.3.206)

Compare Sonnet 148 as it begins: "O me, what eyes hath love put in my head . . . ?" The very essence of a lover's sigh—"O, me, O"—resounds within Romeo's name, as Mercutio makes clear:

> Romeo! Humors! Madman! Passion! Lover!
> Appear thou in the likeness of a sigh.
> Speak but one rhyme, and I am satisfied;
> Cry but "Ay me!" Pronounce but "love" and "dove."
>
> (2.1.8–11)

Even the "me-o" sound in Romeo's name may express keen passion. Compare Juliet seizing the vial of sleeping potion: "Give me, give *me! O*, tell not me of fear!" (4.1.121) Or the sad love song in *Twelfth Night*: "Lay *me, O*, where / Sad true lover never find my grave, / To weep there!" (2.4.64–65). Shakespeare packs Romeo's name itself with suggestions of love and sex. When Benvolio cries, furthermore, "Here comes Romeo, here comes Romeo" (2.4.36), Mercutio responds: "Without his roe, like a dried herring. O flesh, flesh, how art thou fishified!" Again, Romeo's name contains not merely the lover's sigh but also the ovarian roe. Juliet's "O Romeo, Romeo" suggests the longing prelude to asking *where* her lover may be; the name-sound expresses and objectifies her longing, as if part of Romeo's flesh, and Shakespeare gently mocks Juliet (and us?) for thinking names so arbitrary.

As a given name for a male, "Romeo" would seem to identify Juliet's heterosex love-object, or subject. As a name suggesting "Roe me," however, "Romeo" conflates, or starts to switch, genders. Later in the play, Romeo asserts that the beauty of "O sweet

Juliet" has rendered him "effeminate" (3.1.112–13). We can hardly ever run ahead of Shakespeare in sensing how names may seethe with sensual and sexual energy, how language impinges upon nerve and pulse (though, to be sure, the wordplay draws upon cerebral attention to Shakespeare's manipulations of perceptual stimuli).

In her entire speech, Juliet asks just where the essence of Romeo, the object of her love, resides—as if to say: "*Where* are you, in what *part* of you, are you *Romeo*?" She tries to separate out a "dear perfection," a perfect abstraction, as the essence of her love, yet the verse traps her into associating the "perfection" with the sweet and dying odor of the rose:

> What's in a name? That which we call a rose
> By any other word would smell as sweet,
> So Romeo would were he not Romeo called,
> Retain that dear perfection which he owes,
> Without that title.
>
> (2.2.43–47)

(I retain as preferable here the pointing of the 1599 Quarto.[4]) What we think we are about to hear argued, as the verse progresses, is "As the rose 'would' smell as sweet, so Romeo, given any other name, 'would' also smell as sweet. . . ." Juliet's attempt to ascribe a non-sensuous essence to Romeo comes flavored with physicality, slips in a Romeo-mantic sense of smell if not also the "sweetness" of taste.

As Juliet "makes sense" of Romeo's name, so the attentive reader or listener follows her process, incarnating the love sighs of the verse, imagining concretely, internally, the sound and taste and touch of the lovers' affections anchored to dying bodies even as they think to challenge death, killing each other "with much cherishing" (2.2.184). The "concrete universals" of love and art parallel each other, proving themselves universal not in a transcendent Platonic realm, but only in the shared empathies of here-now space and time, matter and sense. Shakespeare brings us to our senses by showing where life lives, in the temporally heard sounds and word-associations of names as much as in their technically singular referents. Life thus lives in existence as much as in essence, in shifting behavior as much as in stable identity, in time-bound experience of taste, smell, and love-passion as much as in disembodied "perfection."

SENSE-READING OF SHAKESPEARE ENGENDERS
APPROPRIATE LITERARY CRITICISM

The concreteness of Shakespeare's language, its sensuous, syn-aesthetic quality, impels readers and audiences away from ordinary consciousness, grounds rational sense in physical sense, reshapes sexual identity, destabilizes gender, and freshens the material world for reinterpretation. When I attend carefully to this concreteness of Shakespeare's language, I may seem to seek "aesthetic" experience limited as psychological response to beauty in its sensuous appeal. I may seem unconcerned about political or philosophical content. A basic postulate of this book states, on the contrary, that careful attention to the sensory dimensions of experiencing Shakespeare may vitally inform political or philosophical criticism. We have already seen how close attention to concrete terms in passages from *Measure for Measure*, *All's Well That Ends Well*, and *Romeo and Juliet* quickly poses issues of gender identity and sexuality. Because he charges so much of his language with sensuous and sensual attributes, Shakespeare inevitably incorporates issues of sexuality and morality into the most immediate, perceptual dimensions of his texts. Only when we ignore the concrete workings of such texts are we likely to stray toward too-abstractly political, unpersuasive readings.

I want to respect aesthetic experience not by celebrating its detached, "nonfunctional" nature but by celebrating the depth at which social significance attaches to concrete being. What tends to turn *The Merchant of Venice*, for example, into a shallow tract treating only anti-Semitism or patriarchalism, is a failure to respect the originality of Shakespeare's intricate amalgams among matter and spirit. To illustrate briefly, the play opens with Antonio's confession that a sadness "wearies" him (line 2) and makes him a "want-wit" (6). Though his friends provide striking images of Antonio's entrepreneurial ennui, of "too much respect upon the world" (74), commentators often restrict his sadness to his feared loss of Bassanio (to Portia):

> At the beginning of the play he was going to lose something much dearer to him than riches, his friend Bassanio.

> At the beginning of the play Antonio is melancholy because Bassanio is about to leave him. . . .

Well then, if Antonio's friend has, in the eagerness of his new plans involving a lady, grown more distant, is not this reason enough for the poor man to be sad—and yet be unable to explain it, without disgrace, to his friends?[5]

Yet Portia, too, is first presented as "awearie of this great world."[6] She searches play-long for accommodations of her material attributes (physical beauty, woman's procreative body, economic wealth) to her nonmaterial value ("the full summe of me" [1437])—as the play searches analogously in so many ways—and thus it seems harshly abstractive to ignore (as not treating Bassanio) the explosive relevance of Solario's attack upon Antonio, the venture capitalist sadly expending himself:

> I should not see the sandie howre-glasse runne   25
> But I should thinke of shallowes and of flatts,
> And see my wealthy *Andrew* docks in sand
> Vayling her high top lower then her ribs
> To kisse her buriall; should I go to Church
> And see the holy edifice of stone   30
> And not bethinke me straight of dangerous rocks,
> Which touching but my gentle vessels side
> Would scatter all her spices on the streame,
> Enrobe the roring waters with my silkes,
> And in a word, but even now worth this,   35
> And now worth nothing.
>
>   (25–36)

Unless one reads with kinesthetic and proprioceptive sensitivity (that is, sensitivity to one's empathic sensations of bodily motion and of internal bodily sensations), one fails to feel the personified ship—mysteriously *he* (*"Andrew"*) and *she* ("her" top, "her" burial)—curving down and kissing at a place below the ribs. Shakespeare elsewhere imagines inanimate wood "kissing" sensually (*Sonnet* 128.6); he imagines lovers "buried" in each other, or self-burying (*Ado*, 3.2.64, 5.2.96; *Sonnet* 1.11); and Antonio could be "dock'd" (if "docks" needs emendation) like *Andrew* in his phallic mainmast. Not that Salerio as a character consciously intends this delicate, barely suggested ambiguity. Rather, Antonio's name (compare the Sebastian-loving "Antonio" in *Twelfth Night* and the sense of "not" or "without" in the prefix "an-"), his way of loving Bassanio, of opening his purse and person, his sense of himself as a tainted wether and weak fruit, his weighing his love for Bassanio *against* Portia's commandment, and so on, all may appropriately read back into this early blurring of sex roles and merchant roles. His "gentle" masculine/feminine vessel is "touched" in such a way as to "scatter" its spicy value uselessly, as if in barren ovulation or wasted seminal orgasm: "even now worth this, / And now worth nothing" (compare "Before, a joy proposed; behind, a dream" *Sonnet* 129.12). Though not an interest-charging merchant (that is, unlike Shylock who seeks to make "barren" money "breed"), Antonio as venture-capitalist who hazards all he has and as apparently homosocial lover, still risks a scattering waste in the material and unreproductive nature of his affairs. One may thus approach a balanced, sense-itive understanding of Antonio's character and his relations to other characters in the play through careful attention to concrete imageries surrounding him.

One who would read *The Merchant of Venice* not as an abstract, political tract but as a concrete, aesthetic experience (informing any political reading) must activate internal registers of perception. Such registers allow the concreteness of Shakespeare's language to resonate without too early or undue abstraction. Much of that resonance, its vast potentiation, belongs to Shakespeare, emerges from his ways of working with words. The confidence that we are reading out instead of reading in comes from the concreteness of our responses and from caring for Shakespeare's particular vocabulary, for Shakespeare's wordplay, for his patterns of usage, for his rhythms, for the language of the age, not for our differing concerns.[7]

I concede at once that attention to one's own responses as also to vocabulary, wordplay, patterns of usage, and time-soaked language may benefit from one's sustained self-examination as well as long acquaintance with Shakespeare and language study. One might question whether general readers or students in a single semester may be expected to participate in such experience. Still, a reassuring answer would stress the relative ease and pleasure of reading aloud, of imagining characters concretely, attending to speech rhythms, investing personal inflections of tone and attitude, and finding physical locations in the body for responsive feelings. Such an answer might face, however, a further question of why critics, including professional Shakespeareans, so often fail to demonstrate that they practice those allegedly easy and pleasurable activities. They are persons who presumably can if they wish revel in a close and subtle experience of text or performance. Why would such critics (or students) substitute in place of concrete experience merely abstract criticism?

The traditional view that interpretation and criticism must be firmly demarcated, as a matter of principle, from direct experience hardly serves to solve the problem.[8] It merely mystifies the category of "direct" experience by making it overintuitive and lacking in awareness. A recent critic who addresses this point, says: "The basic problem in current criticism, as I see it, is that many critics cannot experience—or at any rate, professionally discuss—a play or novel 'direct,' in itself. They have to impose between themselves and it a template, an interpretive model, some kind of 'enchanted glass,' in Bacon's striking phrase."[9] That sounds plausible, and yet the phrase "cannot experience" jars against the phrase "have to impose." The tension between the two phrases suggests the writer's uncertainty whether the critics attacked lack all capacity to read "directly" or, instead, willfully impose distorted "professional" readings upon a "direct" and accurate experience of the play "in itself."

As the massive deconstructive project of recent decades suggests, any critic's assumption that literary experience can be direct (in the sense of providing unmediated access to literary objects in themselves—a kind of naïve realism) runs afoul of work in many disciplines showing ever-tentative, always-constructed aspects of perceptions and concepts. Of things in themselves, particularly of literary texts in word-codes deciphered variously by varied societies and sensibilities, there can be, I concede, few unchallengeable observations. What I want to demonstrate here, however, is that readers not only may choose among kinds, levels, and importance of readerly abstractions (such as character, structure, genre, and theme) but also may learn to perceive more carefully the sensory events from which such abstractions arise. Conceptualizing, interpreting, theorizing, all are indispensable. Still, a reader may practice stepping in front of assumed referents ("Romeo" as a male character, "I" as a defense-oriented identity, "wanting catharsis" as appropriate to *Troilus and Cressida*) toward unfamiliar, more nearly preformed dimensions of reading ("Romeo" as inchoate sound-play, "I" as open awareness, "wanting catharsis" as implicating "not wanting catharsis").

Near the base of such speculations lie, in my opinion, the mingled pleasure and fear of concrete, particular, time-bound, and therefore death-acknowledging experience. To oversimplify, abstraction—whether in the student or critic's hands—often eases us away from painful particulars. Students and professional critics alike sometimes flee to abstraction in search of safety from a painfully arousing or discomforting concreteness of Shakespeare's text and their own responses. That very concreteness provides a focus of sense-reading, and I will look more closely in the third chapter at reasons for such endemic "resistance" to sense-reading.

Reading to experience the sensuous particularities of Shakespeare's text constitutes a version of aesthetic experience. Though one view of aesthetic experience sees in it an attempt to make painful particularities anodyne by purifying them into sensations appreciated solely for their "own" sake without connection to social, economic, political, or moral realms, my version of aesthetic experience seeks to shun that consequence. Notice, please, that aesthetic experience, in my handling, does not aim at detached, "nonfunctional" sensations of sound or imagery. Quite the contrary. The aesthetic experience I would enhance reveals the extent to which Shakespeare infuses content (such as issues of sex and gender or material versus nonmaterial valuing) right down into immediate, concrete texture of his dialogue. At the same time, this way of "making sense" of Shakespeare dares to take unguilty pleasure in artful interplay between sensation and rational sense.

I have now introduced the subject of this book: making sense of Shakespeare through "sense-reading." In the next chapter, I argue that readers and listeners can, if encouraged, make sense of Shakespeare in far more literal and physical ways than are normally assumed. In succeeding chapters, I develop this argument and explore contexts of resistance to sense-reading and strategies of reinsistence upon it.

Making Sense
of Shakespeare

I

Sense-Reading and Resistance

1

Sense-Reading Shakespeare's Sounds

SHAKESPEARE'S METRICAL RHYTHMS AFFECT READERS AND LISTENERS BIOLOGICALLY

IMAGINATION MEANS AS IT MOVES. SHAKESPEARE'S ART ACHIEVES more than abstract meaning as it affects readers in psyche and soma through devices of concretion such as rhythm, soundplay, imagery, paralinguistic features, and stage action. When readers embody imagined readings and stagings, when readers and audiences enter behaviors of characters and actors, then Shakespeare again moves and means concretely.

Take the matter of Shakespeare's meter, the anthem of his rhythm. Today, the dialogue of drama in theatrical, filmed, and televised forms appears almost exclusively in prose, and contemporary poetry appears largely in unmetered forms. Students, and even teachers, rarely associate the force of metered poetry with the musicality of its rhythms. So entrenched have antiformalist, content-oriented, anti-aesthetic modes of teaching and criticism become, that practitioners of such criticism who edited the prestigious Norton Shakespeare (1997), proclaiming itself "an edition oriented toward students," fail even to mention that Shakespeare wrote mainly in metered verse, much less provide any explanation of how the meter works or why its rhythms may be significant.[1]

Immersed as we are in "culture wars," we may not note how utterly anomalous is the present moment of prosodical neglect. For several millennia, the world over, poetry has employed a metrical beat, and that beat has been considered, by poets and listeners alike, a crucial element of its appeal. In his day, Shakespeare was admired for his mellifluous, honey-tongued verse. Shakespeare himself speaks of "the even road of a blank verse" (*Ado*, 5.2.33–34) that makes for easy, regular "walking" and of comically making the blank verse "halt" (*Hamlet*, 2.2.326) against its natural function. Shakespeare never used the word "rhythm," but he seems consistently to associate the "beat" of verse with a muscular, kinesthetic, bodily response, with walking smoothly, or with dancing "trippingly" (*Hamlet*, 3.2.2), or with an appropriate, unstrutting "gait" (*Hamlet*, 3.2.31). He notes the power of Ariel's drum to "beat" for Stephano, Trinculo, and Caliban so as to have "charmed their ears" and left them "dancing" (*Tempest*, 4.1.175, 177, 183). A different sort of drumming "beat" makes a drum in Shakespeare "speak mournfully" (*Coriolanus*, 5.6.156), telling soldiers to trail their pikes, the beat again working kinesthetically. For Shakespeare, birdsong, too, impresses not just with melody but with "beating": Juliet speaks of the lark's notes that "beat" high above the lovers (*Romeo*, 3.5.2), and Theseus describes how two nightingales "beat the ear o' th' night . . . that the sense could not be judge between" (*Two Noble Kinsmen*, 5.3.124–28).

All of these ways in which heard rhythms impinge upon our sense and invoke kinesthetic responses, ways presciently imaged by Shakespeare, have been verified in modern laboratories. It is now "a well-known fact that the perception of rhythm is invariably accompanied by actual movements or kinesthetic motoric impulses in line with the rhythm" that in turn affect the rate of internal processes such as heartbeat and respiration.[2] Metrical accent works on our mechanisms of arousal and de-arousal. It tends to modify the periods of neurological (for example, brainwave) rhythms and to entrain, that is, coordinate, physiological activities having a rhythmic nature. Some poems with markedly regular rhythms are trance-inducing, and hypnotic responses to poetry involve lessened abstract, rational thought, more primary process thought, and more imaginative involvement in inner experience.[3]

Scientific studies show that stressed syllables, during speech processing, receive relatively high allocations of attention, and prosodic features can help convey particular emotions even when intelligibility of words becomes blurred.[4] Our cortical neurons apparently employ and respond to rhythmic timing of "spike trains."[5]

Many laboratory studies of responses to rhythm in music and song have measured changes in muscle tension, heartbeat, blood pressure, skin conductance, shivers, and the like, as rhythms were introduced or varied.[6] These and the other studies cited above strongly suggest that Shakespeare's rhythms produce elaborate, multifaceted, full-body responses in listeners and readers, responses as much a part of engaging Shakespeare as are verbal, discursive interpretation and criticism.

Experts in aesthetic anthropology, biogenetic evolutionary analysis, and sociobiology of ritual concur on ways in which metrical rhythms function physically in audiences such as Shakespeare's. Working backward from the perception that all cultures employ arts fostering species evolution, bio-aestheticists point to art's "fundamental animal pleasures, essential ingredients of life" and to "intensely physical and bodily origins and concomitants of aesthetic experience."[7] These originary pleasures can produce shared emotions, common consciousness, and renewed dedication to group survival. As primary contributors to ritual effects of performance, Shakespeare's poetic and prose rhythms, along with other musical features of his language, help (in biogenetic language) to entrain and coordinate basal biological rhythms within bodies of listeners. Prolonged rhythmic stimuli provoke "simultaneous discharge of both autonomic systems [sympathetic and parasympathetic], generating not only a pleasurable sensation, but under proper conditions, a sense of union or oneness with conspecifics."[8] Physical effects of ritualized rhythmicity depend on systems that integrate the autonomic nervous system with the rest of the body: stimulation of the ergotropic (arousing) and then trophotropic (calming) systems produces autonomic changes in heart rate, blood pressure, sweat secretion, pupil dilation, and gastrointestinal functions.[9] Such rhythms also produce somatic shifts from less to more synchronized EEG, more to less muscle tension, and changed hormonal secretions (from increased epinephrine and norepinephrine to increased insulin, estrogens, and androgens).

Cognitive resolution of tensions in *All's Well* (to present an example of sonic rhythms and its effects) between Helena as inexperienced maid and Helena as agent of Grace for the French King's renewal remain incomplete. Helena's ultrarhythmic, caesuraless, and rhyming/chiming chant, however, in biogenetical terms "by its very rhythmicity, drives the ergotropic system independent of the meaning of words. If the ritual works, the ergotropic system becomes, as it were, supersaturated and spills over into excitation of the trophotropic system, resulting in the same end state as meditation but from the opposite neural starting point":[10]

> The great'st grace lending grace,
> Ere twice the horses of the sun shall bring
> Their fiery torcher his diurnal ring,
> Ere twice in murk and occidental damp   165
> Moist Hesperus hath quenched her sleepy lamp,
> Or four-and-twenty times the pilot's glass
> Hath told the thievish minutes how they pass,
> What is infirm from your sound parts shall fly,
> Health shall live free and sickness freely die.   170
>
> (2.1.162–70)

Conceptually, a reader or listener knows Helena can hardly be the heavenly minister she claims to be, but affectively her chanting couplets (among which these are but a portion) produce a resolution of that tension through rhythm and rhyme. The mind may not be persuaded, but the body in its limbic and autonomic functions is. When the rhythmic effects of Shakespeare's "neural lyre" undermine conceptual resistance to the rejuvenatory message of the verse, one senses a mild trance: antinomies collapse; time and space converge in a momentarily endless present that banishes decay.[11] Such a banishment becomes the result of Helena's speech: a result far different from mere conceptual recognition of her message. Her rhythms "broaden the scope of purely lexical meanings by relating them to a less specific substratum of affective energy."[12]

SHAKESPEARE STROVE FOR SPECIFIC MOMENTS OF METRICALLY INDUCED CALM OR NEAR-TRANCE

I have heard actors (and some English professors) argue—without scientific proof—that iambic pentameter verse, of all metrical forms, seems most lullingly suited to our human heartbeat (with its characteristic da-*dum* sound and internal feel). However that may be, Shakespeare had access to similar theory of physiological effects from poetry and song. The therapeutic, medicinal force of poetry was a common Renaissance topic. "The poet who comforts the sick emotionally might then amend or cure physically, thereby affirming quite literally an image of the poet as healer.''[13] In particular, the calming effects of lyric were noto-rious.

In *Julius Caesar*, the young page, Lucius, lulls himself to sleep when singing for Brutus on the eve of the Battle of Philippi. Bru-tus comments: "This is a sleepy tune" (4.3.269), and, in the econ-omy of Shakespeare's stagecraft, the music and song provide a somewhat trance-inducing interlude. (By "trance" I mean a hyp-notic, psychological state emphasizing rapt attention to inner ex-perience, literalness of understanding and emotional response, variable freedom from inhibition, and correspondingly enhanced suggestibility). The interlude not only prepares for the entering Ghost of Caesar but also provides one of those late-in-play ha-vens, reminders of tenderness among loving souls, that cycle an audience away from and then back to the reflex of tragic waste. Compare Gertrude's pastoral elegy on Ophelia's drowning, or Des-demona's willow song, or Lear's fantasy of reciprocative forgive-ness with Cordelia: "We two alone will sing like birds i' the cage. / When thou dost ask me blessing, I'll kneel down / And ask of thee forgiveness" (5.3.9). Similar moments inhabit Shakespeare's comedies. In *The Two Gentlemen of Verona*, the song "Who is Syl-via?" (4.2.38) offers a lull in the action even as it hauntingly que-ries the mystery of Sylvia's "grace" that shimmers through so many minds in the play. Listening to the song, Julia comments, "It makes me have a slow heart" (4.2.62), and, though editors (in their fashion) tend to gloss "slow" as "heavy" (which is equally somatic in meaning), Julia may well mean precisely what she says: the music has caused her pulse to slow down, her heart to beat more sadly slow. No doubt the ending poetry in *A Midsum-mer Night's Dream*, Marina's song in *Pericles* (5.1.82), the music awaking Hermione in *The Winter's Tale* (5.3.98), and the music and poetry of Prospero's masque for Miranda and Ferdinand all serve similarly somatic and affective functions. They work "to in-duce a state of partial trance, and thereby to free in some mea-sure the emotional life from the trammel of critical thinking."[14] That is, these moments of music promote a fully embodied sanity and calm unachieved by thought alone.

Shakespeare's verse, like any great poet's verse, often induces that "partial trance" of heightened, formal, ritual feeling as it moves the speaker away from quotidian realities of everyday views that are foreign to the trance state. Examples are not hard to find:

> Fear no more the heat o' the sun,
>   Nor the furious winter's rages;
> Thou the worldly task hast done,
>   Home art gone, and ta'en thy wages.
> Golden lads and girls all must,
> As chimney sweepers, come to dust.
>
> Fear no more the frown o' the great;
>   Thou art past the tyrant's stroke.
> Care no more to clothe and eat;
> To thee the reed is as the oak.
> The scepter, learning, physic, must
> All follow this and come to dust.
>
> *(Cymbeline,* 4.2.261–72)

Such meter takes over the speaker and hearer's minds, assimilating the "character's" ideas into the author's overriding voice, and, beyond the author's voice, the voice of living *rhythm*. The meter becomes much of the message. The meter matters and makes matter as it enhances neural, cordial, and respiratory rhythms. It dances us, producing a dancer's "high," that exhilarating and eventually calming immersion in biological rhythms played out through the ear, the swaying body, the circadian and diurnal registries that tell "how many things by season seasoned are" (*The Merchant of Venice,* 5.1.107). Shakespeare thus fleshes out the seasons of a year, of a life, of the body's coming gratingly or gratefully to dust. Characters who chant such verse and poets who produce it yield alike a portion of their reason to inner and outer Forms, or Echoic Energies (some would call them minor gods or spirits) producing palpable immersion in the general dance.

I find it unnecessary to decide degrees to which Shakespeare's rhythms may support semantic meaning or may produce significant responses independent of semantic meaning. It seems obvious to me that Shakespeare's rhythms serve both functions. The beat of rhythm "engages with the body and not just the ears and brain." Rhythm can be much more than "merely a handmaiden to meaning and dramatic situation." As spoken by Helena, Guiderius, and Arviragus in the hypnotic forms above, Shakespeare's rhythms can help us rise at least a little way beyond "alienating social codes of value and standards of behavior, pressures, and demands": "The pleasure of rhythm transcends all boundaries—

class, nationality, race—and even in the feeling of the subject of poetry in his or her ecstasy, the boundary between the living and the dead seems to fade."[15] Yet, even here, I believe, the liberatory response to rhythm issues out of deliberation upon meanings of boundedness itself. There is little point in any critic's attempts to mystify the effects of meter and rhythm into a sublime realm wholly beyond reach of our mental sense-making or of ordinary categories of understanding. Shakespeare's rhythms are pleasurable, no doubt, for many reasons, known and unknown, plain and fancy, practical and mystical. Some hypotheses are easily linked:

> hypotheses that the pleasure in rhythm derives from its associative linking with the rhythm of sexuality, from the degree of its correspondence to the basic rhythms of internal life processes, and from its orientative function as a gestalt are supported by similar observations and complementing theoretical frameworks. Sexuality is but one instance from the overall complex of vital life processes, and orientation draws its importance from its function in making possible the satisfaction of life-supporting needs in general and of sexuality as a particular instance. Rhythm is then pleasure-laden as a result of its multideterminative relations to many and various functions of the human being, which lends it not only the power to arouse tension and provide relief but also to fascinate, bind, and in certain cases dominate the perceiver.[16]

For our purposes, the important point is that Shakespeare's aural (and visual) rhythms, which are almost wholly neglected in classrooms and criticism today, can and should be crucial ingredients of the meaning and pleasure to be derived from reading, hearing, or seeing Shakespeare. Let us resolve to end this era of neglect.

METER JOINS WITH OTHER FORMS OF SOUND-PLAY TO ENACT SHAKESPEARE'S MEANING

Consider how a student or novice reader might read a passage such as Titania's address to Bottom in *A Midsummer Night's Dream*:

> Sleep thou, and I will wind thee in my arms.
> Fairies, begone, and be all ways away.
> So doth the woodbine the sweet honeysuckle

Gently entwist; the female ivy so
Enrings the barky fingers of the elm.
O, how I love thee! How I dote on thee!

(4.1.39–44)

From long years of teaching, I have noted tendencies of students and other readers to overemphasize beginnings of lines relative to ends, to end-stop lines that run over in sentence forms to the next lines (enjambment), to give too little emphasis to parts of most lines, to restrict emphasis to varied loudness and thus ignore resources of pitch, pace, pause, and timbre or tone quality, and to speak the verse too rapidly in a huddled, slurred enunciation. Employing Shakespeare's meter as part of sense-reading involves the elimination of such habits by simple practice open to anyone. To apprehend one step in the practice, note that many readers will (in silent reading or in speech) prosify the first line to something like:

sleep thou, and I'll wind thee in my arms.

To honor the meter requires something more like:

Sleep thou, and I will wind thee in my arms

where the comparison of "thou" and "I," so crucial to the rest of the passage, asserts itself and where the relation between "*th*ou" and "*I*" more clearly echoes in "*th*ee" and "*wi*nd." One needs to read or listen for all of the line, all of its words and syllables, seeking out their interanimations.

Shakespeare's delicate manipulation of relations between sound and sense also creates an association of "sleep *th*ou" with Bottom as "*thee*." As "*thee*" combines sounds of "sleep" and "*th*ou," "thee" incorporates by sound the sense of a sleepy Bottom. Titania's "I," in turn, links sonically to "*wi*nd" and picks up connections to related *i* sounds of "will" and "in" and alliterative assonance of "and" and "arms." By thus associating "sleep *th*ou" with "*thee*" and placing "thee"-Bottom within the enclosing Titania-sounds of "I," "i," "an," and "ah(rms)" (sounds that appear, it so happens in the vowels of her name), the verse *enacts* the process it describes of enfolding the sleepy bottom within Titania's arms. Such sleepy enfolding cannot be enacted, however, without an even, fully enunciated expression that lets the meter do its arousing work, and lulling play.

To suggest, furthermore, how careful attention to sound often discloses new sense, one may note a gentle straining in the verse of meter against grammar. Cradling "thee" inside balanced three-syllable groups—"I-will-wind *thee* in-my-arms"—masks the substitution of "thee" for "arms" as object of the verb "wind." Usually, one would say "I will wind my ARMS *about* thee." To "wind" "thee" directly makes "thee" into something wind-able, like "honeysuckle" (in this context). This vegetative entwisting of Titania and Bottom continues, of course, in the lines:

> So doth the woodbine the sweet honeysuckle
> Gently entwist; the female ivy so
> Enrings the barky fingers of the elm.

So, too, do grammatical entanglements continue to strain gently against reassuring meter, as the first line could be heard through varied anticipations:

1. So doth the woodbine the sweet honey suckle
2. So doth the wood bind the sweet honeysuckle
3. So doth the woodbine the sweet honeysuckle
   Gently entwist. . . .

Are we not supposed to catch by means of such sound-play a sense of Bottom both infantilized to suckling infant and more maturely finding female rings for his "fingers"?

As happens commonly in Shakespeare, oceanic bliss of this kind produces a melding of sexual roles. In the process, moreover, the verse-sounds play their own performative role to suggest that what seems double becomes single and that repetition equals unity:

> begone, and be . . .
> all ways away . . .
> Gently entwist . . .
> Enrings . . . fingers . . .
> So . . . so
> How I . . . thee! How I . . . thee

Constantly, the sounds close and enclose, providing deeper, sensuous workings of the sense. We could term this phonic practice of Shakespeare's (and many other great poets of the language) "message massage."

Unless we read so as to reverence phonic functions of Shakespeare's verse, we risk converting what could be an "experience" into merely the "gist" of meaning, an abstract outline of sense, a flight to general clauses. When Shakespeare invested as much conscious care (or assimilated genius) as we have seen in intricate *forms*—here, precise sound patterns—of his texts, he effectively prevented them from being decoded abstractly. He rendered it literally impossible to read him successfully in the manner that one reads a newspaper or textbook. By writing word-music, he set an absolute requirement that he be approached musically. No other apprehension will suffice.

All it takes to make sense of Shakespeare's musical sounds is a willingness to slow down, to observe, to notice, to care that these words have these sounds in this order. It helps also to believe and practice the belief that one's mind extends below one's neocortex to the sensory apprehensions and rhythms of one's body. One may learn further, of course, how Shakespeare and his age conceived of iambic pentameter and other meters, and one may practice such learning a lifetime, but that applies to hearing or playing any musical composition. Not to hear is not to understand. My concern here, however, is not to provide step-by-step techniques but rather to show concretely just how Shakespeare's (and much other) poetry works against the grain of abstraction, against the tendency of language to lead us away from sensory experience. Thus, one root of Shakespeare's notorious "ambiguity" and "indeterminacy" lies in the particularity of his medium, in the ephemeral, performative nature of its sound-play, syncopations, and tonal choices. Paradoxically, Shakespeare's themes dissolve in schemes and figures; his ideas shimmer their opalescent counterchange within unstable imageries; and every adage measures but adagio. We may as well pay attention, therefore, to Shakespeare's sensory rhythms, for we can never successfully translate Shakespeare into prose or abstract a content remotely equal to his concrete sounding.

2

Sense-Reading Shakespeare's Nonvisual Images

TRADITIONAL READERS HAVE SLIGHTED SHAKESPEARE'S
APPEALS TO VISCERAL AND KINESTHETIC IMAGINATION

ILLUSTRATING HOW SIGHT-DOMINATED WE ARE, WE GENERALLY TAKE
the term "imagery" to include words referring to *any* sensory experience.[1] General lore in our culture subscribes to the truism
that everyone knows how to experience "mentally" a described
sight or sound. If I write "maple tree," you can summon up in
your "imagination" or "mind's eye" the "image" of such a tree.
If I write "a tenor singing," you can mentally "re-hear" or
"imagine hearing" such an auditory "image." Many of us, no
doubt, believe that we have well-developed visual and auditory
memories and imaginations, such that we can vividly "re-experience" things seen and heard or freshly see and hear, in our
minds, new descriptions of sights and sounds. We do not worry,
ordinarily, about whether our literal eyes and ears or other body
parts (other than our brains?) are engaged in such mental re-creation. We may concede, nonetheless, that imagining, say, erotic
sights and sounds may produce physiological changes in us or
that imagining very sad sights and sounds may move us to tears.
Yet these may be considered special cases if we prefer to think of
imagery, particularly aesthetic imagery, as somehow remote from
physiological processes.

In the case of smells and tastes, the exercise of imagination
often invokes immediate reference to or consultation of one's actual nose or mouth. To imagine the scent of a rose, one may focus
upon one's actual nose and even begin to sniff; to imagine the
taste of lemon, one may feel sourness at the sides of the tongue.
Such focusing invokes physical, material, neural activity engag-

ing brain and organs in much the same manner as focusing upon one's foot allows one to sense physically what the foot is touching or how it feels internally. Of all the senses, touch may be the hardest to imagine without some form of bodily consultation or focus or attention. Simply imagining one's own physical movements (without actually moving) may affect, moreover, one's muscular strength and coordination; the "mind" on its own, as it were, can through imaging change the physical constitution of the "body."[2]

But what do we mean by "touch"? Specifically, do we include therein the hordes of visceral and kinesthetic sensations unassignable to any of the other senses? Plainly, yes. Still, this entire portion of sensory experience has largely been ignored by literary observers of imagery. The widely taught *Norton Introduction to Literature* describes the language of poetry as "almost always visual and pictorial" and lets the other senses fend for themselves. The most famous study of Shakespeare's imagery, Caroline Spurgeon's, devotes 1.5 pages out of some 400 to imagery of touch, and then only to external touch. And modern textbook anthologies of Shakespeare, though purporting to give extensive accounts of how his poetic language works, give no hints that visceral or kinesthetic imagery could be of consequence.[3] Consider, nonetheless, how inadequate is merely pictorial imagination to one's mental and physical registry of Shakespeare's full imagery. One has but to turn to any of hundreds of Shakespearean passages depicting nonvisual sensation to feel such inadequacy. Often Shakespeare will contrast duplicitous visual appearance against true inner being, as in Hamlet's invocation of "that within which passes show" (1.2.85) or Claudio's denunciation of Hero in *Much Ado About Nothing*:

> Out on thee, seeming! I will write against it.   55
> You seem to me as Dian in her orb,
> As chaste as is the bud ere it be blown;
> But you are more intemperate in your blood
> Than Venus, or those pampered animals
> That rage in savage sensuality.   60
>
> (4.1.55–60)

We can see in our mind's eye moon and bud, but we slight Shakespeare if we subsume intemperate blood into visual imagery of

Venus and animals. "You are more intemperate in your blood" invites imagination of bodily heat. Just as one may imagine a visual image of moon, bud, Venus, or animal, so one may imagine a nonvisual representation or realization of heated blood accompanying sex arousal.

To modern sensibilities, Shakespeare's imagery of intemperate blood, like his many images of hot and cold blood, may seem simply metaphors pointing to nonmaterial affections. We will be rewarded, however, if in such matters we take Shakespeare as literally as possible for as long as possible. In reading Shakespeare, our internal registries need to be activated, not deactivated. I could have listed a long string of undeniably somatic or visceral images, including:

> Did these bones cost no more the breeding but to play at loggats with them? Mine ache to think on 't.
> (*Hamlet*, 5.1.91–93)

> And I have a rheum in mine eyes, too, and such an ache in my bones that, unless a man were cursed, I cannot tell what to think on 't.
> (*Troilus and Cressida*, 5.3.104–07)

> . . . let our finger ache, and it indues
> Our other, healthful members even to a sense
> Of pain.
> (*Othello*, 3.4.148–50)

> I will not swear these are my hands. Let's see;
> I feel this pinprick. Would I were assured
> Of my condition!
> (*Lear*, 4.7.56–58)

> *Charmian.*   Too slow a messenger.
> [*She applies an asp to herself.*]
> O, come apace, dispatch! I partly feel thee.
> (*Antony and Cleopatra*, 5.2.321–23)

These images in themselves appeal much less to imagined sight than to imagined touch as internal feeling of aching bones and the like. (And notice Hamlet suggesting a theory available to Shakespeare that mere thought may produce *physical* sensations.) The less explicit invitation by Shakespeare (for us to imagine inner sensations) needs specially to be heeded. Thus, when the drunken Stefano in *The Tempest* protests to Trinculo— "Prithee, do not turn me about. My stomach is not constant" (2.2.114–15)—the appeal of the image is not just to our eyes but to our registry of sensations accompanying and recallable from our own upset stomachs in the past. That is plain enough. But often, in reading Shakespeare, we can *choose* whether just to see it or also to be it, whether to visualize or to interiorize. The deposed Richard, for example, imagines clawing his way out of Pomfret Castle, saying:

> Unlikely wonders—how these vain weak nails
> May tear a passage through the flinty ribs
> Of this hard world, my ragged prison walls,
> And, for they cannot, die in their own pride.
> *(Richard II,* 5.5.19–22)

To settle for imaging the *sight* of Richard scratching at the walls is to forego the reward of imaging the *feel* of fingernails tearing at semi-anthropomorphic "ribs," and raggedly somaticized walls (which are "rugged," yes, as editors note, but also more flesh- and clothinglike) in personified pride. To add historical accounts of Richard being starved in prison and the Renaissance proverbs of hunger tearing at stone walls is to add (beyond the kinesthetic tearing of fingernails) a gastric dimension of the stomach searching past ragged ribs for food

What such sense reading depends upon is an alteration in normal reading aims. Instead of aiming for the structured, quickly delivered, seemingly objective *information* often yielded by sight, one must aim for the less structured, often murky and slowly realized, more subjective *feeling* typical of visceral sensations. Sense-reading accepts poetry's, literature's, art's invitation to reconcretize and reenter the world's body, including one's own body, to resist the abstractive forces of language, to materialize perception. Shakespeare in part praises and revalidates our sensory intercourse with life, and to experience that praise and revalidation is one good reason to read Shakespeare.

SENSE-READING ENHANCES RESPONSE TO VISCERAL AND KINESTHETIC IMAGERY

Shakespeare has been coopted in education to teach historical, political, and moral lessons. In the academy, sensations and feelings that might be engendered by training in use of nonvisual imagination have been largely discounted. In theaters, of course, Shakespeare lives emotionally, but, even there, audiences lack training to activate visceral and kinesthetic registers of response. Sense-reading requires that one unbury metaphors and desymbolize both word and world. When Shakespeare somaticizes emotions, we need to follow mental feeling into fleshly feeling. King Henry VI, for example, says:

> I feel such sharp dissension in my breast,
> Such fierce alarums both of hope and fear,
> As I am sick with working of my thoughts.
>
> (*1 Henry VI*, 5.5.84–86)

Consider how easy and habitual it would be for you or I as readers to keep our empathy superficial here, to settle for a quick cognitive translation—the King is upset—and even to doubt he means to report physical sensations in his breast or physical sensations of sickness. It is true that Shakespeare may use "breast" metaphorically as locus of intangible emotions and emotion-tinged thoughts, but he also literalizes the breast as physically sensitive to the feeling of a sigh (*3 Henry VI*, 2.5.117), the feeling of heart or breath throbbing (*2 Henry VI*, 4.4.5), feelings of tightness and release in and from panting exertion (*Coriolanus*, 2.2.122), feelings of coldness associated with fear (*Richard II*, 1.2.34), and so on. In reading or hearing King Henry speak the words quoted above, then, it will behoove us to recall the perhaps adrenaline-inspired sensations that have inhabited our own breasts in moments of mingled eagerness and fear or, if we cannot recall them, to search in our sensory/emotive memories for the nearest analogues and thus actually to focus at least brief attention upon our own breast-feelings. Doing so is valuable for its own sake as an intensification of complex feeling and also as providing better appreciation of Henry's peculiarly childlike mixtures of tentative, wishful hopes and timorous reluctances.

Like the breast, the heart in Shakespeare, as in our common discourse, often stands metaphorically for emotion itself or for an intangible seat of feeling and response, akin sometimes to soul. But Shakespeare often takes the feelings of the heart much more literally and physically than we tend to do. When Troilus, for instance, says, "My heart beats thicker than a feverous pulse"

(3.2.35), we are given no reason to think of "heart" metaphorically. We can focus upon sensory possibilities of "thicker" as "more rapidly" or "with wildly varying strength or regularity of beats," and so on. In our culture, we admit the possibility of feeling physical heartbeats, if not via the heart directly, then through receptors in the chest. But when Troilus says, "I was about to tell thee—when my heart, / As wedged with a sigh, would rive in twain" (1.1.36–37), we may be reluctant to admit the possibility of such direct physical sensation from the heart; we may find no analogue in our own sensory experience. I submit that the sense-reader may profitably take the time to focus upon the reader's heart, while sighing, the same sort of attention or inquiry for sensory information that can be focussed upon admittedly feelingful body parts such as the tongue or chest muscles or lungs. Does a long, slow sigh deoxygenate the blood and slow the pulse in a manner interpretable by the heart as a kind of shutdown? or malign compression or wedging? Such contemplation may render Shakespeare's sense of the feelingful heart less alien. It may also render more accessible Troilus's exquisite sensitivity to the contradictions of sensation, feeling, and thought that throng through him. Later in the play, as he observes Cressida with Diomed, Troilus alleges he will maintain his "patience" through such strange (and perhaps knowingly paradoxical) determination as the following: "I will not be myself, nor have cognition / Of what I feel" (5.2.64–65). As the sense-reader imaginatively contemplates the paradox of refusing cognition to feeling, as if driving feeling back down to preconscious, sensory origins, the reader takes an important step further into the world of *Troilus and Cressida*. It is a world where skepticism and relativism, if not also cynicism, sometimes drive sense to become senseless and feeling to become, "To say the truth, true and not true" (1.2.98).

Making sense of Shakespeare requires that we note the manner in which Shakespeare rarely alludes to physical sensations devoid of emotive import. In *The Winter's Tale*, Leontes jealously observes his wife and his friend holding hands. Leontes tells us in an aside, "My heart dances, / But not for joy, not joy" (1.2.110–11). His heart literally leaps about in expression of his emotive agony. Similarly, however, making sense of Shakespeare requires that we note the manner in which Shakespeare may allude to emotions through a language of the body that deserves to be, at least sometimes, de-metaphored. Later in *The Winter's Tale*, Paulina exclaims:

> Woe the while!
> O, cut my lace, lest my heart, cracking it,
> Break too!
>
> (3.2.172–74)

We could take Paulina's reference to her "heart" as equivalent only to "strong feelings" and the whole expression as equivalent to, no more than, saying "I am extremely upset!" But then we would have refused the somatic invitation of Shakespeare's poetry. Even more blatantly metaphoric references to the heart might be usefully somaticized, moreover, as when Autolycus sings, "A merry heart goes all the day, / Your sad tires in a mile-a" (4.3.123–24). To translate in one's mind "heart" to "disposition" is to begin the gradual, dispiriting crawl out of poetry's bodily home into the desert of abstraction. Physically, a merry heart might be a well-conditioned muscle that beats lightly and freely without strain or pushing, easily sending plenty of blood to invigorate dancing limbs. Just as one may keenly sense, through imagination, the feeling of an incipient shift in posture, a tumescent member, a growling stomach, or a clucking tongue, so also one may imaginatively sense the feeling of such a merry heart.

Shifting focus now from the visceral to the motoric, kinesthetic dimension of imagination, we can note choices available to readers when reading descriptions of characters' movements. When a Shakespearean character describes his own movements, one may choose to view the character externally, through the mind's eye, or one may choose to perform the movements described, through the mind's access to motor memories. Or one can switch between the two views. When Falstaff, for example, complains at Gadshill of having to walk (rather than ride his horse), one can choose either to view Falstaff at a distance or to imagine being very fat and trying to perform the actions of which he speaks:

> If I travel but four foot by the square further afoot, I shall break my wind. . . . Eight yards of uneven ground is three score-and-ten miles afoot with me. . . . I'll not bear mine own flesh so far afoot again for all the coin in thy father's Exchequer.
>
> (*1 Henry IV*, 2.2.12–35)

The advantage of one's objective, distanced, visual imagining is the accompanying disengagement, scorn, and laughter at a Falstaff so imagined. The advantage of one's subjective, internalized, kinesthetic imagination is the intimate, physical knowledge of Falstaff's sensations, which can both fuel one's humor at his expense and also provoke part of that empathy so essential to a fair reading of Falstaff's full humanity.

Even when one has little inclination to extend empathy, much less sympathy, to a Shakespearean character, one may find that kinesthetic imagination may radically vivify one's apprehension of a passage or scene. In *Cymbeline*, for example, the contemptible Cloten, dressed in Posthumus's clothes and intending to murder Posthumus and rape Imogen, imagines his own handsomeness:

> How fit his garments serve me! . . . I dare speak it to myself, for it is not vainglory for a man and his glass to confer in his own chamber—I mean, the lines of my body are as well drawn as his; no less young, more strong.
>
> (4.1.2–10)

Without a performative reading in which one senses the postural pride and self-absorbed preening motions Cloten must be making—running his hands down his ungainly body and flexing his unlikely muscles at "more strong"—one may miss his psychopathic, maniacal delusion as to the very nature of his own being.

Even when a described or implicit motion is vague and invites swift conflation of varied possibilities to sight, a reader's slower testing of kinesthetic possibilities may yield increased understanding of meanings those possibilities convey. In one of the most famous passages in all Shakespeare, for example, Lear responds to the death of his beloved daughter, Cordelia:

> And my poor fool is hanged! No, no, no life?
> Why should a dog, a horse, a rat have life,
> And thou no breath at all? Thou'lt come no more,
> Never, never, never, never, never!
> Pray you, undo this button. Thank you, sir.
> Do you see this? Look on her, look, her lips,
> Look there, look there!
>
> (*Lear*, 5.3.311–17)

To test out in one's performative reading manifold possibilities of what button Lear means, why he cannot undo it, why he wants it unbuttoned, what he is looking at when he says "this," what he means by each "there," and how he moves in response to each reference is to explore within one's very nerves and pulse the vast range of feeling between Lear's perhaps bleak and despairing or perhaps hopeful and heaven-glancing demise, including mixtures thereof.

Despite some obvious attractions, such physically engaging readings of Shakespeare's images as we have been developing here are likely to be resisted and for a variety of reasons. In the next chapter I will consider these reasons.

3

Resistance to Shakespearean Sense-Reading

RESISTANCE TO SHAKESPEAREAN SENSE-READING INVOLVES FEARS OF PAINFUL, AS WELL AS PLEASURABLE, CONCRETE EXPERIENCE

I HAVE ARGUED IN THE INTRODUCTION THAT SHAKESPEARE ACCOMMO-
dates abstract and concrete senses to each other and that we need
to read Shakespeare with special kinesthetic and proprioceptive
sense-itivies to appreciate how he connects aesthetic and social
values. I argued in the first chapter that we need physically to
sense aural patterns of Shakespeare's sound-play if we hope to
move beyond abstract understanding toward concrete and rite-
centered experience, and I argued in the second chapter that we
may add to visual imagination varied forms of nonvisual imagination (mainly visceral and kinesthetic) to enhance our responses
to Shakespeare's nonvisual imagery. Sense-reading makes new
sense of Shakespeare in body as well as mind, in a balanced union
of the two.

If I were to assume that my arguments and examples have persuaded general assent among my readers, I might conclude that
my basic point has been made briefly and that I could better present that point in an article or chapter contributing to a longer
work. One impediment to such a conclusion stands in the observation that I want to instill in readers not a single, discursive imperative—"in reading Shakespeare, consult your sensory
registers of experience"—but rather a complex set of attitudes
and practices that are foreign to the "normal" set in our culture.
In order to convert my idea into action, into changed attitudes
and practices among readers, I need to challenge a number of
generally accepted assumptions concerning relations of mind and
body, ratios of the senses, the nature of images, how readers can
and should read, social functions of art, and the politics of inter-

preting, criticizing, and teaching literature. I need to blend argument and example extensively enough to affect readers below the level of abstractable concepts. If I hope to change reading habits, I need to provide repeated lessons that might work upon "second natures."

I know from years of teaching that ideas requiring practical application may be applauded in the abstract yet resisted in concrete use. "Resistance" is of course famous in psychotherapy. The client who begins a course of therapy may revel in the first days' understanding of her problems. Weeks later, she may find frustration in her seeming inability to change, to *do* the good she "knows." Teachers and students of all behavior-changing arts walk familiarly in such shadows between desire and act, intention and accomplishment. Much more than "laziness" or a distasteful "effort" of accomplishment may be involved. In the case of sense-reading Shakespeare, a host of resistant forces militate defeat.

Imagine, if possible, a more or less typical person in our culture, say, a student, reading aloud to herself or himself such passages from Shakespeare as these:

methinks he should stand in fear of fire, being burnt i' the hand for stealing of sheep
(*2 Henry VI*, 4.2.60–61)

The gods are deaf to hot and peevish vows,
They are polluted offerings, more abhorred
Than spotted livers in the sacrifice
(*Troilus and Cressida*, 5.3.16–18)

He that will think to live till he be old,
Give me some help!
[*Servants hold the chair as Cornwall grinds out one of Gloucester's eyes with his boot.*]
O cruel! O you gods!
(*Lear*, 3.7.72–73)

Anger's my meat. I sup upon myself,
And so shall starve with feeding.
(*Coriolanus*, 4.2.52–53)

How intensely would such a reader be willing to imagine and render such lines? Would she invoke a sensation of red-hot iron in her hand? The smell and touch of spotted livers as well as their look? The precise tenor and volume of Gloucester's agonizing "O"? The innard-consuming rage of Volumnia? I think not, for, beyond the senses of pain and disgust invoked, lie dread intimations of mortality. The power of literary emotion to reveal just how sensitive and vulnerable one truly feels depends upon one's willingness to accept such emotion as part, even if only part, of oneself. Here, aesthetic distance must not equal refusal to accept the emotion.

Even "sweet" lines may be too dangerous to feel completely, to test upon the pulse of one's personal reality. Does "love is not love which alters when it alteration finds" (*Sonnet* 116.2) apply to alterations of divorce or of emergent spouse abuse? What are divorced and abused readers likely to feel in response to such a line? If, having found alteration, their love is altering, can none of them claim ever to have loved? How concretely can one imagine a full range of "alterations" and still receive the comfort of the lines? In truth, much of Shakespeare teaches mutability. Much of Shakespeare "smells of mortality" (*Lear* 4.6.133), yet few of us, I suspect, share Lear's willingness to face and endure the fact.

Fear and disdain of physical self-consciousness—with concomitant sensations of pain, disgust, and gut sadness as interoception (visceral sensing) which tells us so much about how we feel—such fear and disdain often promote a sad view of the body as threatening to "interfere" with mentalized, abstracting, higher life. While of course emotions and feelings generally involve mental functioning, invoke "mind," emotions and feelings often seem remote from cognitive and volitional states of consciousness. "A cognitive emotion is a paradox because the conceptual terrain where 'belief' finds its home differs vastly from that of 'emotion'."[1] Emotions and feelings, in their powers to agitate, remind us that our controls over sensations and even perceptions remain limited. Emotions are both determined and constructed, but "if cognition is viewed as part of emotional experience per se, then it becomes more difficult to examine cause-effect relations among cognitive and emotive processes."[2]

Even our awareness of sensory and neural activity within our bodies appears minuscule compared to the gigantic amount of such activity taking place below that awareness. Our bodies largely live their own lives, and emotions remind us of that, often flooding and taking over our attention, will, and peace.

Emotions produced by art experience, "aesthetic emotions," if you will, invoke physiological changes in pulse rate, glandular activity, body temperature, skin conductance, and, often overt behavior such as laughing, crying, facial expressions, changes in posture, obvious erotic arousal, and the like. They are real emotions. Psychologists and therapists, as we all know, may suggest "purely imaginative" exercises of meditation or reading literature or film-watching to intensify or change "real-life" emotions. Still, emotions of art, like emotions of life, in their full range prove not only enlightening and peaceful but also dark and disturbing. They make us feel physical changes. They unleash the power of unconscious or repressed feelings. They force us to confront terrors of the world, including our fears of varied pleasures as guilt-inducing, chaotic, or overwhelming. They frighten us through their very physicality, their unknown and uncontrollable sensations and energies. And so, in our fear and disdain, we resist or try desperately to control them along with the rest of our bodily life. (Throughout this book, I employ eclectic *theories* of emotion, often combining physiological emphases with causal, valuative, cognitive, and other emphases to underline our resistant fears of the dying and uncontrollable body.)

Fear and disdain of the physical make "modern people see food and body as resources to be controlled. Thus food and body signify that which threatens human mastery."[3] Shakespeare shows how even premodern persons such as Coriolanus and his father-mother Volumnia struggle frantically, manfully, to master the mystery of bodily needs and appetites. Such "mastery" of the body inevitably invokes gendered discourse, for many men "have their masculine identity to gain by being estranged from their bodies and dominating the bodies of others . . . [deeming] serious thought separate from an embodied subject in history."[4] The body as "authorless text," however, cannot be contained or dominated by rationality, by philosophy: "The body is enigmatic because it is not a creation of the mind."[5] The body tells the mind what time is, how loss and decay are to feel. No wonder the mind resists.

We are not brains in a vat. Our "lower" bodies respond with complex kinesthetic and visceral sensations to what we read, no doubt to abstract ideas but particularly to concrete images, expressions of emotion, paralinguistic evocations of pitch, pause, pace, and tone, and rhythms of many kinds. The intellect, let us concede again, rarely works exclusively with the abstract; the intellect participates in feelings, and feelings participate in intellectual thought. In reading Shakespeare, as in life generally, we can engage a range of sensations and activities of rational sense-making. Still, the truth remains that sensing pain, vulnerability, decay, and mortality evokes resistance. Such resistance, moreover, often takes the form of excessive abstraction, the conversion of concrete, discomforting experience to relatively painless, detached notation. Jack Cade's burnt hand loses consequence; Cassandra's evocation of "spotted livers" clicks off into the *idea* of pollution; Gloucester suffers and we do not; Volumnia's self-consuming appetite makes little claim upon our own.

In the face of a general human tendency toward such numbing disengagement, one needs to seek out voices of encouragement. To my voice, I will add the voices of others. Listen. "We do not mean that thought should use no abstractions, but that when abstractions are allowed to usurp the place that belongs to what can only be called the body of the world, they no longer appear as vital components of thought, but as *mere* abstractions."[6] If we hope to regain for ourselves and share with others an appreciation for the sensational and emotive powers of literature, powers that inhere within its claims to effective and original thought, then we must return to the concrete, to what is concrete in our experience of literature. Otherwise we may too closely resemble persons "lost in a world of lifeless abstractions," who have been "seduced by the abstract": they "serve as a warning and parable—of what happens to a science which eschews the judgmental, the particular, the personal, and becomes entirely abstract and computational":

> the concrete is elemental—it is what makes reality "real," alive, personal and meaningful. All of this is lost if the concrete is lost. . . . In particular, as physicians, as therapists, as teachers, as scientists, we are invited, indeed compelled, towards *an exploration of the concrete* [emphasis in original].[7]

MEETING RESISTANCE TO SHAKESPEAREAN SENSE-READING: THE GENERAL CHALLENGE IN EDUCATION

Education, especially "higher" education, teaches resistance to sense-reading. Education eschews the body and the concrete as inferior to abstraction in the same way that spirit in Western thought eschews the body and things of this world as inferior to nonmaterial forms. Still, "if one single formula were capable of curing the ills of our present methods of education, it would be this physical formula: bring the bodies back."[8] What is meant is that persons can work to think of themselves not just from the outside in but also from the inside out. With persistence, students can learn not to think of themselves only in terms of social roles, group affinities, and power differentials.

Allowing for the capacity of all educational proposals and programs to become routinized and authoritarian, would not one appropriately desire to imagine Shakespeare teachers encouraging students in reading and performing Shakespeare with sense-trained emotive and physical response as well as to imagine Shakespeare teachers discussing the ideological status of characters, issues, plays? Within an educational reinsistence upon sense-reading, we might, to be sure, occasionally hear paeans, such as the following, which sound almost as apocalyptically frightening as liberating:

> if the sounds of the words and the rhythms of the language are felt, Shakespeare's voice will call to the voices of eloquence that live in everyone, encouraging their hearts and lungs and resonance. His voice is the voice of individuality, of iconoclasm. . . . The most important element is that Shakespeare provides a speaking language in which vast pain can be articulated—the *lacrimae rerum*. And his articulation is as accessible to the educationally underprivileged as it is to the college graduate. Time and again I have seen, heard and felt Shakespeare's words enter and restore power to a boy or a girl, a woman or a man, whose sense of worth has been obliterated by childhood abuse, social inequality, or racial bigotry. This happens *not when they read Shakespeare, not when they hear Shakespeare, but when they speak the words themselves* [emphasis in original].[9]

Such mystical allegiance to a necessarily progressive, self-esteem-raising Shakespeare could smack of group brainwashing as much as of individual liberation, but the connection of physical engagement in Shakespeare's language with a sensed appropriation of personal power remains challenging.

The full, quirky, surprising, ungovernable life of a particular student's or reader's body as it may respond to Shakespeare stands as a difficult, seemingly asocial center of energy. No wonder students, teachers, and readers fear the strangeness of consulting internal registers of perception. Our bodies generally stand opposed to established educational tasks:

> The conforming child who turns away from his body will find all kinds of signposts (parental injunctions, school routine) to tell him from hour to hour where he should be looking and what he should be thinking about. . . . But the experiences of the child who has learned to tune in on his body cannot be so easily homogenized. The sensations coming from his body are his own, they shift and fluctuate, and they have their own unique patterns. Even when he is in places where others are telling him pretty much what he should be experiencing (in school, for example), his body feelings buffer what is coming from 'out there' and add a unique individual coloring to it all. The child who has discovered and seeks the rich experiences of his own body is already embarked on a more individualistic trajectory. He is already adopting a style of perception that favors seeing things differently— and more originally.[10]

To assess the persuasiveness of these claims for the value of bodily experience, imagine how the student described above could respond to a specific assignment in Shakespeare study. The assignment asks her to focus upon passages in *The Merchant of Venice* concerning Antonio's feelings for Bassanio, particularly as the danger of forfeiting upon the bond begins to appear. What may Antonio be feeling? The student pauses over the following speech by Salerio:

> I saw Bassanio and Antonio part.
> Bassanio told him he would make some speed
> Of his return; he answered, "Do not so.
> Slubber not business for my sake, Bassanio,
> But stay the very riping of the time;   40
> And for the Jew's bond which he hath of me,
> Let it not enter in your mind of love.
> Be merry, and employ your chiefest thoughts
> To courtship and such fair ostents of love
> As shall conveniently become you there."   45
> And even there, his eye being big with tears,
> Turning his face, he put his hand behind him,
> And with affection wondrous sensible
> He wrung Bassanio's hand; and so they parted.
>
>   (2.8.36–49)

Not only might such a student wonder at hints that acting for Antonio's sake would "slubber" (muddy, despoil, daub, make dirty) such "business" as courtship—wonder if or why Antonio feels Bassanio's care of Antonio as dirtying his suit to Portia. Not only might she remember that Gratiano employed the term "ostent" a bit earlier in the play (2.2.187: "well studied in a sad ostent") to mean *play-acting* and that the term goes back to physical stretching (possibly here suggesting love action)—as if Antonio could feel pain at the thought of Bassanio's love for Portia and an accompanying need to portray it as only a "convenient" show. Such a student might also physically try out the action of putting a hand behind herself to wring another's hand "with affection wondrous sensible." She might then discover how uncertain will be one's posture and how fluid one's feelings while performing that movement, how many possibilities there are, ranging from stooped humility to grimacing and bent-legged pain to martyred uprightness and so on. The vast mystery of Antonio's nature, orientation, mood, and desire would then have been more nearly appropriated in a truly personal manner. Antonio's double-signaling in the passage—"Oh, you go have a happy time; don't think of how much I am suffering"—would find physical embodiment and so become ten times more memorable as well as ponderable than if it went by in abstract notation.

No teacher can definitively describe meanings of Antonio's strange gesture or the workings of thousands of cues in the text upon an individual reader's body, emotions, thoughts. Only at the level of high abstraction, moral teaching, or ideological generality can the meaning of Antonio become narrowed into "merely faithful friend," "homosexual rival with Portia for Bassanio's love," "wealthy capitalist ready to buy Bassanio's love," "Caucasian Christian martyring himself at hands of demonized Jew," and so on. We need to recognize the appropriative, liberative powers of the body "to discard class merely by performing calisthenics," or "to absorb the artifacts of culture into its own interior matter, its self-experience of gender and race, its endless separation into parts (hands, tongue, skin) and reacquisition of wholeness."[11] Shakespeare belongs to our bodies as much as to our minds, or, to put it more realistically, we cannot know Shakespeare except through the integration of body and mind. In studying Shakespeare, as in much education: "Any attempt to disassociate ourselves from our bodies should be immediately rejected." As the body absorbs cultural artifacts into its interior matter, the body helps to digest and rework relatively inert words and images into human form, personal thought and feeling, individual life. "The images the old stories give . . . these are meant to be taken slowly into the body."[12]

The student depicted above as being unusually sensitive to his or her body signals might be called a "bodyreader." That student's individuating and creative powers are often dampened, in the course of education, by definitions of useful knowledge as abstract, discursive, and public, by misdefined ratios of the senses, and by pervasive dullings of body-sense. How does the first effect, the abandonment of personal knowing, come about? One explanation goes like this:

> The bodyreader who is still alive and well in many elementary classrooms where language experience, directed reading-thinking activities, and phonics provide a rich and varied sensory and interpersonal ground for learning soon gives way to the reader who discriminates the private self from the public text. Meaning is either in here or out there. When it is in here it is identified with feeling, sensuality, and imagination that cannot be communicated and cannot be negotiated into any statement that deserves or attains the status of knowledge. When it is out there, it belongs to the text and to the teacher, and understanding means that the reader stands under the text, under the gaze of the teacher, and learns to anticipate and repeat the interpretation that is an index of comprehension.[13]

Theories of human intellectual development such as Piaget's may be interpreted as privileging "higher" order abstraction and formal operations over concretion and sensory reference to the point that healthy relations obtainable between emotion and intellect are endangered.[14] "Is emotion, then, any different from intellect? The two are very closely related. There is a great deal of intellect in emotion and emotion in intellect; however, whereas people deal intellectually with events and matters at a distance from themselves, once the self is involved, emotion is the faculty in use."[15] Despite the undeniable significance (and, often, pleasure) of abstract thought, Shakespeare endures not primarily because he appeals to such thought but because he appeals to bodily feelings and the emotions organized upon them; an educational system that "teaches" Shakespeare but fails to honor and explore that fact is disreputable.

Sense-Reading Activates the "Lower" Senses, Senses Often Denigrated by Educators

The sometimes invidious distinctions in learning between what is "out there" and what is "in here" or between intellectual "distance" and emotional connection to a "self" are fostered partly by learned, or mis-learned, ratios of the senses. We are generally taught in our culture that sight and hearing—the brain-level senses—are vastly more important than other senses and deserve to be educated at the expense of attention to lower than brain-level senses. Sight and hearing allow the world to be held at a distance; we can see and hear far-off things and experience their distance rather than the "in-hereness" of retinal stimulation or tympanic vibration. Sight in particular seems to go out from us, as Renaissance discussions of eye-beams suggest. We think of sight and insight as penetrating their objects, and "we tend 'to reach through the sensation to the object' when we perceive things, instead of heeding the way the sensations present themselves to consciousness, or attending to the differences between sensations in different modalities."[16] Hearing is more inflowing though it enables us to triangulate and guess the distance of objects separate from our bodies. The other senses, as conventionally defined, take place near the surface of our bodies. Smell can give us information about surrounding matter at varied distances, but we also "feel" smells with our noses and mouths and throats. Taste and touch require our bodily contact with more palpably felt matter. Unfortunately, we tend to be taught as children that the fifth sense, touch (lowest in physical placement and in common esteem), involves primarily the surface of our bodies. We think we "touch" mainly with our fingers and other parts of our skin. The whole internal dimension of touch is largely ignored; indeed, "touch" seems hardly the right word for the gamut of internal registers we all possess.

It comes as something of a truism to observe that "our particular Western culture stresses sight and hearing, while touch, taste, smell, and kinesthesia are grossly undereducated."[17] Notice the addition here of at least "kinesthesia" to touch. Actually, we need to reconceive our senses, especially "touch," to include a host of internal registries such as receptors for pressure, heat, and pain, the proprioceptive sense of body position, the visceroceptive sense of internal organ states, information from the autonomic nervous system, and so on. "Scientific investigators, freed of the restraint of conforming to an outmoded world view, can now describe a number of major sensory systems in addition to the five that had been so firmly rooted in thought since the Renaissance."[18] No longer need we privilege the "conquering" and "male" sense of sight over the "homey" and "female" senses of smell, taste, and touch; no longer need we imagine or pretend that our interoceptive senses are largely unconscious, inactive, or remote.[19] In reading, all our senses can come into play, and, when they do, our reading becomes that much more lively, feelingful, momentous.

The internal sensoria register lively patterns of activity during the reading process. It is a "fact that silent reading is accompanied by electrical activity in muscles required in the production of speech sounds, though no oral speech is directly observable."[20] If a silent reader devotes part of attention during reading to perceiving activity in laryngeal muscles, such activity will be distinctly sensed. Feeling follows focus. Sensate focusing, in particular, when combined with emotional arousal, turns attention inward and enhances esthesia, the ability to feel sense impressions.[21]

In addition to the subvocalizations and the "heightened covert oral behavior intimately associated with the performance of linguistic activities,"[22] reading invokes complex eye-muscle movements that probably provide kinesthetic codings or translations of motions described in texts.[23] The same sort of empathetic transcoding may be true for eye movements and postural shifts of spectators at a play. Researchers can measure changes in rates of heartbeat and respiration, in skin conductance, and in muscle tension as readers respond to successive images and narrated events in texts. "Instructions to imagine an emotional event or feeling state prompt more than the activation of semantic memory; they initiate processing of associated efferent information [carrying impulses from the central nervous system to effectors, nerve-endings that activate glands and muscles]. Even if overt responding is inhibited, such processing produces effector activity which is detectable in psychophysiological measurements."[24] Such results should go without saying since we all know that such grossly observable behaviors in response to reading as laughter or tears must overlie a full range of subovert physiological responses in the "lower" body.

Less obviously, researchers have shown that readers can be trained either to intensify or deintensify measurable somatic responses to written images. In one experiment:

> Groups are administered imagery scripts and instructed to imagine vividly the events described. Subsequently, they are asked to recall their images and to report to a trainer all the details of the experience they can remember. The trainer then reinforces the subjects specifically for response details (i.e., actions the subject was performing, visceral and somatic responding), priming him or her with instructions to include more such material in subsequent images. In a series of studies, we have contrasted this training procedure with a type of training more oriented to the "mind's eye" view of imagery. In this latter procedure, subjects are reinforced postimagery for only stimulus detail (i.e., the characteristics of the external scene as presented to the receptors). . . . The results strongly supported our primary hypothesis. That is, response subjects showed greater physiological activity during imagery than did stimulus-trained subjects. . . . Training amplified response, increasing the strength of the subject's efferent signal to a level that could be readily measured.[25]

That is, emotional activity increases when not just the thinness and silence of sight dominate reading but when teachers encourage whole-body response. We need, however, a new vocabulary for such "imaging," sometimes called "narrative imaging" to suggest a reader's concrete perceptions of situation, action, and relations as they inspire full bodily empathy and emotive response. Perhaps we need a new term such as "somage" (Latin *soma* plus *ago)* or "somatic image" to stand for the internal bodily imaging or body-take we experience in response to the complete range of what is now called "imagery," including material that appeals to any of our senses.

The researchers cited above also grouped subjects who had not been "trained" to respond to imagery and then presented fear-inducing texts (depicting encounters with poisonous snakes) and anger-inducing texts (depicting unjust verbal abuse) in two ways, first, by reading the texts aloud, and second, by dramatizing them: the drama "generated heart-rate change in untrained subjects that was significantly greater than that shown by text-prompted imagery."[26] Thus the same words when enacted and not just read generally produce more palpable emotional response.

Other studies have shown that the mere act of focusing attention on bodily sensations as one reads or imagines can change levels of arousal, activity of the facial corrugator muscles, heart rate, and skin conductance and that persons who imagine vividly report relatively more intense emotional responses than do those who imagine poorly.[27]

Psychophysiological ingredients of attention in reading are of course extremely complex, invoking systems of arousal, activation, and effort. "Indeed, linguistic performance may vary as a function of arousal or attention systems."[28] It is not my purpose to advocate a single, selective focus of attention in reading Shakespeare, but rather to urge not only precise visual and aural imaging but also inner, visceral, and kinesthetic registry. Vision and hearing often produce, relative to the other senses, more abstract, more "refined" hedonic response in aesthetic experience; "it seems fair to say that those two senses are intrinsically the least affective."[29] We need to explore these currently more affective modalities while recognizing that "change in the *functions* of the different senses" may in time require that "the very distinction between distance and contact senses must be reconsidered."[30] Again, "abstraction" per se is not the enemy; "abstract concepts are the foundation for both imaginal and verbal experience."[31] Still, abstraction in reading (or criticism) that limits itself to a single mode of attention and selection may give up too much that is interesting in the reading experience. "In the process of abstraction one is always faced with the question of how much abstraction is possible while retaining the essence of the problem of interest."[32]

If we wish, then, to make the reading of Shakespeare (and other imaginative texts) vivid and memorable, we will alter our classroom allegiance to current sense ratios that favor the employment of sight so disproportionately to all other senses, and we will increase the proportion of classroom attention that goes to concrete features of text and response, as opposed to abstract ones. Not only do "people learn concrete words more easily than abstract ones," but also "people remember pictures more easily than concrete words, and actual objects more easily than pictures."[33] It behooves us as well to consider possible benefits of dwelling more intently on concrete and specific experience in the earlier stages of reading Shakespeare because that may render propositions and abstractions derived from such experience easier to learn and more memorable.[34]

Shakespeare amounts, finally, to behavior. Shakespeare cannot be abstracted as knowledge apart from behavior. "The only relations among objects that can be known are those resulting from the way in which we behave with respect to those objects."[35] Until we think of Shakespeare as our own, personal behavior, how can we hope, in Gloucester's words (*Lear*, 4.6.149), to "see it feelingly"?

Tragically, the teaching of imaginative literature seems to be getting more, not less, abstract. Even attention to visual images has eroded. "In literature classes, a context in which imaging was once valued, it is rarely advocated. . . . [T]here is little support in literature classes for the production of visual imagery by the college student," and this remains true despite the fact that "the visual modality of imagery is only one among a number of sensory modes that come into play during reading; auditory and muscular imagery are others."[36] Still, even though readers' careful attention to imagery aids memory, makes spatial description more clear, concretizes the fictional world and makes it more immediate and comprehensible, gives the reader greater control of the fictional situation, adds pleasure to reading, and probably helps teachers improve reading instruction,[37] there are further opposed factors (connected with our hierarchy of the senses) that help account for antisensory abstractions of our Shakespeare classroom and reading practice.

For one thing, "a successful career as a student calls for endless hours of sitting (with body almost immovable) while absorbing information from books. The body is largely superfluous to the whole scholastic enterprise."[38] In one study, researchers found that

> boys who went on to become good students and invested in intellectuality were typically afraid of the body world in their younger years. Their parents instilled in them anxiety about potential body damage, and their teachers noted that they avoided activities in which there was the possibility of getting hurt. In other words, intellectuality and body security were found to be in opposition in boys. One could interpret the intellectuality as a compensation.[39]

By organizing our senses into a false hierarchy of "lower" and "higher" and by privileging the abstract affinities of sight and

concept-making, our educational systems have rendered incalcu-
lable harm.

Resistance to appropriate sense-reading of Shakespeare will
not diminish, furthermore, until the teaching of such sense ratios
and of their meaning changes. Particularly in the teaching of art
experience (including the study of Shakespeare and other imaginative writers), students need to learn that the full interactive
medium includes their bodily sensations of tone and visceral feeling, sensations that must be felt below the neck. Students need
to understand that "almost all persons in our society have lost
the proprioception of large areas of their body"; genuine and
strong feelings involve and aggregate within our organs, muscles,
and nerves as they interact with our minds, and it is for this reason that "the important part of the psychology of art is not in . . .
the critical consciousness, it is (where the psychoanalysts do not
look for it) in the concentrated sensations and the playful manipulations of the material medium" including the responder's
body.[40] Such pervasive denigrations of "lower" bodily senses as
are outlined above achieve specially pernicious effects when combined with the particular, culturally bound habits of silent, private reading that most of us employ. Indeed, a profound silencing
and privatizing of the whole reading process followed upon the
invention of printing.[41] All readers used to read aloud and no
doubt conceived of reading stories somewhat in the fashion of
oral audiences who "clapped and danced and sang collectively, in
response to the chanting of the singer," but this sort of interactive, full-body responsiveness disappeared with the introduction
of typographic culture that changed reading to a visual, sound-
less, and relatively incorporeal process, effecting "a shift in the
ratio of the senses."[42] Whereas Shakespeare's style carries a
"heavy oral residue in its use of epithets, balance, antithesis, for-
mulary structures, and commonplace materials," not to mention
its incessant concretizing of abstractions, and whereas "oral
memory has a high somatic component" while "vision, the dis-
secting sense" often takes us out and away from our bodies,[43] our
own silent, visual, nonoral readings tend to discount and immobi-
lize full-bodied response. We are even taught by grammatologists
that written texts cannot speak and are hostile to spoken language.

The shift from oral to print culture thus further unbalances the
ratio of our senses in favor of sight and promotes resistance to

sense-reading. Partly motivating such a shift, however, lie bodily fears, as noted above, of vulnerability and pain. These fears, together with anxiety against uncontrollable excitement and emotion, assure that resistance to sense-reading will not easily give way.

The general educational challenge to sense-reading has been partially addressed by specific modes of literary interpretation and criticism. Next, we will look at two of those modes, note their own fashions of resistance to sense-reading, and place that continuing resistance within wider cultural contexts.

4

Further Contexts of Resistance to Shakespearean Sense-Reading

I HAVE OUTLINED THE GENERAL NATURE OF SHAKESPEAREAN SENSE-reading and of personal and educational resistance to it. I consider now how such resistance functions in oral interpretive and reader-response criticism, in Western aesthetic traditions, and in recent doctrines concerning social construction of identities.

ORAL INTERPRETERS URGE SOMATIC ENGAGEMENT IN READING LITERATURE, BUT LACK METHODS TO ACHIEVE SUCH ENGAGEMENT

Two groups of educators—oral interpreters and reader-response critics—appear poised to direct readerly attention to psychosomatic components of reading Shakespeare. The poise turns out, however, to offer more appearance than reality, for neither group provides a means to apprehend Shakespeare concretely.

Building upon centuries of educational attention to rhetoric and elocution, oral interpretation survived past the middle of this century in speech departments and margins of English departments, often under clouds of suspicion for overstressing unscientific elements of empathy, delivery, and emotional response. As late as 1966, oral interpretation was defended in these terms:

We prove the "truth" of literature both in our minds and, in the rhetorician's phrase, "on our pulses" as we make the full sum of responses which a sensitive reader can undergo when he opens to himself the situations in literature. Because the enjoyment of literature demands this full engagement, it has continued to be an important part of living. Because interpretation, too, demands this full engagement, it has continued to be an important pedagogical and critical instrument for studying literature. Unlike the silent student of literature, the oral interpreter seeks overtly to translate his engagement into vocal and bodily behavior, thereby sharpening his own engagement and encouraging his audience's empathic responses.[1]

Some oral interpreters cagily attacked doctrines of aesthetic disinterest and, by implication, the notion of an affective fallacy (the notion, as mentioned above, that accounting for one's subjective responses helps little to interpret or evaluate the literary object):

> We can judge the weight of a stone without lifting it because our visual response to the stone stimulates through our imagination (recollections of past experiences with stones) kinesthetic sensations of muscular tensions. . . . [M]ost of us still cling to the notion that we enjoy direct, lively sensations in life, but only the pale reflected image of those sensations in literature. Generally, however, we underestimate the power of literature to affect us directly. Indeed, we may not want it to move us deeply; in that case, when the images threaten to transcend their mirrorlike flatness and to become solidly real, we seek refuge in further abstractness; we become more "educated," and a consciousness of words as words replaces the images evoked by the words, and consequently we are at a further and safe remove from life.[2]

In a neo-Blakean manner, such oral interpreters insist: "the spiritual life is based on a sensory contact with the concrete world. . . . Even the sedentary practice of reading literature involves neuromotor responses of widespread intensity."[3] When attitudes are seen as dispositions to act, then naturally kinesthetic sensations are seen to derive from attitudes, and, further, "if the representation in words on the page is to be understood with the vividness and immediacy that characterized the author's impressions gained from the primary data of human experience, should not the symbolic movement of the reader, his motor activity as he responds to the text, assist the process of symbolic thinking which understanding of the literature necessitates?"[4]

Though they may theorize about bodily engagement in imaginative readings, these oral interpreters describe, nonetheless, little physiological response beyond muscular tensions. They provide few instructions for somatically engaging dramatic texts beyond attention to bodily movements suited to giving speeches and beyond general invocations to remember organic sensations.

Like most of us, perhaps, they seem unsure how to summon up a full range of somatic responses.

READER-RESPONSE CRITICS FAIL, SIMILARLY, TO EXPLORE PHYSICAL DIMENSIONS OF RESPONSE

What is meant by the reader's "response"? If "response" were defined in old-fashioned ways to mean the capacity of literature to enhance judgment or "prudence," then even a seemingly antiquated Tudor literary theory would be adequate to the concept:

> Historical knowledge of the humanist emphasis on the activity of reading and judging suggests an analogy with modern critical interest in "reader response"—if by this we understand the assumption that the meaning of a work of art does not exist as a timeless object, but is produced in the reader's interaction with the text, that is, in the act or reading. It also makes clear that reader-response criticism could only be seen as new and fashionable when the assumption of the humanist rhetorical tradition had been forgotten.[5]

Well, that's not quite true, for today's reader-response critics do include in their consideration textual, experiential, psychological, social, and cultural varieties of response. They do not consider, however, psychosomatic response to concrete features of literary texts.[6] Reader-response critics may pay generalizing lip-service to "a multitude of motor and sensory responses to the movement, rhythm, and imagery of the work,"[7] but they focus, as a rule, on other matters such as psychoanalytic concerns[8] and questions pointing away from the body: "How shall subjective feelings and motives be converted into publicly negotiable issues, and what knowledge does this conversion yield?"[9] Earlier stages in acts of reading remain unexplored; "those interested in literary response have, for the most part, deflected attention from the act itself to other things associated with it."[10]

That education in literature and drama might work in the other direction, teaching students how to feel, and feel more intensely, what goes on in their bodies in response to reading is a possibility rarely considered. The reader-response critic more likely assumes: "the bringing of a reading experience under conscious scrutiny requires its translation into verbal language."[11]

Readers, nonetheless, obviously can cry or laugh or feel tense or relaxed in response to Shakespearean drama and know they feel so without requiring their own verbal language to name their feelings; they can, moreover, exhibit their responsive tears, laughter, facial expressions, postural shifts, and other motions to the conscious scrutiny of others and use no verbal language. And readers can be taught to attend, consciously, to their nonverbal responses and even, as we have seen, to increase the measurable intensity of those responses. Indeed, to bring imaginative reading under full conscious scrutiny requires its translation into nonverbal language, into bodily languages of internal feeling and, sometimes, physical performance.

Some reader-response critics work in the general direction of reprivileging somatic response when they distinguish between "efferent" or referential, information-based reading and "afferent," "aesthetic" reading or "the full absorption in the rich experience of thought and feeling during the reading itself."[12] They may even deplore the loss of aesthetic sensibility among teachers of literature. "I would go so far as to assert that a large number of our literary critics have also lost the ability to read aesthetically. A great deal of academic criticism, even some that comes under the heading of 'reader-response criticism,' is efferent moralizing,"[13] When such reader-response critics turn their interest to nonverbal responses, however, they may too easily shrink back and introduce "a note of caution" that "articulation of nonlinguistic process is done through language" such as ticking off numbers on bipolar scales (tragic-happy, bitter-sweet) or writing poems about poems.[14] They also tend to fear that "focusing primarily on the unique, aesthetic response fails to account for the ways in which social and cultural forces constitute the meaning of response"[15] without considering the means and degrees to which such (preinterpretive) response, as argued above, itself creates and informs social and cultural forces.

Because so much reader-response criticism spends itself in refuting premises of text-centered criticism and in attempting to establish an equally disorienting reader-centered or "lectocentric" criticism unmindful of textual resistances to subjective associations, some have speculated "that reader-response criticism, on the evidence of its own premises, suggests that it has a past rather than a future."[16] Still, renewed or developing emphasis, in literary study, upon what actually may happen within readers as they read imaginative texts seems salutary when it amounts to less than a call for unthinking dominance of readers over texts. "Learning to read is learning that what is appearing in the text has everything to do with you and what you are doing on your end. Rather than learning to disengage from pragmatic events, literacy requires learning how to become purely and attentively entangled."[17] Yes, sometimes "reader-response theory is a gesture toward opening up dialogue with students and problematizing questions of authority,"[18] but the problems and entanglements need not be free-associational or privatizing or subjective in a pejorative sense. By carefully exploring relations among fictional images or actions and reader empathy (including somatic response), critics and teachers can help readers understand and alter sharable relations among perception, affect, and association.

Consider, for example, the following two extracts from Shakespearean dialogue:

> thou wouldst not think how ill all's here about my heart
> *(Hamlet, 5.2.210–11)*

> But wherefore could not I pronounce "Amen"?
> I had most need of blessing, and "Amen"
> Stuck in my throat.
> *(Macbeth, 2.2.35–37)*

On a stage I would see Hamlet accept misgivingly the challenge to duel Laertes or Macbeth declare his guilt over the murder of King Duncan. I might not think of these passages as containing imagery, in the conventional sense. I might also see on the stage or imagine in my own reading each character touch himself in a gesture alluding to heart or throat as invoked in the respective sentence. Certainly the most casual, superficial reading of each passage requires some notion of what each character is feeling and thinking. If I slow down for a moment, however, to ask myself what each character may physically feel in the moment and how that feeling may connect to the character's emotions and thoughts, then I embark upon a much more precisely empathic journey, a journey that intertwines objective and subjective elements.

Let us read Shakespeare in part to educate our senses, to make sense sensible. In the second chapter, I argued briefly that it sometimes aids in reading Shakespeare to take references to the "heart" as mixing the metaphorical and the literal. Extending the argument, it will be appropriate to note that, though greeting cards, songs, and ads may deaden heart-reference into the deadest of metaphors for "luv," Hamlet's references to his heart, for example, may be usefully perceived much more literally and materially. Not ten lines into the first scene of *Hamlet*, we hear of a man "sick at heart," and soon in the second we are warned of "a heart unfortified." Hamlet, himself, may be Shakespeare's most heart-conscious protagonist. In his first scene, he intones: "but break my heart, for I must hold my tongue." Yet when he does relieve his stuffed, full heart, he feels sullied to "like a whore, unpack my heart with words." Upon seeing the Ghost, he fears internal disintegration: "Hold, hold my heart!" and he longs to wear the commeddled blood and judgment of Horatio "in my heart's core, ay, in my heart of heart." He berates Guildenstern for seeking to pluck at the heart of his mystery, yet he fears that his heart may lose its "nature" when he talks to his mother whose heart he tries to "wring." Aboard the ship to England, Hamlet felt a "fighting" in his heart that kept him from sleep, and he goes to the duel with an illness, as we've seen, all "here about" his heart. This "heavy sickness in the heart" of Hamlet has been identified as one of "certain universal forms of visceral response."[19]

As Hamlet dies, he hopes that Horatio may hold him in his heart even as Hamlet's heart "cracks." In our or any age, readers find it disturbing to follow Hamlet toward a physical and emotional heart conflict. Still, to refuse the invitation of the words, "how ill all's here about my heart," toward somatic investigation means to miss an enlivening connection with Hamlet and his play. Does he touch near or draw a circle around his heart? If so, where? How large? Drawn how? With which arm? Which finger(s)? Why? What parts of the body are implicated in "here about"? What do they feel? Does a sense of illness spread out from the in-fighting heart to an "all"? To the general censure taking corruption from that particular fault? Or are we to imagine other aspects of the body—the humors or the vital spirits, perhaps—surrounding the heart with their own dis-ease? Compare Macbeth wishing to "cleanse the stuffed bosom of the perilous stuff / That weighs upon the heart" (5.3.46–47) or Lear, who would "anatomize" Regan to find "what breeds about her heart" (3.6.75–76) to make it so "hard."[20] What sort of "feeling" for life and its archetypal morbidity may be embodied here? How may the reader best physically attend to Hamlet's visceral depiction of heart illness? How might such attention change the reader psychosomatically? By such contemplation, Hamlet and the reader come more nearly to know each other, to merge in feeling and experience. This contemplation yields a way of learning that reaches below discursive concepts into sensate experience, into the anatomy of change, a readiness for dying and death more profound than an intellectualized formula. Shakespeare's sense of heart feelings encourages us to search below modern mechanistic reductions of heart function (a visualized pump). Through Shakespeare, we can reengage our internal sense of the feelingful heart, responding intimately to each motion and emotion.

Macbeth's unpronounced "amen," similarly, appeals little to our visual senses. We might imagine an actor swallowing or gesturing when he describes how "amen" stuck in his throat, but a radical shift to internal registry on the part of spectator or reader could allow a deeper exploration of the experience. Instead of explaining the passage away by moral abstraction—"he thus expresses guilt"—the reader could accept the invitation to enter its *sensations* of guilt in breath cut off, throat constricted, and "amen" (meaning, of course, "truly" and going back to root idea of "strengthen") literally "stuck" between lungs and mouth, body and head.

Macbeth was first imaged as spent swimmer about to "choke" his art (1.2.9); he "unseamed" Macdonwald to the "chops" and took off his head. When Macbeth imagines killing Duncan his function is "smothered" in surmise (1.3.142). Before he murdered Duncan, he mocked his own speech: "Words to the heat of deeds too cold breath gives" (2.1.62). The somatic image of amen stuck in the throat organically suits Shakespeare's kinesthetic rendering of Macbeth as one who unnaturally divides head and body, who employs "the best o' the cutthroats" (3.4.17), who cuts off heads and threatens hanging, who sees a ghost's bloody head and an apparitional head, who ends onstage himself only as a bloody severed head. Macbeth cooled and smothered the warm breath of life, counting it finally no more than the words of an idiot, "signifying nothing." When I work, through psychophysiological engagement, or sense-reading, to enter "his" life process or to psychosomatically imagine it mine, then I can find myself exploring authentically how my ambition may literally cut the access of my mind to my action. At the very least, I ground concretely in experience the discursive abstractions of moral interpretation.

Reader-response criticism would seem to provide an ideal stage upon which to play out creative attention to such bodywork. Reader-response critics tend, however, to show as little understanding of precise relations among perception, affect, and association as tends to be shown by other critics. Thus our physical display and correlates of affect are commonly oversimplified:

> Affect is a kind of raw emotion and is usually describable in very familiar terms—anger, love, jealousy, indignation, contentment, and so on. Such feelings are usually accompanied by physiological correlatives—changes in heartrate, perspiration, respiration, and the like—and they are easy to spot for that reason. Affect is also what most people are most likely to tell you about when you ask them how they are feeling about something. Affect is usually easy to notice and easy to communicate—provided one is willing in the first place, of course.[21]

On the contrary, physiological correlatives of affect may prove exceedingly subtle and manifold, extending far beyond pulse, sweat, and breath, and feeling anything but "raw." While reading the "amen" passage, for instance, I can cough, clear my throat, swallow, sense minuscule tightenings of thorax or eye muscles or stomach, catch my breath, or simply sense what "stuck" feels like in any of a thousand ways. Macbeth's behavior is known by my behavior. The halted "amen" amounts to behavior, not in itself an abstract conception. A reader's responses thus touch physically upon affect, and any verbal translation of it will only rawly approximate the physical condition.

RESISTANCE IN CRITICISM TO SENSE-READING OCCURS WITHIN WIDER POLITICAL CONTEXTS

Why should it matter whether oral interpreters or reader-response critics believe they can uncover agreed-upon "empathic responses" or affect that is "easy to communicate?"[22] It matters because such claims push us back toward the old abstract universals of discursive content in Shakespeare, particularly the content of festive, cooperative harmony. We risk dulling the edge of our personal freedom when we are asked to believe that Shakespeare's meter stimulates "the lower levels of the nervous system" in such as way as "to reinforce the cognitive functions of the poem, to improve the memory, and to promote physiological and social harmony"; we risk imposing our own response upon everyone's if we think that "our ethnocentric bias may be partly overcome by . . . recognition of the underlying universals in poetic meter."[23] "Recognition" of cross-cultural rhythmic patterns and responses in the abstract is very different from reinforcing physiological and social "harmony" within and among bodies of individual readers. We can hardly jump, with any logic, from the proposed cultural affinities to such suggestions of law-and-order "harmony." Strongly perceived poetic rhythms may be integral to social *protest* chanting or to individual persons marching to the beat of *different* drummers. One who responds forcefully to Shakespeare's rhythms may find the affect more, not less, difficult to know and to communicate.

To convert sense-reading of Shakespeare into the old "festive" social harmony actually resists the claims of sense-reading itself. To participate in Helena's metrically healing rites for the French King may well lead me as a spectator to experience how profoundly "she" destabilizes power relations of gender and social class in the play. It may also lead me to perceive vividly how a boy actor of Helena's part can recuperate the old relations of gender (her success is really a man's) or how the ritual healing serves finally a regressive marital order (Helena will have to serve Bertram in their marriage).

A performance of *All's Well* may promote, then, conservative social norms, or it may promote progressive ones, just as rituals of many kinds may serve structure or antistructure, the current social order or a more creative reorganization.[24] Perplexingly, both ends may be served together. In the same fashion, making sense of Shakespeare by attending to bodily responses could lend itself to conservative functions, radical functions, or both. These ideas (of recuperation and regression) may of course precede, accompany, or follow a temporal experience of reading or hearing Helena's rhythmic incantation. Individual readers or hearers will move through a wide array of combinations in arousal and dearousal, excitement and sedation, and it would seem foolish to imagine that a "rhythmic" element in Helena's chant could be separated from all the other sensuous and cognitive appeals of her speech and then made to play a wholly independent part in causation of response.

Devoting more attention to sensory components of response to Shakespeare could lead some practitioners toward reactionary uniformities of speaking, feeling, performing, appreciating. I concede that such a result is rightly to be feared. Such fear borders the argument "that the unification of aesthetics and politics should be resisted rather than welcomed—not because aesthetics is an unimportant aspect of liberated society, but because the aesthetic practice cannot be trusted to contribute to the realization of a liberated environment."[25] Still, I refuse to translate such anxiety into a reason to cease exploring the body's role in nominally "aesthetic" response to Shakespeare or other art. The struggle of ordinary people not only to control but to understand and enjoy their own bodily life must accompany, if not precede, any genuine or widespread social liberation. Though Western history finds itself replete with that precise struggle, the struggle remains in its formative stages. Coming to our senses seems to be the last thing we dare to do. Yet many great artists such as Shakespeare demand no less for their appreciation.

No doubt, Shakespeare's art, like most art, serves varied social and individual functions. Even bio-aesthetic response to Shakespeare cannot be reduced successfully to ritual coordinates of group cohesion and survival, to "fellow-feeling," or to psychobiological empathy. Shakespeare's intractable ambiguities arouse and calm us as much as his formal art and thematic solutions do the same. "This kind of alertness to the strange and unexplained as compared to the familiar (and therefore presumably safe) has obvious biological survival value,"[26] both on social and individual levels, but the alertness stimulated by Shakespeare may also provoke alternative waves of fear and ecstasy, of thoughtful agitation and meditative awareness, in body-consciousness. Behind comic celebrations of familial and social reproduction lie tragic fears of individuated death, fears muted in turn by intimations of life extension through love or fame or art or spiritual survival, intimations shadowed in turn by the primacy of ever-aging temporal sense. Shakespeare's master theme of mutability plays itself out by exploring joys and limits of catharsis, of bearing the burden of the time. Not just through theatrical performance but through individual reading, Shakespeare daringly displays how it feels and what it means to be alive and making sense through fallible yet miraculous senses.

In order to read and study Shakespeare sensuously, however, and in order to overcome personal or social resistance to sensory readings, a reader needs to find authority for reassociating cognitive and bodily functions. Such a reader can hardly proceed before she or he achieves the working belief that body equals mind in value and that rational sense feeds upon, even as it informs, bodily sense. What can foster such achievement?

RESISTANCE TO SENSE-READING INVOKES WESTERN TRADITIONS OF CONTEMPT FOR THE BODY AND TRADITIONS OF ICONOCLASM

Histories of sensory repression in the West appear infinitely diverse. Just how Judaic notions of vertical ascent, Greek dualism of body and mind, Roman contempt for the body, and Christian salvationism intertangle to influence Renaissance and modern attitudes toward the body need not, however, trouble us here.[27] Suffice it to observe that "the fear of losing an identity that one feels is connected to the body"[28] must motivate appeals to nonbodily identity such as Shakespeare's Sonnet 146: "Poor soul, the center of my sinful earth . . . Shall worms eat up thy charge? Is this thy body's end?" Though Shakespeare expresses traditional contempt of the body, he nonetheless follows an alter-sacral instinct to embody soulful abstractions. Yes, we hear in Shakespeare such expressions as:

> I do betray
> My nobler part to my gross body's treason
>
> (*Sonnet* 151.5–6)

> Not sleeping, to engross his idle body,
> But praying, to enrich his watchful soul
>
> (*Richard III*, 3.7.76–77)

> I will not do 't,
> Lest I surcease to honor mine own truth,
> And by my body's action teach my mind
> A most inherent baseness
>
> (*Coriolanus*, 3.2.120–23)

In context, however, dense ambiguity surrounds such expressions. The larger context of Shakespeare's life was devoted to sensory entertainments of theater, the aural pleasures of honey-tongued verses, onstage embodiments of ghosts, gods, goddesses, and spirits, and the whole "cherishing of particularity which is so remarkable a feature of these plays' poetry." All these suggest how far appreciation of Shakespeare must remain from disembodied, abstractive knowledge. Cutting against the grain of Western spiritism, Shakespeare's "is a new kind of poetry, attentive to the minutiae of natural life at earth and sea level."[29]

Not only throughout Shakespeare, but throughout the Renaissance, images evolved "from a conceptual to a perceptual representation of reality," and the concern for realism "can be traced," for example, "in the evolution of the drawings of the heart: at first it is just delineated; then shadowing gives it relief; later the main artery is shown; finally it becomes the gory palpitating organ that we know."[30] A dark side of such anatomizing realism inheres in doubts that delving into physiological substrates brings us closer to sources or order. It is a despairing Lear who believes that to "anatomize" Regan would be to look for her "hard" heart (3.6.75–77). No cause of such psychophysiological hard-heartedness could be found in the amoral natures of Regan, Goneril, and Edmund. Nor could it be found in the nature dissected by Renaissance anatomists such as Vesalius who sadly removed more life from his artistically posed standing figures as he examined them ever more closely: often, "the anatomist would like to insure the morality of the world, but ends up confirming its essential materiality."[31] Shakespeare's anatomists, such as Lear and Jaques (in As You Like It, 2.7.56, 5.4.184), pursue their searches for life in matter much farther and more ambiguously than that, however, and they, like Shakespeare taken in toto, end up only hinting at an animist's hope for unquenchable sparks of divinity in all loved things, all subjects of gratitude: "Look there, look there!" (Lear, 5.3.317; compare As You Like It, 5.4.183–84).

No doubt Shakespeare participated in ideological eruptions of the Reformation and in paradigm shifts that drove divinity, ultimate value, in anatomizing fashion, out of individual and social bodies. Shakespeare, though working in poetic and theatrical media that assume iconic harmonies between image and idea, costume and character, nonetheless persistently questions idolatries of imagination whereby concrete things of this world are made to outshine abstract themes of the next. Could it be that "the plays of Shakespeare often dramatize a suspicion of their own figures"[32] or that Shakespeare, with as great sophistication as skepticism, reveals how imagination makes us "apprehend / More than cool reason ever comprehends" (*Midsummer Night's Dream*, 5.1.5–6)?

As Shakespeare participates in the paradoxical fascination of iconoclasts with the power of images nearly to yield their proto-types to sensuous apprehension, he defines imagination in irre-mediably sensuous terms. Any failure on our part, as readers of Shakespeare, to grasp the sensuous reality of our reading as phys-ical and emotional behavior attached to material tones, rhythms, and image-generated emotions must remain simply that, our fail-ure (though one sited within massive contexts of social resis-tance). Thus, "the chief obstacle in the way of understanding response . . . is our reluctance to reinstate emotion as a part of cognition."[33]

Despite our reluctance to experience his informative feelings, we can struggle to let Shakespeare's materializing imagination reflect "our mode of embodied inherence in the world."[34] We can work to break the resistance offered by our general, cultural icon-oclasm. Study of iconoclasm demonstrates that "the reality of the image does not lie, as we might like to think, in the associations it calls forth, it lies in something more authentic, more real, and infinitely more graspable and verifiable than association."[35] Sig-nificant apprehension of art, particularly an art as materially fo-cused as Shakespeare's, accrues in experience here and now, in immediate sensory and intuitional response, immediate not in the sense of instantaneous but rather in the sense of meditation-ally clear, receptive, open, and true to body-stance. We could put this more fancifully by saying that the anima of the icon turns out not to reside in a realm of abstract forms. The full icon inhabits concrete space between its matter and the center of our bodies, bodies whose reality increasingly eludes us, "for the body has cer-tainly been among those objects which have been effectively hid-den from history."[36]

CONTEXTS OF ICONOCLASM AND REFINED MANNERS FURTHER
INDUCE RESISTANCE TO SENSE-READING AND SUBSTITUTE
EVALUATION FOR EXPERIENCE

Shakespeare emerged at a particular historic moment in which cries of antitheatrical iconoclasm increased yearly. Such cries closed English theaters during the Puritan revolution. After the reopening of the theaters, the same iconoclasm evolved into the long "civilizing process" whereby sexual arousal, vocal interaction with actors, touching of statuary, and other physiological responses to art were "refined," "elevated," and "etherealized" in middle- and upper-class "manners." Lower-class, childlike, or animalistic response even now is discouraged through educational stress on rational thought, moral conscience, and critical consciousness. Such controls "now interpose themselves more sternly than ever before between spontaneous and emotional impulses, on the one hand, and the skeletal muscles, on the other, preventing the former with greater severity from directly determining the latter (i.e., action) without the permission of these control mechanisms."[37]

Consider, to exemplify our loss of sensuous response and our need for its recapture, the kinds and degrees of audience arousal once promoted by endings of Shakespearean romantic comedies but now abstracted into after-play debates on gender inequalities in Shakespearean marriages. Truly, "the words of Mercury are harsh after the songs of Apollo" (*Love's Labor's Lost*, 5.2.518–19), for most of the plays end not in invitations to divisive debate but in characters' happy prospects of the "bride-bed" and "issue there create" (*Midsummer Night's Dream*, 5.1.398–400). *The Merchant of Venice* ends with expressed desires to "go to bed," the wish to be "couching" (5.1.303–5); *Much Ado* ends with a dance celebrating Benedick's conversion to the imploration: "Get thee a wife, get thee a wife" (5.4.120); the last words of *The Merry Wives of Windsor* (5.5.239) present a semi-adulterous image of Ford as "Master Brook" who "tonight shall lie with Mistress Ford"; the epilogue to *As You Like It* (15–16) "charges" that between the men and women in the audience "the play may please," plainly including sexual play in the charge; of course *Twelfth Night*, *All's Well*, and *Measure for Measure* as well as the romances end in wedding and wedding-night prospects. Such plays, as the epilogue to *As You Like It* makes plain, stand as invocations to men and women in the audience to "go and do likewise." Audience applause is made, moreover, to signify a physical assent to the arousing message or working of the play. That is rendered most apparent in the close to the epilogue of *Henry the Eighth* (13–14) when the epilogue figure declares it is "ill hap" if the men "hold" when their ladies bid them to "clap" (meaning to applaud but also to strike, thrust, join erotically), thus conflating clapping hands and sexual play.

One can of course resist these comedic seductions to arousal, arguing, for instance, that it's the males who promote the bed-going in unfair satisfaction with their patriarchal power to push women into degraded marital status and life-threatening pregnancy, but that might sound a bit like the observation that a ballerina cannot be found beautiful so long as she wears more revealing costume than her male partner or permits him to toss her about. The ending of *The Taming of the Shrew* presents a special case in point. Petruchio exits, taking Kate specifically "to bed" (5.2.188). While modern audiences have every right to be appalled at Petruchio's abusive treatment of Kate earlier in the play,[38] it remains a shame to treat Kate's long speech of apparent submission as vile degradation and to miss the way its likely sarcasm and innuendo contribute to the arousal of the couple's exit. Kate's bawdy punning, for instance, at the close of her speech is set up by her earlier reference to women's "hands" when she says to each listening woman (5.2.156–57) that her husband "craves no other tribute at thy hands / But love, fair looks, and true obedience." We mistake to read or hear the text abstractingly, as if "at thy hands" could mean only "at thy service" when "hands" and "tribute" in Shakespeare so easily suggest a physical, even genital connection (compare *2 Henry IV*, 3.2.305–7). Kate's closing four lines continue the double entendre:

> Then vail your stomachs, for it is no boot,
> And place your hands below your husband's foot,
> In token of which duty, if he please,
> My hand is ready; may it do him ease.
>
> (5.3.180–83)

It would hardly "do" Petruchio "ease" (terms themselves used bawdily elsewhere in Shakespeare) to present a hand to be stepped on; but if Petruchio's "foot" were associated with playing footsie (in modern parlance but ancient activity) or with "no boot" as including, possibly, his member (compare *Love's Labor's Lost*, 5.2.666; *Henry V*, 3.4.50), then the anatomical talk could find its sensual mark. Whether or not we approve of Kate's (or Petruchio's) "solution," we can recognize its relevance to the arousing endings of Shakespeare's comedies. To censor the sensuality, as editors routinely attempt to do by glossing "stomachs" only as abstract "pride" and "boot" only as abstract "profit," is to attempt the very iconoclasm assailed above.

Shakespeare knows, and cares, how theatrical images affect watchers viscerally. Hamlet, despite his lofty, patrician statements about eschewing audience laughter in favor of them considering "some necessary question of the play" (3.3.42–43), himself puts on the play within the play precisely to cause an observable *physical* response in Claudius. Hamlet assumes that plays can probe "to the quick" and make guilty spectators "blench" (*Hamlet*, 2.2.598). Lucrece gazes upon a painting of the fall of Troy (*The Rape of Lucrece* 1492, 1564): "feelingly she weeps Troy's painted woes" and "tears the senseless Sinon with her nails." King Claudius stands up to interrupt the play depicting his guilt. Leontes is struck motionless and speechless by the "statue" of Hermione. And Gower, as Chorus to *Pericles*, insists that lords and ladies have read the story "for restoratives," for healing in their lives (1.Chorus 8). How ironic it is that such sensory response has now been fairly emasculated by the growth of aesthetic theory that insists upon a mentalized "disinterest" of aesthetic response and by the dominant skepticism in poststructuralist and social creationist theorizing that reduces response to preferences of power groups, ignoring the point that, "no matter how we are pressured to repeat or conform, our existence as embodied subjects means that, in the final analysis, the individual always sees the world from a position which cannot be wholly colonized by the structure of broader social existence."[39]

In contrast to abstract philosophic, political, or theoretical discourse, Shakespeare's dramatic art demands, moreover, the utmost in embodied, psychophysiological, emotional, behaviorally active response. Not only were his texts written to be spoken aloud and physically acted but also an actor or reader can hardly hope to apprehend the reach of Shakespeare's images without sensuously exploring them. When, for example, after the discovery in *Macbeth* of the murdered King Duncan, Banquo declares (2.3.132) "In the great hand of God I stand," no abstractive translation could possibly replace the value of physiologically imagining what it would be like actually to stand in the enclosing hand of God. To bring kinesthetic and receptive memories into play, feeling what it is to breathe within secure embrace, radiant warmth, a high platform of support, the vast hands of divine protection around a tiny infant (again, not of woman born or cradled?), or whatever sensations embodied subjects summon up, is to begin appropriating and liberating the image for both vital and individuated experience. Shakespeare, through Banquo, invites a paradoxically physical appropriation of spiritual power. Whereas Macbeth's analogous image might be " 'Amen' / Stuck in my throat" (2.2.36), a proprioceptive image of being unable to breathe the spirit, to feel the wind of spiritus, an interior connection to God, Banquo's image of standing infolded in God's hand fits with Duncan's statement to Banquo: "let me infold thee / And hold thee to my heart" (1.4.31–32). Macbeth's fear or pride encloses and bottles up his Amen, whereas Banquo is enclosed, planted in a place of spiritual nourishment and reward.

If I hope to gain any fullness or intricacy of response to such a sensuously imbricated text as Shakespeare's, I must circle back from meaning to "me-ing." I must let the text speak to me personally, as nearly as possible, in *its* way even as I speak to it in mine. To know there, I must go there, opening myself always to original, strange, unobvious complexities or tics of the text's invention that, paradoxically, I can apprehend only by employing sensory and cognitive manifolds genuinely my own, weaved into the fabric of my own experience, my own body and mind, my incarnation. And always my more abstract interpretations must honor, reinforce, make flower the hedonic or painful sensations that constitute my perception, my attention, my open, receptive, meditational apprehension.

PHILOSOPHICAL CRITICISM AND SOCIAL CONSTRUCTIONISM IMPROPERLY RESIST SENSE-READING

In our era, those who doubt or question possibilities of somatic engagement with art such as Shakespeare's often verge upon polite despair, academic ennui, wistful wishing:

> Must the aesthetic charm, then, gradually disappear from the interpreted work of art, and leave us but an intellectual construct, one with a fascinating, fallacious, teasingly evasive mode of being? . . . Given our broadened historical perspective, however, there is now more helplessness about interpretation as it stretches toward an infinity of statements and contaminates art itself. . . . I have sometimes thought that design perception and interpretive brooding were separate gifts, and that we have genuine criticism only when interpretation reinforces perception or does not erode it. The ideal act of

criticism would circle back, in that case, to the design (the partial or complete object) that stimulated it.[40]

Notice how, even here where we see an avowed attempt to preserve aesthetic charms that antedate interpretive brooding, such charms are received through perception not of surface or texture or temporal/affective experience but only of "design," a spatial, inert, Platonic form that remains thoroughly desomaticized. How can the sensuous nature of artistic perception ever be defended if the body cannot be reached?

Actually, "design" as the disposition of parts cannot be apprehended without reference to "the embodied origins of imaginative structures of understanding, such as image schemata and their metaphorical elaborations."[41] Our sense of designational relations such as center-periphery, part-whole, and depth-surface originates with, depends upon, and is constrained in its freedom by our bodily experience of space, gravity, interiority, and the like. The same embodied schemata organize conceptual bases for artistic depictions of emotions that can only be apprehended by implicit reference to internal bodily states. Anger, rage, and wrath in Shakespeare, for example, must dependably be imaged in the same terms of body heat, internal pressure, redness in face and neck, agitation, and interference with accurate perception as are employed transculturally to register the physiological effects of anger.[42] Otherwise, we wouldn't know what Shakespeare was talking about when he speaks, as he does, of blazing, flaming, sweating, bursting, spitting, hot, red-looked, fiery, swelling, eyeless or eye-rolling anger, rage, and wrath. Our common abilities to make physical sense of such imagery "suggest that our concept of anger is embodied via the autonomic nervous system and that the conceptual metaphors and metonymies used in understanding anger are by no means arbitrary; instead they are motivated by our physiology."[43] We absolutely must refer to our bodies, to somato-sensory awareness and to visceral attention, if we hope to understand both the shape of designs and the sense of emotions.

Perhaps much of the foregoing argument seems obvious, but, if it is obvious, why then are physiological engagement and internal bodily sensations so generally elided from accounts of aesthetic experience? Why the firmly philosophical resistance? The underlying answers, as suggested earlier, probably have something to do with widespread fears of death and bodily decay. To such fears we have responded with idealist philosophy, salvationism, and historical "refinements" of manners. We have tried to link wealth and education with the deferral of death by transcoding class divisions into an upper-class, idealized, classical, outlined, spiritualized body versus a lower-class demonized, grotesque, visceral, decaying body.[44] Cultural authority has in part tried to defend itself against time, pain, and mortality by pushing them "downward," by splitting mind and body, by distorting ratios of the senses, and by connecting high elite art with unbodied response and low popular art with embodied response.

Another significant philosophical (and often political) position from which the possibility of sense-reading Shakespeare may be attacked is that of social constructionists who would claim that the knowledge pertinent to reading literature in the twentieth century "is discursive and subjectless."[45] On the contrary, as suggested above, I know why Shakespeare describes anger as red-looked and bursting because I have physically, internally experienced the visceral sensations of an embodied subject who has become red and bursting with anger. I did not make for myself that experience and much of its necessarily concomitant cultural meaning; my body made it for me, and for Shakespeare (and surely how anger makes us feel and the words generally hauled up to describe it are part of its "meaning" in any culture). And so I partially reject a cultural materialist's claim that "the point of Shakespeare and his plays lies in their capacity to serve as instruments by which we make cultural meaning for ourselves."[46]

I applaud these critics' demands for liberation from repressive constructions of meaning, including imperialist, sexist, patriarchal, reactionary, objectionably prejudicing interpretations of Shakespeare. But I deplore the loss of partly sharable realities in concrete, sensory body-hold or world-bite that the abstractive acceptance of discursive meaning-making, as quoted above, implies. We "need to study the biological and affective foundations of our social constructions of reality. . . . It cannot be assumed that somatic states necessarily remain neutral until some social interpretation or value is assigned to them. Some somatic states may have intrinsic qualities that command attention, expand consciousness, and actually suggest their own interpretation. . . . What constrains people from developing limitless differences is not simply social convention, but also the sensory and communication system of the species."[47] Truly, the senses are bearers of culture, but also "the senses are shapers of culture."[48]

The reference to expanding consciousness may suggest an inherently progressive position, one imperfectly reconcilable with my previous claims about the malleable politics of sense-reading. I hope not to underestimate anyone's capacity to flee from fearfully mortal freshenings of somatic sensations and prereflective perceptions encouraged by Shakespeare. I hope, at the same time, to recognize and rejoice in our counter-capacity to accept embodied vulnerabilities revealed by Shakespeare (and other artists) and to make them a foundation for expanded responsibility and growth. By appealing to our sensuous imaginations (including our sense of rhythm), Shakespeare, like other artists, "seeks to engage our whole being rather than cognition alone."[49] Our whole being as embodied subjects grounds our creativity. "The contents of the embodied subject's perception and consciousness are stylized: that is, they are given unique inflection by virtue of being absorbed into a unique personal history. . . . The style of expression is a direct manifestation of the individual embodied subject *qua* individual embodied subject. Such stylization *changes* the significance of the material it is giving expression to" (200–201). Herein lies, I believe, a useful critique of the (Foucaldian) "treatment of the self as merely the effect of discipline and technologies of the self."[50]

When we attend physically, then, to Shakespeare's rhythms or other sound play or to his abiding somatic imageries, we may experience both shared and specially stylized perceptions of our embodied histories, our lives. This blend of shared and individuated bodily reference, in turn, configures empathy and helps us sense likely, appropriate, "natural" ranges of tension between common and uncommon perceptions, conventional and unconventional responses, shared and special creations. None of this argument means to deny, however, the full entanglement between perception and culture, sense and sensibility. We may recognize cultural and subcultural relativities in sense-ratios and sensory deployments at the same moment in which we appeal to sharable dimensions of body focus and sensory awareness. We can, moreover, concede our excessive Western "visualism"[51] as a springboard for nonvisualist responses to Shakespeare. Even critiques of Western visualism imply, after all, standards of cultural development, standards at least implicitly cross-cultural.[52] Some of us may tend to forget how incessant is body-reference in the reading of imaginative texts such as Shakespeare's. The jealous Othello says to Desdemona:

> O thou weed,
> Who art so lovely fair and smell'st so sweet
> That the sense aches at thee, would thou hadst ne'er been born!
>
> (4.2.69–71)

Not much "sense" can be made of such a passage except by one who has experienced an ache associable to that of which Othello speaks or who can sensuously imagine its location, feel, and power. Would personal recall or else imagination of such an ache be available, however, to a culturally wide range of persons? To, say, a eunuch? Shakespeare apparently thinks so. He makes Cleopatra ask the "unseminared" eunuch, Mardian:

> Hast thou affections?
> *Mardian.* Yes, gracious madam.
> *Cleopatra.* Indeed?
> *Mardian.* Not in deed, madam, for I can do nothing
> But what indeed is honest to be done.
> Yet I have fierce affections, and think
> What Venus did with Mars.
>
> (*Antony and Cleopatra*, 1.5.13–19)

Here, not only are fierce heterosexual affections thought to survive below or beyond effects of castration but also a myth image from paint or word-sounds is thought to feed and gratify fierce affections, passions, sensory arousals. Did Shakespeare not think of his own images similarly available to and sensibly stimulating diverse attenders and readers of his works? Would it not be folly for us to take works designed by a master-artist on such a premise and belief, works proven to provoke common laughter and tears from diverse responders in diverse settings, and for us then to deny a core of sensational response? Do we not diversify out of shared origins?

That Shakespeare, like life, sometimes means differing things to differing people (or peoples) provides no reason for assuming that Shakespeare, or life, rarely means sharable things to differing people. Part of the importance of art lies in its refusal to become pure thought, interpretation, or evaluation. Art refers us continually to shared immediacies and fundamentals of sensory, bodily living. "Art is a way of integrating the selective, verbal, analytical purposive part of the mind with the more primitive intuitive unconscious that is not simply what is denied or repressed, but includes the basic biological wisdom, the body-intuitions of the race, and does not set the self off sharply from what surrounds it. . . . There are some universals in human experience, and in human physiology that underlie the esthetic response."[53] Another way to put this is to say that art, unlike most philosophy (including much poststructural and constructivist thinking), works through concrete universals, connecting our reflective thought with our prereflective experience as embodied subjects: "in order for the individual to be at home with himself or herself, the needs of the mind and of the senses must both be satisfied. Art is a major satisfaction of this need in so far as it brings rational and sensuous material into an inseparable and mutually enhancing relation. . . . [Indeed, sensuous and] aesthetic appreciation *itself* points us in the direction of . . . philosophical significance."[54]

When Shakespeare invokes for our aesthetic recall the body heat of anger or the knotted arms of sorrow or the physical heart's engagement in jealousy and love, or when we experience the rousing and calming cycles invoked psychosomatically within us by cadences of Shakespeare's prose and verse, or when we explore which vocal and postural expressions of Shakespearean mood or character "feel" appropriate in our own embodiments, then we can appreciate the human body as "a shaping factor in social representations rather than as the resultant mould."[55] Such behavior would still be countertraditional, however, working against a vast educational, societal, religious, political apparatus that shuns body wisdom and denigrates sensory life. "Idealist and objectivist Western world views have tended to emphasize our 'mental' (rational and practical) side, considering the 'body' (senses and emotions) as inferior, something to manage and restrain rather than as the very stuff of which our life-in-the-world is composed and through which our thought is mediated."[56] Not only is bodily expression denigrated by such labels as "nonverbal communication" that accord it in logocentric thinking a peripheral, negative position,[57] but also "in our culture the careful analysis of body experiences (in the form of report symptoms) has been left almost entirely to the physician. Poets, dancers, artists, psychotherapists, and chiropractors have also taken a fair amount of interest in such experiences—but only unofficially and under a vague cloud of suspicion."[58]

Such suspicion assumes many origins and forms, from fear of dying and decay to fear of irrationality and distraction. Although generations of study of psychosomatic illness and recovery teach us that our bodies express keen and truthful opinions of our lives, values, attitudes, we still find endemic in our society the expression of such fatuous bromides as the following: "That the events of the inner body are hidden from us is further proof of the kindness of Nature, which spares us the physical self-consciousness that would interfere with practical and philosophical life."[59] To counter such gross yet wisdespread belief in the wisdom of routinely separating physical self-consciousness from higher life, the sensuous study of materializing imaginations such as Shakespeare's could contribute much.

Shakespearean new historicists, cultural materialists, and others who often follow Foucault's extreme antisubjectivism tend to write of "the" body, rarely of their own bodies. They are externalists, not internalists. They believe "there is no unmediated access to the body,"[60] but they rarely stop to ask: "access by or of what agency? brain? nerves? feelings? thoughts?" The brain is bodily substance as are the nerves. Feelings and thoughts are bodily events; they themselves occur inseparably from their own physical media. There's nothing nonmaterial sitting around asking for nonmaterial access to the body. All "access" is in a material medium which itself mediates cultural ascriptions of meaning. A Foucauldian Shakespearean will argue that bodily functions can be "experienced [sic] only in terms of culturally available discourses,"[61] thus not only suggesting that babes in the womb "experience" no bodily functions but also suggesting that my "experience" of my laughter or tears while seeing or reading *Hamlet* does not include my nondiscursive sensations of rhythmic contractions in my diaphragm and chest muscles (bodily functions). A Foucauldian Shakespearean may ostensibly recognize "the body as a cosmic structuring principle" and that bodily experience is not just interpreted through culturally available discourses but rather itself "provides conceptual frameworks for understanding."[62] Still, the reader or viewer's body remains in such discussion firmly excluded from consideration even though its material sense of weight, compression, rhythm, and the like conditions the very metaphors and rhythms available to Shakespeare (as well as the anxieties or pleasures such metaphors and rhythms confer).

Extreme historicism of Shakespeare, promoting mainly era-specific meanings, belies the obvious facts of continuity among eras and across cultures. It is fine to estrange and defamiliarize Shakespeare so long as we recognize that millions of persons worldwide are *still interested* in him and may well have broadly human, if not "universal," reasons for being so, reasons based in part upon bodily, sensory affinities.

A seminal discussion of new historicist principles is in the first chapter of Stephen Greenblatt's book, *Shakespearean Negotiations: The Circulation of Social Energy in Renaissance England*.[63] Greenblatt asks how plays by Shakespeare "acquired compelling force" (5), and he proposes adopting the term "energy" as a term derived from Greek rhetorical traditions, a term we can use "provided we understand that its origins lie in rhetoric rather than physics and that its significance is social and historical" (6). Here, however, is where the rabbit goes in the hat, for in the very next paragraph, Greenblatt asks, "What is 'social energy'?" (6) and promptly associates it with the production of "physical and mental experiences" (6), "with the capacity to arouse disquiet, pain, fear, the beating of the heart," and so on (6). Thirteen pages later, still *asking* the enormously problematic question, "What then is the social energy that is being circulated?" (19), he includes "sexual excitement" in his answer. By thus making "social" energy, despite his initial denial, all-inclusive of physical energies such as beating hearts and sexual excitement, Greenblatt seems to deny the relevance, or perhaps even the existence, of any nonsocial energy within responders to Shakespeare. By sleight-of-hand "social" energy turns out either to include or to neutralize the significance of the very "physics" or physical, nonsocial world *apart from which* social energy ostensibly had been defined in the first place.

The beating of our hearts and the occurrence of our sexual excitement in response to Shakespeare's rhythms and images takes place, of course, *within* a context of social practices including language training and the whole manifold of our education concerning human behavior. Those social practices are not, however, the sole cause of our heartbeat or arousal. Social energy in no sense accounts completely for the production of such phenomena. Without the huge tide of diurnal and biological rhythms, physical and presocial rhythms, surrounding and infusing us bodily, Shakespeare's rhythms would cause nothing to happen. Our sexual responsiveness, likewise, is created out of our biological heritage, from reproductive physical energies we share with other living creatures. Our response to Shakespeare's imagery depends absolutely upon the physical evolution and deployment, over presocial millenia, of capacities for smell, taste, touch, inner sensation, and the like. Society and culture do not produce the energy, moreover, for exercise of such senses; that energy is produced, physically, by cell and soma. Society, social practices, can of course affect the expression, use, outcome, or meaning ascribed to such energy, but society and social practice are hardly the producers, the originators, of it.

It does make a difference whether we think the energies of our response to Shakespeare "lie in rhetoric rather than physics" (6) and are produced exclusively by social practices, or whether we think forces best viewed as larger, deeper, more ancient, and more physical than rhetoric and social practice account for those energies. If we restrict our focus, in responding to Shakespeare, merely to energies of mind treating rhetoric, social texts, semantics, and sign systems, then, I believe, we risk engaging in a kind of hurtful hubris or pride. We forget or ignore or deny that such social energy is itself shaped, constrained, and ultimately dissipated by nonsocial energies, by meterological, geological, and solar energies as well as molecular, cellular, and biological energies. Social energy circulates at the thin intersection between macrocosmic and microcosmic metasocial energies, energies that originate outside society and impress themselves, by their own rules, upon society. Social energy is a relatively local, small derivation from such metasocial energies, and one of the chief functions of poetry, drama, and aesthetic experience generally is to help persons sense, attend to, come to terms with the huge informing energies—of inner sensation, feeling, growth, and aging, and of outer reality in wind, rain, time, and earthly change—that originate and circulate above and below everyday social realms. Aesthetic experience thus differs from other cultural experience (social, political, moral) insofar as it reveals the ephemerality and contingency of culture itself compared to the wider world or, we might say, to a hugely autonomous inner and outer cosmos.

Shakespeare, like other verbal artists, helps us perceive and think about social energy encoded in language with all its rhetorical devices. As Stephen Greenblatt implicitly concedes, however, the rhetorically encoded social energy manifested in poetic "traces" (6) only *seems* to "produce" by itself such "physical . . . experiences" as "the beating of the heart" (6). In truth, it does so only in a very limited sense. It does not itself create the heart or the fact that it beats. Nor does it (Shakespeare's language) "produce" the reader's sense of rhythm or melody or capacity for arousal through imagery. It *engages* the reader's preexisting, physical, nonrhetorically created senses.

Reading Shakespeare thus invokes both 1) a rich field of discursive mentation in which hugely complex thoughts and feelings mingle as the reader interprets the text, and 2) a lively and vivid play of rhythmic, auditory, visual, and internal sensations and sense memories. In experiencing other arts such as dance, painting or sculpture, or music, we can recognize the nonverbal, nondiscursive dimension of the art experience: we sway with the dance, look at art and sculpture, and listen to music partly, or sometimes largely, to experience life nondiscursively, to clarify and purify sensation. In the same way, experiencing the rhythms of Shakespeare's words differs from thinking with verbal, rhetorical thoughts through or about his words. Such experience is not, moreover, the sort of "social practice" that new historicists such as Greenblatt are addressing. Such experience of rhythm is closer to experience of heart rhythm, breath rhythm, or kinesthetic rhythm: rhythms largely independent of social creation but more nearly in the hands of, here comes the taboo word, nature. And, even if our physical experience of Shakespeare's rhythms, melodies, images, and the like is never wholly unmediated by or undefined by verbal thoughts, certainly such experience can be *relatively* unmediated or undefined by verbal thoughts. To enjoy that relative absence of discursive mediation (as well as to enjoy richly mediated verbal interpretation), is, indeed, one of the chief reasons we go to Shakespeare or to any great poet. We want to amplify our discursive, interpretive mediations, but we also want to amplify our nondiscursive, sensory immediacies. We paradoxically employ poetic language partly to step in front of it as well as past it. In addition to information, we seek sensation. We make intellectual sense and we make physical sense.

II

Beyond Resistance to Sense-Reading

5
Working Beyond Resistance

Aᴌᴛʜᴏᴜɢʜ sᴇɴsᴏʀʏ ʀᴇᴀᴅɪɴɢ ᴏꜰ Sʜᴀᴋᴇsᴘᴇᴀʀᴇ ᴍᴇᴇᴛs ʀᴇsɪsᴛᴀɴᴄᴇ, as we saw above, sensory reading of Shakespeare also finds support, as we shall see below. Some of the support comes, to be sure, from countertraditional sources. Indeed, a confluence of radical biological and psychological investigation and medical innovation in the West, Eastern meditational practice, and other streams of interest in mind/body engagements has grown to river of revelation. Readers of imaginative, emotion-laden literature such as Shakespeare's may now find themselves, in particular, more free than before 1) to connect Shakespeare's imaginative forms and their own physical responses, 2) to explore their emotions as sensate phenomena, and 3) to incorporate Shakespearean narrative as body fable or as exhibiting "dreambody" dimensions. In this chapter, I will justify these three assertions through reference to secondary sources and examples from Shakespeare. Though I anticipate academic resistance to the notion that better reading of Shakespeare requires "body-training," I hope to persevere both in the tragic spirit of Gloucester in *King Lear* who, as noted above, learned to see it feelingly and in the comic spirit of Grumio who would knock at his listener's ear with a "sensible tale" (*Taming of the Shrew*, 4.1.64).

Bᴏᴅʏ/Mɪɴᴅ Pʀᴀᴄᴛɪᴛɪᴏɴᴇʀs Sᴜᴘᴘᴏʀᴛ Rᴇᴀᴅᴇʀs' Cᴏɴɴᴇᴄᴛɪᴏɴs ᴏꜰ Sʜᴀᴋᴇsᴘᴇᴀʀᴇᴀɴ Fᴏʀᴍs ᴛᴏ Pʜʏsɪᴄᴀʟ Fᴇᴇʟɪɴɢs

As discussed in the third chapter, some reader-response critics distinguish between "efferent" (or "informational") and "afferent" (or "aesthetic") reading. Efferent reading, in an analogy to outgoing, motor activity, moves attention away from "the work itself" and the experience of reading it toward an abstracted conglomeration of ideas; afferent reading, in an analogy to inflowing, sensory input, moves attention inward toward the moment-to-moment, aesthetic dimensions of the reading experience. This employment of physiological terms does not, however, create an exact analogy to what actually happens in efferent and afferent pathways of the central nervous system.

> We must resist immediately the logical tendency to view these afferent and efferent divisions as being in any way *opposed*. . . . Sensory and motor activities are everywhere and at all times interpenetrating one another to create the homogeneity of conscious experience. It is difficult to imagine a stream that flows two directions at the same time, but this is just what the nervous system does. The failure to sufficiently appreciate this unity of seeming opposites leads us into separating too absolutely afferent from efferent, sensation from behavior, attitude from activity.[1]

Inflowing, sensory, aesthetic reading thus produces not only changing breath rate, heart rate, perspiration levels, and the like but also myriad kinesthetic, muscular impulses toward expressive behavior. These changes and impulses evoke feeling states that we then interpret as emotions.

We have been encouraged for some time, of course, to understand that viewers of artistic works are kinesthetically engaged. On fire to reach the deepest core life of spectators, Artaud proposed "to return through the theater to an idea of the physical knowledge of images."[2] When Hermione and Leontes come together at the close of *The Winter's Tale*, "we not only see the embrace, we sense what it *feels* like."[3] A tendency for viewers of artworks to change posture to imitate perceived forms, moreover, or at least to feel the impulse to do so, has also been recognized.[4] We know, too: "The set [attentive focus] of an audience is so important that when, for example, spectators of a film are led to concentrate on observing the technique of the film or on judging its contents in a detached intellectual manner, they fail to experience the tensions involved in the various atrocities presented."[5]

Some critics have searched years for terms to describe how poetic language functions as "gesture" for readers: "motion as meter moors gesture to meaning"; language as gesture in meter and punning inveigles us, we are told, into "feeling the pang, the inner bite, of things forced together."[6] Yet, despite such sporadic

critical attentions to the "inner bite" of imaginative experience,
it seems to be the bodyworkers, the physical and psychic therapists working in wake of precursors F. Matthias Alexander, Wilhelm Reich, Elsworth Baker, Alexander Lowen, Fritz Perls, and
the like,[7] who most daringly argue "that words and images are
connected to muscular patterns, that the body speaks, and that
fantasy is preparation for action."[8]

Let us approach applied theories of the bodyworkers by means
of a Shakespearean example.

> *First Witch.*
>> When shall we three meet again?
>> In thunder, lightning, or in rain?
> *Second Witch.*
>> When the hurlyburly's done,
>> When the battle's lost and won.
> *Third Witch.*
>> That will be ere the set of sun.   5
> *First Witch.*
>> Where the place?
> *Second Witch.*
>>> Upon the heath.
> *Third Witch.*
>> There to meet with Macbeth.
> *First Witch.* I come, Grimalkin!
> *Second Witch.* Paddock calls.
> *Third Witch.* Anon.   10
> *All.*
>> Fair is foul, and foul is fair.
>> Hover through the fog and filthy air.
>
>   (*Macbeth*, 1.1.1–12)

Any reader attends of course to plot and so notes news of a battle
and the Witches' plan to meet Macbeth, but the reader, or more
likely re-reader, needs to attend closely to other dimensions of the
passage. Here language achieves gesture and not only gesture but
also posture and not only posture but also an invitation to empathic, internal, physical feeling.

Where does tragedy begin? With unnatural instability and with
hidden, traitorous equivocation. With questions designed not to
be answered. The first line appears sonically balanced and stable:

$$\text{When} \qquad\qquad\qquad \underline{\text{gain}}$$
$$\text{sh}\underline{\text{a}}\text{ll} \qquad\qquad \underline{\text{a}}$$
$$\text{w}\underline{\text{e}}\ \text{thr}\underline{\text{ee}}\ \text{m}\underline{\text{ee}}\text{t}$$

The internal sounds of "we three meet," phonically gesturing their threeness and centering the seven syllables of the line, appear to be bracketed by paired sounds in syllable positions 2–6 and 1–7. But how are we to hear or say the line, actually? Do "when" and "-gain" rhyme? If so, then "-gain" and "rain" become off-rhymes (as "heath" and "beth" may off-rhyme?). Either way, two sounds (among the threesome of "when," "-gain," and "rain") won't match (unless, perhaps, we employ Elizabethan pronunciation and probably not even then). What seems clear proves unclear. Normal expectations for "when" to meet (expectations of a set and appropriate time) face abrupt challenge in the second line. The disturbing prospect of "meeting" in foul weather may overlie, in an attentive reader's mind, furthermore, unnatural separations of thunder, lightning, and rain. Is the First Witch thinking of meeting either in thunder and lightning or else in rain, as if these might occur separately? Or is the First Witch further separating the three items into three discrete possibilities, as if we could have thunder without lightning? Does "in," furthermore, mean "within the point of"? Or simply, "during"? What kind of creature would meet "in" lightning? And where? Of course we think of thunder and lightning as data for the distancing senses of hearing and sight; being "in" rain provides a contrasting, tactile experience. How does the prospect of meeting "in" rain connect to the prospect of otherwise meeting "in" lightning "or" in thunder? Plainly the second line of the play baffles the first line and disorients one's accustomed senses of time, space, and causality. Similar disorientation occurs in the second two lines where first one imagines Witches meeting when hurlyburly is "done." Immediately one finds that "done" suggests no ending, because the Witches look beyond allegiance to either side in the hurlyburly battle. "Done" remains inconclusive if the same battle that's lost is also paradoxically won. "Done" and "won" rhyme, but a reader's point of view hovers uncertainly.

Sounds in the next group of lines also chime in ways that produce sonic and semantic confusion:

Where	the	place
Upon	the	heath
There	to	meet
With	Mac	beth

Which vowel sounds in the third column match: *ea* and *ee*? *ea* and *e*? all four? Are we to hear or speak with a Scottish or other accent? Could "meet" pun on "mate" (note how "place" and "meet" are given metrically similar positions in the text, possibly pulling their sounds into alignment)? What sort of "meeting" or "mating" have the Witches enjoyed here before? In the comedies, "Journeys end in lovers' meeting" (*Twelfth Night*, 2.3.43) that includes mating, but here the sexuality, gender, and procreational status of the Witches portends, in its accreting murkiness ("And like a rat without a tail / I'll do, I'll do, and I'll do" [1.3.9–10]), the confusion of an unsexing Lady Macbeth and of her husband too full of the breastlike "milk" of kindness (1.5.17).

Bafflingly, the Witches stand, in body and in spirit, at margins of humanity. They could choose to meet (or mate?) "in" thunder or "upon" the heath (or under it if they wished?); they hear from far off the to us silent voices of their familiars. They speak of a toad as "calling." They unnaturally separate thunder, lightning and rain; they unnaturally join winning and losing, fair and foul. Their last image in the scene (perhaps the most emphatic kinesthetic image) yields "hovering" in "filthy air." They are there when clear sight dims, when black fog and choking smoke of battle insinuate a loss of natural, peaceful rhythms in time and place, season and kingdom. Their term for battle is "hurlyburly," enacting nonuniform repetition (compare "pell-mell," "topsy-turvy," and "helter-skelter"), signifying mutiny and turmoil and going back etymologically to senses of diarrhea and vomit. If we were to follow the Witches kinesthetically to feelings of "hovering," we could spread our arms and sense an effort to balance shifting elements. If we follow the Witches into interoception, or organ feel, we sense disgust, an urge to "hurl," a predecessor feeling to that stimulated by the poisoned entrails of their famous cauldron or by Macbeth's willingness to have "nature's germens tumble all together, / Even till destruction sicken" (4.1.59–60).

One advantage of reading Shakespeare over watching a performance is that a reader may more assiduously work past sight and hearing to less explored senses, to "unoccupied" channels of perception.[9] Such channels include proprioception and gut feelings.[10] Because "many people are not aware of their physical bodies" in any consistent or revealing sense, they live out their "inner body sensations and connected fantasies" mainly through dreams, art, and unconscious behavior.[11] Preoccupied as most of

us are with sight and hearing—and, often, accompanying intellec-
tualizations—we miss opportunities to feel and respond to inner
body feelings. Those who have studied the imagery of *Macbeth*
have focussed attention mainly upon visual images of clothing,
blood, babies, or light and dark. More viscerally responsive readings allow smell, taste, disgust, nausea, and purgation to enter.
Thus the Witches do not *originate* so much as they help to *express*
a text-pervading sickness of destruction. Banquo doubts whether
he saw the Witches or had merely "eaten on the insane root"
(1.3.84). We can taste Lady Macbeth's milk turning to "gall"
(1.5.48). We are assailed by Macbeth's talk of bringing "the poisoned chalice" to his own lips (1.7.11), by sensations of hope
being "drunk" (1.7.37), by reminders of Macbeth and his lady
drinking spirits (2.1.32, 2.2.1), by "drugged" guards (2.2.6), by
the disgusting "filthy witness" of blood (2.2.51, 65), by the Porter's readiness to "cast" or vomit (2.3.40), by Macbeth's descent
to the unpalatable "lees" or dregs of life's wine (2.3.97), by horses
eating each other (2.4.18), by Macbeth's regurgitory vision of
"rancors in the vessel" of his peace (3.1.68), by the Macbeths' inability to eat their meals save in fear (3.2.19), by Macbeth's call
for "good digestion" (3.4.38) just as he spies Banquo's "gory
locks" rising between him and the banquet table (3.4.51).

   The one thing even schoolchildren know of *Macbeth* is the
"trouble"/"bubble" couplet of the cauldron scene, that deep hot
center of the play. A central sense of the cauldron scene is disgust—primal, infantile disgust: trouble in the bubble. I cannot
hope to appreciate this play until I connect my decimative appetite, my unconscious, Macbethian urge to dismember and feast
bloodily, with Macbeth as "butcher" (5.8.70) who "unseamed"
his enemy "from the nave to th' chops" (1.2.22), bloodied the
feast of life, of social order, and cut a crimson path through Duncan, guards, Banquo, Lady Macduff and son, to the Witches' am-
putative stew. Such a connection seeks no reduction of the play
to a single emotion but rather a reverencing return of art experience from "head" trip to whole-body life. The play swerves from
bloodlust through disgust (adding the Witches' "infected" air
cursed by Macbeth [4.1.138], and the "smell of the blood still"
[5.1.49] driving Lady Macbeth insane) to the "purge" (5.2.28; cf.
5.2.57) of the close. By ironic sleight-of-hand, Shakespeare converts ambiguously emetic or enematic pressures of the middle
section to the final, phlebotomus "med'cine of the sickly weal"

(5.2.27). Physiological roots of metaphors for catharsis and purgation deserve, then, to be taken seriously as explored through readers' literal "ruminations" (etymologically, throat and stomach work).

Such poetically medicinal purgation of course "solves" our sense of life-threat only temporarily. The sense of disgust at decay and mortality—the sense that vibrates so importantly, but neglectedly, through *Hamlet, Lear, Macbeth, Timon*, and *Coriolanus*—ever returns, for "disgust, a universal emotion, can be understood as a defense against a universal fear of death by humans"; and while such fear concerns the body, such disgust concerns, ultimately, the soul, the part of us we hope to preserve beyond death.[12] Paradoxically, however, Shakespeare's care for the soul demands for its apprehension that "base" sensation of salivating, nauseating disgust so graphically evoked in *Macbeth*.

Readers may respond with gut feelings even when Shakespeare's text seems to bypass taste, digestion, or disgust. The opening scene of *Macbeth* seems shaped in aural terms of rhyme and pounding meter and in heady terms of abstract disorientation: "fair is foul and foul is fair."

> But from the body's point of view, the emotions we feel are the information our guts arrive at after processing the energy around us in a preconscious way. We moderns are so devoutly trained to believe that information can only arrive in the form of data to be processed in the brain that we forget how much information is offered by, to, and through our other faculties.[13]

Notice how, for example, lines of the Third Witch continually interrupt patterns begun by the other two Witches; the two opening couplets are not continued but capped off by a third rhyming line from the Third Witch. Then, a new pattern is started by the First Witch taking a half-line, "Where the place?," and the Second Witch also taking a half-line, "Upon the heath." If the Third Witch were to enter the pattern, she might say something like, "There to face . . ." with all the Witches then chanting, perhaps, "the thane, Macbeth!" or some such; instead the Third Witch mismatches "Where the place?" with "There to meet." Readers and listeners are made to hover between the precise mathematics of line distribution among the three Witches (2, 2, 1; 1/2, 1/2, 1) and the phonic disruptions of off-rhyming and Third Witch depatternings. (And again, "I come, Grimalkin / Paddock calls" might be expected to yield a line from the Third Witch metered and rhyming thusly: "da dum da dum da dum da . . . alls," but instead she says merely, "Anon.") Does such disequilibrium jostle the inner ear toward the motion sickness of attempted hovering in filthy air? Perhaps. Such queasiness afflicts all who find imbalance in the inner ear disturbing to abdominal peace.

Process-oriented psychology argues that "amplification" of signals in one channel or mode of perception can often lead to abrupt channel-switching to a more normally uninhabited, less conscious or primary channel.[14] A reader who focused upon the swaying, aural/semantic hoverings of "lost and won," "fair is foul," "cannot be ill, cannot be good" (1.3.132) might feel daze, imbalance, grogginess. The occupied aural channel could produce spillover into normally unoccupied proprioceptive and interoceptive channels. "When situations become too extreme or painful in one perception channel, when they reach their limit or edge, the experience switches suddenly and automatically from one channel to the other."[15] In like manner, the Witches at the opening of *Macbeth* beckon us into a ritual world of chanting, incantatory verse, of "meeting" in ritualized space through gnomic verse, chiming sounds, heavily-metered, mind-beating, hypnotic poetry. The apparent order of that ritual introduction proves, however, to be not an orientation but a disorientation, not the order of rationality, but the order of a mind-numbing tom-tom. We can't think; we can only go along, into a world where, indeed, what's fair is foul, where eye and hand, conscience and act, brutally sever themselves to serve ambition. Mere statement of such disorienting paradox could never by itself produce nervous effects; Shakespeare employs language not merely as idea but as psychosomatic experience. As Artaud expressed it:

> let there be the least return to the active, plastic, respiratory sources of language, let words be joined again to the physical motions that gave them birth, and let the discursive, logical aspect of speech disappear beneath its affective, physical side, i.e., let words be heard in their sonority rather than be exclusively taken for what they mean grammatically, let them be perceived as movements, and let these movements themselves turn into other simple, direct movements as occurs in all the circumstances of life but not sufficiently with actors on the stage, and behold! the language of literature is reconstituted, revivified.[16]

Body/Mind Practitioners Also Show Why and How Self-Directed Movements Can Enhance Readers' Engagement with Emotions in Shakespeare

To let Shakespeare's words "turn" into physical motions, and into kinesthetic and interoceptive sensations, is to let them gain emotion and to risk tragic pain and catharsis (or perhaps disturbing pleasure) inside us. "To move is to feel."[17] If we would connect Shakespeare or any imaginative literature to its ancient roots in rites, to its medicinal, cathartic past, we must return our experience to outer and inner movement, to motion and, hence, emotion. To base cathartic purgation only upon already purified, intellectualized notions of pity and terror is to forget the physical bases of fear, disgust, and sickness, the badges and burdens of our mortality that partly motivate tragic rites. It will mean precious little to me that Hamlet, for instance, finally registers his disgust at the stench of death—"And smelt so? Pah!" [*He throws down the skull.*] (5.1.200)—if I fail to register my own disgust. That "Pah!" must be mine upon reading *Lear*, as well

> *Lear.* Pah, pah! Give me an ounce of civet, good apothecary,
>   to sweeten my imagination. There's money for thee.
> *Gloucester.* O, let me kiss that hand!
> *Lear.* Let me wipe it first.
>
> (4.6.130–33)

If disgust at the smell of mortality wafts up from the Witches' cauldron, Yorick's skull, Lear's hand, to motivate in part the tragic revelations of Macbeth, Hamlet, and Lear, why should the characters in the plays (as we assemble their reality) or the actors of their parts gain physical, bodily access to the sensation and I, as reader, be left with merely a disembodied, abstracted "recognition" of what that "pah!" means? That spitting exclamation of disgust is really mine for the asking. I could argue that the "pah!" seethes subliminally in the muscles of my face, throat, abdomen—whether or not I admit it to myself. "All of my muscle cells—both alpha and gamma—are continually *felt* by the mind as they work, whether most of these 'feelings' ever reach my conscious awareness or not."[18] Yet I may make a more profound connection to the spitting, face-scrunching, shoulder-hunching, stomach-crunching "pah!" of disgust and to its edged abutment upon other channels of perception if I intentionally "make a somatic caricature of the pattern and then attempt to identify both the feelings that accompany this organization and the image that it creates."[19] After doing that, I am free to reflect upon the caricature and images to employ the significance and pleasure of disengaged reflection. Such reflection may in turn prompt a new enactment and engagement, which may call for further reflection, a process of somatic and psychic interaction with the text that will often reduce the need for further caricature and reveal what (for the reader) can constitute appropriate norms of perception and feeling.

When the reader of Shakespeare purposefully activates her or his reading so as to make it somatically engaged, say, by employing facial and postural movements of disgust while reading "pah!," then the reader in consequence changes the measurable (and probably immeasurable) activities of her or his autonomic nervous system. Numerous studies have indicated that intentionally deploying one's facial muscles into (cross-culturally demonstrated) patterns of anger, disgust, or sadness stimulates changes in brain waves, in heart rate, in skin temperature, and in neurochemical reactions that arise from externally imposed, unintended incitements of such emotions.[20] In addition, consciously produced facial expressions "can enhance the experience of emotions produced by other means."[21]

Researchers have shown, moreover, that certain movements of head or arms or both can affect both our memory for and our emotive evaluation of language. Vertical head movements produce better memory for positive terms and more agreement with given arguments. Horizontal head movements produce better memory for negative terms and less agreement with given arguments. Approach behavior, such as pressing arms upward or making embracing motions, yields more positive assessment of given stimuli than the more negative assessment of the same stimuli experienced during avoidance behavior such as pressing arms downward or pushing away.[22] There is, in other words, a marked tendency in humans toward congruence of movement and perception and, beyond that, a drive toward motor-conceptual compatibility.

Why should reading Shakespeare, then, mimic in any way the passive, unathletic nonactivity that accompanies undramatic perusal of newspapers and textbooks? Let face, voice, gesture, posture, and bodily movement (locomotion) all activate and enhance your making sense of the Bard's actionful drama.

Purposefully employing one's voice tonally to express positive or negative states can elicit responses of the autonomic nervous system indicating emotional arousal.[23] We could speculate, further, that a reader's physiological mimicry or enactment of tragic protagonists' successive emotions of rage, loathing, and grief or (in muted form) anger, disgust, and sadness might enhance the hedonic, strangely exalting outcome of Shakespearean tragedy.[24] The intensifying heat and pressure of rage or anger so typical of the early and middle stage of the tragic journey (an unavailing and perhaps inappropriate attempt to "dominate" death) gives way to the expectorative, rejecting disgust, and the cooling-off sadness of the close.[25] There is some evidence to suggest that warmed air in our nasal cavities may be relatively less pleasurable than cooled air as such air varies cerebral temperatures that influence release of emotion-linked neurotransmitters.[26] If we as readers follow the tragic hero through the compressive, constrictive heat of anger and the explosive "letting go" of disgust ("pah!") and then move beyond to the more open, in-breathing coolness of sadness at the close, we may be helping to create physiological correlates of our cathartic intimations. A. C. Bradley suggested that Shakespeare's tragic figures "are too great for the little space in which they move," and so they vanish "into freedom":[27] as readers we can follow that progress from compression to release not only with our minds and metaphors but with our whole being. We can reach below conventional vectors of "mind" to an underself of considerable potential growth.

We are free also, of course, to *reject* Lear's anger (or Cordelia's or any character's); we needn't empathize equally with every emotional expression. There will be, nonetheless, somatic correlates (in coolness, say, or kinesthetic drawing back, or feeling for renewed balance) of sensed injustice or of determined disengagement. We may, indeed, experience intersecting waves of anger *at* and anger *on behalf of* Lear or Hamlet or Othello, to name but three likely targets. The important thing is to recognize and accept all opportunities for one's neural complicity, one's muscular interaction, one's sensory dance with the text, actors, mise en scene.

It may perhaps be pertinent at this point to add the caveat that my use of the term emotional "experience" is not intended to equate all emotion-related physiological change with conscious perception of that change. Most minutiae in physiological changes of heart rate, breath rate, skin conductance, muscle tensions, organ states, and the like, that are associable with emotive response to Shakespeare, may indeed remain unperceived by readers or spectators, at least unperceived in any fully conscious or verbalizable form.[28] Persons who enhance their proprioceptive awareness, however, are likely to experience their reading or seeing as more emotional. In a recent study measuring physiological responses to slides depicting pleasant and unpleasant images, for example, "good heartbeat perceivers consistently showed more facial expressions, for a longer duration, and at a higher intensity level than poor perceivers. This finding points to a relationship between visceral perception and degree of emotional expressiveness," and it lends "partial support to the Jamesian peripheral theory of emotion in which proprioception and emotional expression are causally related."[29] Our "feelings," then, here including our emotions, inevitably embrace both mind and body. They question the very division suggested by those two terms, and readers who wish to experience Shakespeare feelingly will be well-advised to include bodily feelings in their attention.

6

Undermind Shakespeare: Sense-Reading as Self-Shaping and Play-Shaping

BY SENSE-READING PERFORMANCE FEATURES AND CHARACTER SIGNS, ONE MAY AMPLIFY SHAKESPEARE'S SOMATIC PATTERNS

I HOPE THAT I NOW HAVE CLARIFIED FOR YOU WAYS IN WHICH APPLIED theories of contemporary body/mind workers may help overcome abstractive resistance to sense-reading. Sense-reading concentrates upon antiabstractive moving and feeling as underparts of mind, as employing inner, trunk-body senses. In general use, " 'mind' usually refers to seeing and hearing. The idea of body is usually a composition of feeling and moving."[1] Shakespeare, like other great imaginative artists, both appeals to and makes his subject this undermind body of feeling and moving. I trust it will be clearer, moreover, why I say that Shakespeare works, just as a musician works, in media that require temporal performance for significant experience. "Music, like dance, is nothing if it is not actual performance, and performance is nothing if it is not muscular. The muscles are the Muses. . . . Rhythm, phrasing, pitch, and tone are all direct manifestations of muscular control, and our aesthetic response to them is solidly linked with our perception of the sophistication of these efforts."[2] As we have been witnessing, Shakespeare, through a sophisticated array of performative features, rouses a commensurate array of inner responses. Thus incantations in *Macbeth* hypnotically overpower audience defenses against deep feeling and assist in the eventual purgation or catharsis.[3] Particularly if we amplify the somatic messages of *Macbeth*—such as the tympanic disequilibrium, the restless, hovering, equivocating, unnatural, dismembering, stomach-churning, nightmarish "doing"—we will discover how the play may "pattern proprioceptive experiences, organizing body behavior. . . . Visions, dreams, and myths use our physical bodies as a dramatic stage upon which the individual organs are actors."[4] Macbeth tries to suppress "body" and become "head," fighting death and time in a shadowy, filthy battle, losing all feeling in the process, a process we can follow closely and make a source of purgation and growth.

After embracing Shakespeare's immediate appeals to our undermind responses, we can discover in his plays appeals to more indirect bodily processes. *Hamlet*, for example, presents a classic dream or myth of the repressed, suicidal youth suddenly confronting a hugely powerful figure (the Ghost) who invites him to act with explosive physical violence. Recalling worldwide stories of a genie released from a lamp or the spirit Mercurius rising from an unstoppered bottle,[5] the spirit asks the depressed and angry Hamlet to release him from "tormenting flames" (1.5.3) through Hamlet's act of regicide. We could see this father/ghost figure in archetypal terms as Mercurial god of the unconscious and body (individual and social) "cooking" with pent-up energy deep within the protagonist who (as both creature and culture) is aware only of feeling still, downcast, heavy, suicidal, "rotten." As in all the stories, the messenger energy associated with Mercury (compare Hamlet imaging his ghost/father as "herald Mercury" [4.5.59]) releases extreme emotions of rage and revenge, and the protagonist's task is to harness this sudden eruption toward productive ends, to match its force to appropriate deeds, to suit its inner words to outer actions.

Kinetic analysis of Hamlet as a character suggests, at least in part, opening tendencies to be still, heavy, cold, downcast. Any given reader might interpret textual signals somewhat idiosyncratically, "kinesensically,"[6] but some agreement can reasonably be expected within a central range. Do not Horatio and Marcellus, at the close of the first scene, think of Hamlet as receiving their address passively? They will impart what they have seen "unto young Hamlet" (1.1.176). The Ghost, they think "will speak to him" (1.1.177). They will "acquaint him" and "find him" (178, 182) as if he may be stilly waiting, and we do find him silently standing by while Claudius and others conduct state and private business. The clouds are said to "hang" on him (2.1.66) as if he droops; his eyes are down, probably refusing eye contact (1.2.70–71). He confesses to sigh, cry, and carry "dejected havior of the visage" (1.2.79–81). Once by himself, he immediately exclaims (1.2.129–30):

> O, that this too too sullied flesh would melt,
> Thaw, and resolve itself into a dew!

Hamlet of course professes himself suicidal, but bodywork and process work teach us to care for his *manner* of expression: he appears to feel cold, frozen, imprisoned in a defiled or over-solid body. Shakespeare associates dew with tears, and with beneficent refreshment, morning, youth (compare *Hamlet*, 1.1.173, 1.3.41), and God's mercy (*Henry VIII*, 2.4.78; *Cymbeline*, 5.5.355). With "a dew," Hamlet might be punning upon "*adieu*" (compare *Henry V*, 4.4.6–9; the English probably anglicized "*dieu*" into the sound "dew"). Less consciously, he may pun upon the underlying meaning of "*á dieu*," that is, he wishes his flesh would go "to God" (who is the explicit subject of the lines immediately following in the speech). Yet his will is grammatically absent from his speech; he expresses no sense of agency or personal cause to bring about the melting, thawing, resolving of his flesh.

If someone says, "My arm hurts me," then he is the object of the verb "hurt," while his *arm* is evidently doing the hurting. The arm is in some sense the *agent* of the verb. This is in contrast to a statement like "I hurt my arm" where *I* am the agent of the hurting. These two sentences reflect fundamentally different processes. In the first one, I am the victim of the hurt; being hurt is a *secondary process aspect*. It is happening to me, while I am a passive recipient of the hurt. In the second case, the hurting of the arm has a primary process character, since I am identifying myself as the one being responsible for the hurt.[7]

We could say, then, that though Hamlet professes he wants to die, he doesn't yet identify with, fully occupy, his body's consequent transformation. He doesn't will his fate. He's not "in touch" with the heating, angry forces within him. They can melt his cold passivity and produce the "dew"/"dieu" of the Ghost's ministry. In the course of the play, Hamlet will heat up, melt, and flow into action, rage, sea change, readiness, scrambling swordplay, and eventual liquid death by "potent poison" (5.2.355). All this could be worked out in great somatic detail, but the point here is merely to sketch how our own bodily mimicry of Hamlet's apparent bodily process—his sighing, his held tongue, his ever-vulnerable heart, his sense that he is the polar opposite of Hercules, his fore-gone exercises—can help us make real his depression and his difficult breakthroughs to action.

Hamlet is, among other things, the story of what happens when mind truly engages body, when a person confronts in full the facts of his mortality. In his first soliloquy, Hamlet reaches toward death to change his relation to life; "life is kindled whenever 'death' is present."[8] His fantasies of death expand to include the Ghost, the Pyrrhus speech, the play in the play, and his graveyard meditations. Certainly, "death fantasies prevail in people of all ages. In my experience most of these fantasies try to create radical changes in life at a time when the ego feels blocked against the apparently inflexible forces of the world" (79), including the force of fleshly mortality. Hamlet is no "special case," which is why his story appeals so widely; his story is the story of every body, an anatomy of oncoming death. Whoever I am as reader, Hamlet's story is mine and Hamlet's body is mine: for part of the play he appears slumping, immature, energyless, out of breath, ectomorphic, oral, voluble, head-centered, cyclically depressed, heartbroken.[9] I, or any reader, through adjustment between close engagement and aesthetic distancing, can achieve an appropriate bodymind perception—a psychophysical learning—that integrates a character out of Hamlet's cues. As spectators, furthermore, we can cooperate with the actor to create the same "internal imprint . . . which possesses us, in mind and body."[10] To our ideas about Hamlet, we can add "a fuller, physio-neural awareness of the *feel* of thinking."[11]

We may note, for example, in Hamlet's contempt for "the funeral baked meats / [that] Did coldly furnish forth the marriage tables (1.2.180–81), in his contempt for the King's "rouse" and "heavy-headed revel" (1.4.8, 17), and in his contempt for "the fatness of these pursy times" (3.4.160) Hamlet's nearly anorexic rejection of physical appetite. To him, Claudius is like a "mildewed ear," a fetid swamp upon which Gertrude is seen to feed, gorge, "batten" (3.4.63–68) as on "the bloat king" (3.4.189). While sense-reading, we can test the inner body feel of Hamlet's twinning nauseas against food and sex, test the close-in meaning of his possibly "anorectic asceticism": "anorectics act as if the words 'whore' and 'nun' were synonymous for them."[12] "Get thee to a nunnery, go, and quickly too" (3.1.141).

Anyone may work through such kinetic analysis of the early, ectomorphic Hamlet (as played by numerous thin, relatively frail actors) to a more endomorphic Hamlet at the close (as played by other, more burly actors), a Hamlet bulked out with "sea-gown scarfed about" him (5.2.13), muscled through "continual practice" in sword-fighting (5.2.209), perhaps even literally "fat" or sweaty as Gertrude seems to suggest during the duel (5.2.289). The latter figure is certainly a more physically active Hamlet than seen in the first part of the play, a Hamlet now proclaiming "the readiness is all" (5.2.220) and possibly finding a way to suit the Ghost's suspect word, "revenge," to Hamlet's more spontaneous, intuitive, un-conscience-stricken, whole-body responses at the close.

Sense-reading thus allows for both microanalysis and global perspectives, but it also heightens awareness of that extended middle range of play reading wherein the reader works along from scene to scene, attending to every sort of clue, including somatic imagery, and testing the accumulating patterns of excitement against varied registers of internal body-feel, emotion, and cognition. To the attentive sense-reader, the first scene of *Hamlet* presents cold, huddling sentinels straining eye and ear beyond mortal bounds, assaying a fearful extension of their senses beyond the bourn of mortal body and yearning for some answer from past those outer limits. After the Ghost appears but speaks not and attention turns to the former, frowning King and to the "state," we hear of "eruption" and "sweaty haste" and "posthaste"; we hear of Fortinbras's "mettle hot and full," of his soldiers "sharked" up for "food and diet" and an enterprise with "stomach" in it. That is, the sentinels, perched on outward wall or parapet, evoke a mood of chill stillness in which the vulnerable body, "sick at heart" (emulating a moon "sick almost to doomsday with eclipse") questions the ghostly beyond and waits for inflowing response. Within and below lies the Claudian "state"— hot, sweaty, rummaging, hasty in "toil" and "task"—about to face off against its appetitive, stomach-defined rival. Those above in the castle waiting stilly for news from the outer world of spirits contrast strongly against those moving on the ground below, physically smiting in "angry parle" or erupting, casting forth, pricked on, sharked up with outflowing energy.

In the second scene, Claudius smoothly spins somatic metaphors that suggest how the "discretion" of manly will may overcome the "nature" of the senses:

> it us befitted
> To bear our hearts in grief and our whole kingdom
> To be contracted in one brow of woe,
> Yet so far hath discretion fought with nature.
>
> (1.2.3–5)

> The head is not more native to the heart,
> The hand more instrumental to the mouth,
> Than is the throne of Denmark to thy father.
>
> (1.2.47–49)

> 'Tis unmanly grief.
> It shows a will most incorrect to heaven,
> A heart unfortified.
>
> (1.2.94–96)

> Why should we in our peevish opposition
> Take it to heart?
>
> (1.2.100–1)

> This gentle and unforced accord of Hamlet
> Sits smiling to my heart.
>
> (1.2.123–24)

The "heart" of Claudius seems "fortified" by his will to make it work in smooth concert with head, hand, and mouth so as to advance all necessary shows of state—combining in one face "an auspicious and a dropping eye" (1.2.10), dispatching Cornelius and Voltimand in "haste" (1.2.39), releasing Laertes, confining Hamlet, and sweeping off to "the King's rouse" (1.2.127). Hamlet's opposed de-arousal, his appeal beyond all "shapes of grief" (1.2.82) to "that within which passes show" (1.2.85) starkly exposes the overmanipulated, overpoliticized sense-work of the King.

At the root of many great works of art lies a question as to how our senses work and how it *feels* to be human. Opposed to Claudius's fortified, smiling heart is the heart of Hamlet, ready, quite literally, to "break" (1.2.159). Hamlet's appeal to that within which "passes" (or "passeth") show hints at kinesthetic etymologies of stepping a *pace* beyond or stretching past the boundaries of social form, and it allies Hamlet with the straining crew upon the parapet. Horatio had to unfortify his ears (1.1.36) so that Bernardo and Marcellus might "assail" them (1.1.35), and Hamlet fears Horatio might "do my ear that violence" (1.2.171) to hear ill of Horatio. Once unfortified, Horatio found himself "harrowed" with fear and wonder so that he trembled and looked pale (1.1.48, 57). The opening of *Hamlet* presents an argument between the sensitized and the desensitized, the in-gatherers and the outgoers, those who fear and wonder in known vulnerability and those who attack or give advice in unknowing armors of fortified desire.

The sense-reader who attends carefully to the opening sense-argument of *Hamlet* must not only attend but also "go beyond" to muse, meditate, and absorb, psychophysiologically, the play of the play. In part this absorption is accomplished through activated reading that may include vocalization, gesture, and postural or other movement, but also this absorption is accomplished through hundreds of slowly learned mediations, in reading and pondering the play, between empathy and distance, engagement and detachment, sensory and cognitive poles of emotion.

In part because *Hamlet* is long and wordy and because Hamlet thinks so much, we as readers are often seduced into overintellectualizing and overanalyzing to the detriment of feelingful experience. If we search instead for the essential emotions of the scenes and only ponder what we feel once we have truly felt it, then we are more likely to discover how emotion can connect what analysis divides. Thus the third scene introduces an Ophelia who seems able to discount her brother's cynical counsels to fear the "contagious blastments" (1.3.42) of Hamlet's affection, but then we observe Polonius contemptuously dismiss the validity of his daughter's love relation with Hamlet ("You do not understand yourself"; "Affection? Pooh!"; "Think yourself a baby"; "Go to, go to"; "Do not believe his vows") even though Ophelia has declared their love "honorable" and countenanced "with almost all the holy vows of heaven." To feel (and preferably produce) the harsh dissonance in tones of father and daughter, to feel (and imitate) the slumping pathos of her "I shall obey, my lord" ("lord," not "father") is to invite the sort of emotion that may connect all the first scenes of youth harrowed out of innocence and into grief by the elder generation.

To the stoical Horatio's early trauma of fear and trembling

caused by the usurping (1.1.30), frowning Ghost of Hamlet, Sr., we add Hamlet aghast at the cynical counsel and manipulations of his mother and uncle and teased into his own doubt and fear by news of the father/ghost he associates with "hell" (1.2.25) and "foul deeds" (1.2.262). Then we see Ophelia cut off from love unfeelingly by her father and Hamlet commanded to revenge-murder by his father, a "cursed spite" (1.5.197) and, in a plainly parallel scene, Polonius laying "sullies" on his son that "soil" him with the "working" or handling (2.1.42–43). To feel a whole youthful generation torn away from its own learning and love and forced to live only for concerns and demands of the parental generation is to feel the very stream of grief that flows through much of Shakespeare (compare *Titus Andronicus*, *Romeo and Juliet*, *Hamlet*, *King Lear*, *Coriolanus*, many history plays, and even romances such as *The Winter's Tale*) and flows, of course, through much of the world's history. I believe it is when we reach within ourselves for deeply empathic response, that which passes show, by a caring sensory contemplation, placing the experience of Horatio, Ophelia, Laertes, and Hamlet (not to mention Fortinbras and Pyrrhus, who also live only in relation to their fathers' deaths) within our personally experienced grief over lost parental or other cherishing, that is when we find a means to make the play *Hamlet* "touch upon the deepest synapses of grief in our own lives."[13]

Hamlet remains, of course, an enormously complex play, emotionally and cognitively, one not to be reduced to simple vectors of unilinear thought or feeling. Thus the early (and to some extent continuing) grief in and for the younger generation in *Hamlet* facing shocks of parental betrayal and death leads to waves of both defiant and accepting action that dominate the close. The point is, however, that sense-reading, far from diminishing our experience of the play, impels us to make the famous "interrogative mood" of the play much more than a grammatical mood, to serve as well as observe each "antic disposition," and to help the play impart physically and emotionally as well as convey cognitively its "sense of mortality" as a literal sense within us.[14]

THE SENSE-READER'S BODY SHAPES SHAKESPEARE'S MEANING

I think it unlikely that I can establish a genuinely insightful relation to Hamlet or his play before I establish an emotional, passionate relation: "if you try to reach the station called Insight before you pass through the town called Emotion, you never reach your destination."[15] In more literary terms:

> from the point of view of catharsis, cognition, in the wider sense of the word, is only possible after we recognize the role of emotions. Most formalists, disputing this, stipulate the separation of emotions and cognition. They think that cognition and detached ideation are enough for a meaningful aesthetic response. Their separation of emotions and cognition is artificial and ultimately detrimental to our understanding of the function of art. The aesthetic response that is catharsis presupposes the unity and interrelatedness of the emotions with the intellect; understanding, which comes from the exercise of the intellect, therefore results from the exercise of emotions. It is a phenomenon that even the Formalists cannot deny.[16]

The sort of emotion here addressed rises from physical affect and cannot inhere in our experience of words alone. "We content ourselves with words—treacherous, contradictory, fleeting—to tell us about ourselves, to invent ourselves. But it is essential for us to feel within our bodies who we are, that we are."[17]

Consider your own memory of reading or studying *Hamlet*: if you have memorized passages, then of course your memory contains that verbal component, but is not much of your memory of the play nonverbal? Don't you remember the look of the castle; your visual images of the characters and their actions; your kinesthetic participation in Hamlet's rushing after the Ghost, Claudius rising at the play in the play, Ophelia floating downstream in song, Hamlet and Laertes wrestling at Ophelia's grave; the duel with rapiers; Hamlet's immobilizing death? You may recall your feelings of sympathy, disgust, fear, triumph, and the like, but do you need any remembered words to trigger them? Do you remember the words as such of what you have read or heard discussed or written about *Hamlet*? Like the memory of a whole childhood, which is not a memory of who said what or what words were read but is a memory of the look and sound and feel of things, a prevailingly nonverbal memory, so, too, the memory of a play is mainly memory of sensory images, emotional responses, and evocations of attitude and mood, nonverbal memory. Given that, it behooves us all both to *enact* Shakespeare's text and to *somatically imagine* Shakespeare's text in the most vivid and inward detail we have time and care for.[18]

To reach undermind Shakespeare, furthermore, we must move beyond the receptive process of sensing our somatic responses to his images. It remains true, of course, that "images are the primal language," producing through brain activity cascades of changes in heart, lungs, gastrointestinal, and immune systems,[19] but each of us also contains bodily profiles and literally organic dispositions that help shape our responses.

> Our Weltanschauungen arise from our organs. The human spirit owes its existence to them, being capable of thinking solely in the language of the organs, and in such categories as provided by the viscera, the muscles, and the skeleton.
>
> The brain is no exception, acting as but one organ among many that serve the intellectual/spiritual function. . . . It remains enmeshed in its dependence upon natural functions and carries out its singular activity much as does the indefatigable and stubborn heart. No matter what philosophical, political, theological, or scientific theories find their origins in us, the brain seems to play no greater part in their creation than the other organs.[20]

To those for whom Weltanschauungen arise from organs, the authority of Shakespeare is undermind and also undermined, at least to the extent that such authority would be dictated exclusively through external culture such as formal education or theatrical production. Bodyreaders, though of course obligated to learn as much as their means admit about Shakespeare's language, times, theater, and the like, take responsibility for personally, corporally contributing to the experience of reading Shakespeare's texts, for incarnating them. Such incarnation reaches far below wordy debates over interpretive preferences or political nuances; it reaches to the inner, emotive, nonverbal memory that is most of what we have left when verbal experience is long past.

7

Practice

Specific, repeatable practices to make sense of Shakespeare may alternate between or combine the preanalytic and the analytic. Some of the practices I discuss here build upon those adduced in earlier chapters. Others suggest new issues and methods. Throughout, I am indebted equally to decades of experience in reading, seeing, and teaching Shakespeare and to hosts of body/mind theorists and practitioners. I hope that you as reader may find yourself challenged to experiment and to find appropriate excitement in your own sense-reading of Shakespeare.

To Visual and Aural Imagination of Sights and Sounds Add Corporeal Imagination of Smell, Taste, Touch, and Inner Sensation

I began the Preface to this book with an appeal for synaesthetic responses to the first lines of Shakespeare's Sonnet 18. Let us explore further:

> Shall I compare thee to a summer's day?
> Thou art more lovely and more temperate.
> Rough winds do shake the darling buds of May,
> And summer's lease hath all too short a date.
> Sometimes too hot the eye of heaven shines,   5
> And often is his gold complexion dimmed;
> And every fair from fair sometimes declines,
> By chance or nature's changing course untrimmed.
> But thy eternal summer shall not fade
> Nor lose possession of that fair thou ow'st;   10
> Nor shall Death brag thou wanderest in his shade,
> When in eternal lines to time thou grow'st.
>   So long as men can breathe or eyes can see,
>   So long lives this, and this gives life to thee.

"Thee" and "a summer's day" may be compared in other than visual terms. Indeed, Shakespeare's term, "temperate," for both "thee" and the "day," suggests attributes of mild temperature or warmth. Youth and day appeal not just to eye but to other sensors as well (for example, to "thermo-receptors"). "Rough winds," similarly, cannot themselves be seen, and the invitation of "temperate" to activate inner sensation may easily extend toward kinesthetic empathy for the shaken buds. Merely *seeing* buds roughly shaken might convey little sense of unpleasantness, whereas sensing the feeling of being oneself roughly shaken strengthens the "image."

Many poetic images, in truth, that could be skimmed over visually will appeal more keenly to nonvisual senses (providing one doesn't skim there, too). By noting synaesthetic interchanges among two or more senses, the reader or hearer or speaker can activate sensory registers deepening poetic experience. Consider the line, "Sometimes too hot the eye of heaven shines": that the sun itself is hot matters little: that it makes *us* hot matters much. We could assimilate "hot" sun to a visual sense of brightness in order to accommodate visual meaning of "shines," but the discomfort even of a "hot" eye itself is not felt as sight of something but as neural pain within the eye. Shakespeare's verbs in the latter part of the sonnet, furthermore, generate a kinesthetic undertow beneath the visual surface: "declines," "untrimmed," "lose possession," "wanderest," "breathe." To wander in shade is to reduce or obscure visual acuity, and so that line invites a shift from visual picturing to kinesthetic empathy, a muscularly felt sense of wandering that continues in the paradoxical next line. In that line, do the "eternal lines" strangely grow *toward* time, rather than its opposite, eternity? Or are they "addressed" *to* time? Visual and nonvisual imaginations are both challenged to provide sensory equivalents of that suddenly cosmic journey.

The couplet, finally, hints that the breath of poetic speakers, as well as their seeing eyes, gives "life" to the poem and to the youth: that is, "so long as men can breathe" means more than "so long as people live on earth"; it means "so long as poems are spoken aloud and thus given life through living breath." There are, then, a remarkable number of appeals in this sonnet to nonvisual senses, and it behooves us to attend to them if we would hope to respond fully. Sense-reading unpacks the way words appeal to our varied organs of imagination.

One reason Shakespeare can be exciting to read inheres in his ubiquitous employment of cross-sensory correspondence. Certain common cross-sensory or "cross-modal" correspondences are well known to researchers in perceptual psychology: for example, pitch and brightness (higher is brighter), loudness and brightness (louder is brighter), or loudness and size (louder is bigger).[1] It is not unlikely that diurnal rhythms dictate infant associations of coordinated increases in brightness, loudness, size, activity, warmth, and the like. Night tends to be itself and also to render its inhabitants (such as pregnant mothers) dark, quiet, nonexpansive, still, cool. Underlying gradients of *intensity* in neural activity reach across apparent division in sensory *modes*.

Shakespeare's Sonnet 73, aligns late season, low temperature, absence, evening, dim light, movement to indoors, rest, being consumed, and farewell. Varied sensory inputs are here equated in terms of shifting levels of intensity, de-arousal, sedation.[2] Shakespeare's complexity, however, cross-matches verbal reminders of sustained energy and force at key locations such as ends of each quatrain ("sang," "seals," "nourished"). The persistent images connecting the speaker to *intensifying* light (in yellow leaves, sunset, glowing fire) against darker and darker backgrounds provide a sensory basis for the couplet's surprising assertion of "love more strong" and of the youth, not the speaker, being the one to "leave." Ostensibly the speaker is dying away, but there is an undersense of color and warmth associated with him and evoked repeatedly, qualifying through sensory stimulation the semantic, logical assertion of their eventual eclipse.

Shakespeare's crossings of sensory modalities often challenge speakers, readers, and hearers to delve beneath accustomed primacies of sight and listening over other senses. When, for example, in *Coriolanus*, Volumnia says:

> The breasts of Hecuba,
> When she did suckle Hector, looked not lovelier
> Than Hector's forehead when it spit forth blood
> At Grecian sword, contemning
>
> (1.3.41–44)

—she offers for visual comparison breasts and forehead. Still, beneath that visual comparison, surges the muscular drama of sucking turned to spitting, as if a mouthful of milk converted in an instant to spat blood, as if the mother's breast itself *became* the infant-turned-warrior's forehead. This is an experience and a meaning of the passage that urges deep contemplation of Coriolanus as orally deprived and contrived, as lost in a world of wounding mouths and mouthing wounds, of infantile dependency and vulnerability transmogrified preternaturally into spitting disgust and contempt.[3] Again, to "see" the whole image "feelingly" requires more than the mind's eye; it requires the mind's mouth muscles and taste buds.

A similar attention to interweavings of "primary" and "secondary" senses provides a pattern for Macbeth's "tomorrow" speech (5.5.19–28). There, *hearing or seeing* the "word" (5.5.18) "death" (5.5.24), the "syllable" of "recorded" time (5.5.21), the player's spoken "frets" (5.5.25), and the furious "sound" of life's "tale" (5.5.26–27) links synaesthetically with *acting or doing* the creeping pace or way, the walking of the shadow, the strutting of the vain actor. That is, the insignificance of life as idiotic sound is played out in a differing sensory mode, the kinesthetic mode of petty creeping, walking, and strutting. Sound without significance matches motion without meaning. The jumble we see and hear implicates the jumble we enact with our creeping, strutting limbs.

Shakespeare's familiar associations, furthermore, of colors with specific emotions—red anger, green and yellow jealousy, black despair (empty life as a "shadow"), and so on—are in part culturally specific and in part attributable to universal human experience.[4] The mere fact that there are great cross-cultural overlays of such synaesthetic experiences reminds us to take the associations seriously, explore their sensuous logic, and not skim by or ignore them as merely arbitrary or capricious. To color Shakespearean emotions, when invited by the texts, as literally and specifically and concretely as possible will no doubt enhance their significance.

READ ALOUD

When I read aloud, I match my own breath to that of the character speaking. I can breathe in and out precisely when I believe she or he breathed in or out. I can choose physically vocalized pitch, pause, and pace to embody my self-version of the charac-

ter's embodied speech. If I add posture, gesture, or other movement, I have started a good way along the path to lively sense-
making, the incarnation of a "fictional" being.

Reading aloud lets one express and communicate to oneself "a
relatively large number of highly differentiated emotional states
on the basis of vocalization alone."[5] One may of course doubt conceptually what precise emotion a character seeks to express, but
physical vocal work itself allows for infinitely more rapid and
subtle experiment and adjustment than attempts to find verbal
labels for emotion can allow. A likely alternation between spontaneous and self-conscious voice production in the reading of
Shakespeare allows, moreover, for a complex interplay between
discovering a character's emotions and learning how one registers one's own—even in such relatively slight matters as "shifts
away from fundamental frequency, or tension indexed by a shift
from a chest to a head register."[6]

In the process of reading aloud Shakespeare's blank verse
(most of his writing), though I must always follow "the twin authorities of meter and sentence"[7] or of rhythm and meaningful
phrasing, I want to let my visual and aural awareness of line integrity provide a continuing, carry-through pulse for the text. As
a silent reader, I may become overimpressed with grammatical
and syntactical units and exigencies (though even a silent reader
may "go down into the workings of the throat, mentally to reen-
act the poet's imitation of speech").[8] As an enactive reader, I
want to give in to the cascading cycles of rough-averaged three-
second lines. Such relaxed alertness allows me to tune up rhythmically, with local and far-reaching hedonic consequences. It lets
me experience much more lengthily sustained patterns of excitation than the ones I continually cut short through anxiety or
defensiveness.[9] I sink to an undercurrent of enter-trainment
in which "the curious subjective effects of metered verse—
relaxation, a holistic sense of the world, and so on—are no doubt
attributable to a very mild pseudo-trance state induced by the auditory driving effect of this repetition."[10]

As a text-dominating, semantically based, silent reader, I might
assemble, for example, the first line of Macbeth's famous speech
thusly:

Tomorrow, and tomorrow, and tomorrow,

but as an oral reader unwilling to trust an abstract, concept-centered shaping of the line, I may smooth it out, lengthen it to a more musical, phonically organized form:

Tomorrow, and tomorrow, and tomorrow.

Suddenly (or gradually) the "and"s—as usually unstressed, subordinate conjunctions now given prominence (partly through meter and partly through the tortuous negotiations of repeated "-nd t" soundings)—become a dramatic enactment of the whole tedious "and"-ness within Macbeth's sere view of life. In similar fashion, if I lean against the enjambments in a blank verse passage, pausing just a little, allowing but not overdoing line unity, then I vocalize and embody more of the music of Shakespeare's verse, feeling the syncopations of phrase and sentence lengths against the reassuring steadiness of line lengths.

In my experience, stage and film actors often fail to honor the line integrity of Shakespeare's iambic pentameter, with its possibly silent "sixth foot" or slight pause marking what might be called its subtactile rhythm. If, in an actor's reading, "the irregularities are too numerous or occur too frequently, the hearer simply misses the characteristic quality of blank verse, and Shakespeare becomes (what it often is on the stage) a kind of metrically chanted prose. The silent foot, actually or in a hearer's imagination, determines the felt character of the pentameter line, when it is felt as a line."[11] A nonprofessional reader, on the other hand, one who speaks the lines aloud and seeks actively the felt character of rhythmic line units, may add substantially to significance and pleasure in the reading experience.

Consider an association of Shakespeare and shouting. Shouting is emphatic speech. Shouting attempts to communicate with heightened emotive, and sometimes, cognitive, impact. The main acoustic features of shouting are elongated vowels that tonally dominate syllables, simplified and systematic pitch differentials, exaggeratedly organized and rhythmic stress patterns,[12] and amplified loudness. These happen to be chief features, also, of much musical expression. They are ways of making acoustic signals more significant to hearers. Shouting often expresses, of course, an extreme of surprise, fear, rage, joy, or other emotion. Its lack of subtlety in employment of the features just mentioned distinguishes it from poetic and musical employments of those same features, but the analogy of Shakespeare and shouting helps teach basic elements of speech that cohere in his lines and emphasize their difference from "normal" speech.

For many readers, reading aloud provides learning by doing. Shakespeare teaches and requires not only a more musically emphatic vocalic delivery but also a more athletic enunciation of consonants, a more strenuous workout of tongue, lips, teeth, throat, than many are accustomed to. Of course, there is no need to emulate British Received Pronunciation, for Shakespeare never spoke that way, sounding instead more like "a funny mixture of West Country, Ireland, a bit of American. . . . American is actually closer to Elizabethan English than our current English speech. [Current English speech is comparatively] genteel, yes, that's a good word. Elizabethan English is rougher—isn't it?—and tougher."[13] Of course, an occasional emulation of Shakespearean sounds may provide not only the musical/emotional effects intended by the author but also a feel for possible puns ("creeps in this petty pace from 'die' to 'die' "?) and syllabification. Shakespeare wrote "sheriff" as "shrieve," for instance, and it often needs to be pronounced as a one-syllable word in his uses; hearing modern-spelled "burden" as old-spelled "burthen" opens up many puns in Shakespeare on "birthing"; "line," "loin," and perhaps "learn" begin to intermingle, and so on.

We see Shakespeare productions, furthermore, that spend huge amounts of money emulating Elizabethan architecture, costumes, and props. They employ old-style musical instruments so as to achieve more original, "authentic" sounds. We rarely hear, unfortunately, the more original, "authentic" sounds of musicality in the pronunciation of Shakespeare's verse, a musicality that remains accessible to modern popular audiences but is strangely denied them. It's up to individual readers, apparently, to create and feel that music for themselves.

One may well ask: "How can anyone ever dream of 'translating' Shakespeare into 'modern English'?"[14] Such translation into modern English becomes, however, the activity of everyone who reads with modern pronunciation in ears or mouth. "That would do, perhaps, if one were merely interested in the contents of Shakespeare. (It is, by analogy, in the contents of the Bible that we are interested, not in its exact syllables.)" (1.xii). Yet what *are* the "exact syllables" of Shakespeare? Are they unsounded elements that provide silent access to abstract ideas as "contents" of the plays? "But who can bear to have nothing more than the contents of Shakespeare's plays? What translation, even merely from one form of English into another form, could possibly reproduce the exact music and thunder of Shakespeare's syllables, and without that—" (1.xii). Still, what *are* the "exact music and thunder" of Shakespeare's syllables if not their sounds as he spoke them or imagined them being spoken? Was Shakespeare not a musician of the word? Did he not care what precise agglutination of sounds renders his verse honey-tongued? Who will have the temerity to assert that such "exact" music and thunder need not be sought in their particular, original, intended forms? And how can one predict the possible effects within readers, even now, of hearing and producing that exact music and thunder? Would it not be worth a try?

Some may argue that an attempt to speak Shakespeare authentically would be too taxing. But when one speaks to a friend, to a baby, to a police officer or judge, or to a foreigner, one varies one's tones, vocabulary, and other elements of expression considerably. Many songs are characteristically sung with styles of pronunciation that differ elaborately from the singer's ordinary pronunciation. All these methods have to be learned. Millions of people find it worth a try to learn nonnative languages in order to communicate with others and to appreciate their cultures, including their poetry and drama. Actors of course often learn a wide variety of very precisely intoned "accents." In the teaching of English literature, Chaucer is generally taught in the "original" sounds and Spenser is spelled and, presumably, spoken in special ways. Many novels, stories, and plays contain dialogue written in dialects that readers are expected to approximate, forming and hearing sounds quite different from their own native dialect.

A rough guide to Shakespearean pronunciation can be presented easily. Witness:

Here, in summary form, are some approximate suggestions for pronouncing words in Shakespeare that are not similarly pronounced today. These examples can be applied to similar words: for example *way* and *say* have the same vowel sound as *day*; *night*, the same vowel sound as *wide*.

    folk (sound the *l*)
    gnaw (sound the *g*)
    knife (sound the *k*; *i* as in *wide*, below)

brush (rhymes with *push*; *r* somewhat trilled)
dull (rhymes with *pull*)
seam (pronounced *same*, with open *a*)
old (pronounced *auld*)
now (pronounced *noo*)
house (pronounced *hoos*)
soul (pronounced *saul*)
know (pronounced *knaw*, with sounded *k*)
own (pronounced *awn*)
tune (pronounced *tiwn*)
rule (pronounced *riwl*; *r* somewhat trilled)
day (pronounced *die*)
time (pronounced *toime*)
wide (pronounced *woide*)
join (rhymes with *line*)
creeping (pronounced *craypin*, with open *a*)
dissention (in four syllables, without *sh* sound)
persuasion (in four syllables, without *zh* sound)[15]

What such a guide lacks in completeness or perfect accuracy it makes up for in encouragement to find the flavor and tone of a more authentic, tunable Shakespeare in the mouth and ear. Such a guide will not, for example, explain why Shakespeare may rhyme "love" with "prove" or "remove," but it may nudge one to take the *u* sound of "luv" as in "brush" or "dull" (above) and lengthen it to approximate the vowels in "push" and "pull," thus bringing such words as "love" and "glove" much closer to the even-further-lengthened vowels of "move," "prove," "remove," "approve," and so on.

Such phonic adjustments as these may significantly enhance both meaning and emotion in reading a Shakespearean text such as the famous Sonnet 116:

> Let me not to the marriage of true minds
> Admit impediments. Love is not love
> Which alters when it alteration finds,
> Or bends with the remover to remove.
> O, no, it is an ever-fixed mark   5
> That looks on tempests and is never shaken;
> It is the star to every wandering bark,
> Whose worth's unknown, although his height be taken.
> Love's not Time's fool, though rosy lips and cheeks
> Within his bending sickle's compass come;   10

Love alters not with his brief hours and weeks,
But bears it out even to the edge of doom.
    If this be error and upon me proved,
    I never writ, nor no man ever loved.

If we assume, as seems likely, that Shakespeare's contemporaries pronounced the word "love" along a range including, approximately, "luv" and "loove,"[16] then we set the stage for a phonetic drama in the poem whereby the first "love" (second line, third word), even if pronounced "luv" (as would be common today and was perhaps rapidly prevailing in Shakespeare's day) becomes chastened, as it were, to change in pronunciation to rhyme, in its second appearance, with the word "remove" (fourth line). This teaching is reinforced in the couplet when "proved" draws "loved" into being pronounced "looved."[17]

Through the requirements of rhyme, the poem covertly tells us that we are talking about an old-fashioned or simply old kind of love. To read with roughly Elizabethan pronunciation is to lengthen and often open the rhyme and chime sounds so that the distance between *ark*, *ak*, and *eek* sounds ("mark," "bark," "shaken," "taken," "cheeks," "weeks") lessens, and the words arguably work through this phonic harmony toward a more stable lexical, semantic bonding than would our modern forms of them achieve. In Elizabethan pronunciation, the poem is allowed to *enact* a musical blending and binding of sounds that evoke a singly assertive mood, momentarily keep irony at bay, and delay the couplet's sounding "grandly hollow."[18] "Come" is allowed to rhyme with "doom," and the line "But bears it out even to the edge of doom" brings vowel-sound relations of "But," "out," "to," and "of" into greater alignment and smoothes the vowel sounds of "bears," "even" ("e'en"), and "edge" toward a single openness. If you will practice such a reading aloud, you may find personal proof that such rhyming and chiming through Elizabethan pronunciation allow the poem to succeed more conclusively as a phonic, tonal evocation of affirmative mood than as abstract, logical proof.

Reading aloud with either old or new pronunciation will, moreover, help provide sense-experience of a peculiar, wakeful lulling or pretrance arising from Shakespeare's repetitions: "love . . . love . . . Love's . . . Love . . . loved"; "ever . . . never . . . every . . . even . . . error . . . never . . . ever." Such performative reading becomes at once curiously arousing and quieting, as does much work with music. The reading aloud takes work, feels more chancy and exposing, but also allows sounds to assert strong appeals to feeling. Such a reader emphasizes "incongruities between tongue, lip, and eye, the slips between sense and senses that are activated by rhyme."[19] Such a reader also approaches that athletic rest in motion, or grace under pressure, that Shakespeare uniquely and "trippingly" provides.

Hamlet, as everyone knows, asked the players visiting at Elsinore to "study a speech of some dozen or sixteen lines" that he would "set down" (2.2.541–42), thus indicating his intent to write down the speech and have the literate players study it through reading. Hamlet did not, however, let the matter rest there, for he took the added step of intoning the speech aloud to the players. He even went on to admonish them: "Speak the speech, I pray you, *as I pronounced* it to you" (3.2.1–2, my emphasis). If Shakespeare can imagine his amateur playwright so intent upon securing the precise pronunciation he himself provides, cannot we imagine Shakespeare requesting similar care for his own pronunciation? As students and general readers, may we not find some means to honor that presumed intention? I fervently hope it may be so. Then we may read and hear Shakespeare in the same sweet-sounding, euphonious mode in which we read and hear Chaucer, Spenser, Burns, Twain, and Hurston. The words will not sound to us exactly as they sounded to the authors, of course—any more than our ears can capture Bach's intended sounds—but the older pronunciation will aim toward whatever long-term continuity in cultural forms and responses may be allowed by history.

Work with Patterns of Excitement

Whether reading aloud or silently, I need to risk, at least occasionally, the buildup of energy, tension, and sensitivity that results from sustained reading of whole scenes, acts, plays. I need to breathe deeply as I read (often changing postures, standing, or walking about), probably the single-most important change in my ordinary reading habits, creating access to emotion and particularly to the disturbing intensifications of both positive and negative emotions that I habitually cut short. A Shakespeare play, like a tom-tom session, provides a ritualized invitation to build up and intensify exceedingly strong emotions. It resembles a Shamanic dream. We don't want to break off the dream, wake up, or interrupt it with excessive analysis while it takes place. Even a philosophic critic will sometimes admit: "the play's thinking about man and Nature is irreducibly experiential, a process we live through. Here, once again, we see how different this unfolding, often jarringly contradictory process of 'poetic-dramatic thinking' is from the linear process of logical-discursive thought."[20] Let us dread what is read just with head.

Because the streaming energies of argument and desire, ambition and loneliness, within my body have been painful in the past, I've developed barriers (Kurtz) or conditioned tendencies (Heckler) or patterns of constriction or explosion (Keleman) or armoring (Lowen) to contain my sensitivity to rising excitation.[21] But if while I read, say, a Shakespeare scene, I gently yet firmly resist distraction or evasion, if I come back to a deep-breathing and relaxed alertness, and if I physically enact each character, then I more nearly accept Shakespeare's implicit invitation to explore a variety of foreign, "other" patterns of excitement. I teach myself new ways of moving, feeling, and being: to refuse or adopt, as later reflection warrants. Yet I can hardly hope to approximate the experience of Portia, Othello, Lear, or Cleopatra until I participate in their embodied presence, until I "feel their health and their sickness inside."[22]

Such contact will require much work, but simply making an initial effort to accept physical, emotional contact with character and action, to drop habits of intellectualizing that evade risky feelings, will accomplish much. We need not translate or interpret our temporal experience into spatialized structure and content; we can trust the process itself, trust the more immediate, temporal, affective workings of the plays to reveal the life of the characters and the potential for reenactment in our lives. We can always label and consume Shakespeare, but these differ from engaging in experience right now. To feel how Banquo may stand in the hand of God or Macbeth unsay "Amen" or Antonio shake hands behind his back or Coriolanus defend his body from exposure or Othello writhe in a foaming agony of betrayal or Cleopatra nurse the fatal asp or Hermione move from statuesque stillness is "to recover our senses,"[23] to participate in "the most profoundly civilizing of processes—the education of the senses."[24]

Simply the physical stance I adopt toward my reading may affect my responses. If I signal to myself when I read Shakespeare that I do not want to engage my patterns of excitation, if I read when sleepy or tipsy or distracted by television or when slouching or fidgety, then I cannot expect much significant psychophysiological response. On the other hand, I may accept that "body attitudes infiltrate the 'feel' of the world" and that "people tell different kinds of imaginative stories when they are lying down and when they are sitting up," so that "one could say that simply altering the position of a person's body in space can influence the way in which he uses his imagination."[25] Accepting such bodily involvement in the work of "imagination," I will understand why I. A. Richards, reading about the bite of centipedes, leaped out of his chair when a falling leaf struck his face,[26] and I will experiment with how I may act my way into new modes of feeling and being by echoing or mirroring possible tones, postures, and movements of Shakespeare's characters.[27]

To give a practical example, I suggest that you as reader try reading aloud the following lines while slowly lowering your brow:

> Alive in triumph, and Mercutio slain!
> Away to heaven, respective lenity,
> And fire-eyed fury be my conduct now!
> (*Romeo and Juliet*, 3.1.121–23)

Now, read the lines while slowly raising your brow. It may or may not have worked for you, but researchers have shown that raised brows usually accompany rising voice pitch and lowered brows usually accompany falling voice pitch.[28] Subjects have found it difficult to lower brows and raise pitch at the same time. Thus, "facial cues provide emotional 'color' to what is being said" (483) and in far more literal and complex ways than ordinarily imagined. Might facial involvement, even in silent reading, intensify, alter, or enhance perceived "tones" or dialogue? We stand at the threshold of freshly rewarding reading methods.

Because reading is a physical process, environmental as well as personal conditions affect response. Changes in lighting, ventilation, temperature, seating and table arrangements, outside sounds, and the like all may produce changes in reading response. A sense of time pressure may produce a wildly differing reading from that encouraged by its absence. May one read comedies with a speed inappropriate to a good reading speed for tragedies? How much Shakespeare will one read at a "sitting" or "standing"? How often will one slow down for meditational musing upon a passage? With what results? May isolating oneself as reader suit tragedy better than comedy? When will one wish to share reading aloud with others, and why? Does looking down, literally, upon one's text suggest a differing relation to it than might be gained by looking levelly at it or up to it? Might wearing bifocals help produce a more scrutinizing frame of mind? Could varying states of dress at all affect ranges of formal or informal feeling while reading? (One may recall that, during his exile, Machiavelli dressed in formal robes to read the Greek and Roman classics.) Will a hungry reader attend more closely to food imagery? Will a recently bereaved reader fail to appreciate some of Shakespeare's comedy? Are some forms of crying at sad scenes pleasurable and some forms unpleasurable?[29] Are post-menstrual surges of interest in erotic scenes discernible?[30] Does advancing age enhance appreciation of Shakespeare's later works? These are but a few of the myriad questions that might be creatively addressed by interdisciplinary teams of Shakespeareans and psychologists. Even common readers may profitably ponder such questions, if only to extend engagement with and controls over the reading experience.

BECOME AWARE OF KINETIC SIGNS

Despite the emphasis above on giving in to the text, reading Shakespeare (or any imaginative literature) requires that readers work back and forth between varied modes of engagement and detachment.[31] Yet engagement and detachment can become intertwining states. One of my arguments here is that amplified engagement can produce rewards of detachment. By exaggerating the tonal and gestural dimensions of a text, a reader brings intuitive and spontaneous parts of the play (and of the reader's self) to light.

Troilus and Cressida contains, for example, a brief scene (4.5.232–71) in which Achilles and Hector survey each other's persons (in the Greek camp well before their last meeting). Part of it goes as follows:

Achilles.
> Now, Hector, I have fed mine eyes on thee;
> I have with exact view perused thee, Hector,
> And quoted joint by joint.

Hector.
>   Is this Achilles?

Achilles. I am Achilles.   235

Hector.
> Stand fair, I pray thee. Let me look on thee.

Achilles.
> Behold thy fill.

Hector.   Nay, I have done already.

Achilles.
> Thou art too brief. I will the second time,
> As I would buy thee, view thee limb by limb.

Hector.
> O, like a book of sport thou'lt read me o'er.   240
> But there's more in me than thou understand'st.
> Why dost thou so oppress me with thine eye?

>   (4.5.232-42)

Though Hector acts gravely assured in much of the play, still he fails to follow his own counsel when the Trojans deliberate on the war; he unwisely spurns warnings of Cassandra; and he foolishly disarms himself after capturing the armor of a Greek soldier whom he has "hunted" for his "hide" like a "beast" (5.6.30–31). In his conversation with Achilles, he asks questions and uses subjunctives and tag-ending qualifiers, suggesting subliminal subordination to Achilles. A wide range of tones might then be fitting for Hector's question: "Why dost thou so oppress me with thine eye?" Should Hector sound disdainful? Or genuinely curious? Or struck with intimations of dread? Does he seek eye contact with Achilles? Or shun it? Does Hector shudder, lower his shoulders, bend, or sink down upon uttering the verb "oppress"? Does he later recover his equanimity? Because readers and actors will play this exchange in variegated styles, any reader owes it to herself or himself not merely to skim cerebrally over lightly imagined possibilities but to explore the full body's instinctive contribution to a personally engaged reading of the text. As soon as one attaches posture, gesture and tone to "oppress" one discovers a good deal about degrees of anger or fear that feel appropriate in that moment, and a fascinating interplay between internal feeling and rational response can ensue. My Achilles may tap complex vectors, psychophysiological components, of anger and fear ready to rise in me; and your Achilles may do the same for you. And this can happen not according to anything so conceptually stark as an "identity theme" in each of us,[32] but rather according to a blend of historical knowledge, linguistic competence, Shakespeare study, body type, patterns of excitation and holding, mood of the moment, energy level, age, gender, physical experience, conception of prebattle rituals, unconscious feelings, thoughts, and attitudes concerning fighting, staring and being stared at, kiting, intimations of fate, and so on.

Shakespeare's texts are filled, paradoxically, with holes. Those holes defy clear interpretation, leading instead darkly down and mazelike toward the text's and our secondary process, to regions where discovery requires access to energies much more spontaneous and body-centered than conceptual analysis can reach. To look at one other example, consider those amazing moments before the gulled Malvolio picks up a letter he thinks is Olivia's. He has been imagining marriage to Olivia and dominance over Toby and the rest:

> *Malvolio.* Calling my officers about me, in my
> branched velvet gown; having come from a daybed,
> where I have left Olivia sleeping—
> *Sir Toby.* Fire and brimstone!
> *Fabian.* O, peace, peace!   50
> *Malvolio.* And then to have the humor of state; and
> with a demure travel of regard, telling them I know
> my place as I would they should do theirs, to ask for
> my kinsman Toby.
> *Sir Toby.* Bolts and shackles!   55
> *Fabian.* O, peace, peace, peace! Now, now.
> *Malvolio.* Seven of my people, with an obedient start,
> make out for him, I frown the while, and perchance
> wind up my watch, or play with my—some rich
> jewel. Toby approaches; curtsies there to me—   60
> *(Twelfth Night,* 2.5.46–60)

If one desires, one may find suggestions here and in the broader passage that Malvolio's sexual appetites are working mightily in the scene, present through conscious and unconscious display. Olivia presumably sleeps after Malvolio has tired her with lovemaking on the "daybed"; later Malvolio claims to recognize in the letter Olivia's "very c's, her u's, and [or 'n] her t's" (suggesting "c-u-t" or, the same thing, "c-u-'n-t"). And so, above, when Malvolio says, "I frown the while, and perchance wind up my watch, or play with my—some rich jewel," a reader has many options. Malvolio could be kinesthetically expressing the frown, winding of the watch, and "play" with . . . well, what? It could be his steward's chain (Toby earlier admonished Malvolio (2.3.118–19), "Go, sir, rub your chain with crumbs"). It could be his staff. It could be a jewel, in a ring or somewhere else. It could be that Malvolio's hand strays downward to suggest masturbatory fantasy at "play with my—"; or Malvolio might not physically display any of these behaviors. Still, the reader who experiments either with alternate physical motions or with inner kinesthetic attention to varied possibilities will learn much about her or his own styles of humor, defenses and preferences, and resultant feelings and situation.

As awareness meets the body in motion or attends to inner feelings, not everything it finds is the product of conscious planning. Consciousness finds itself offered fruits of unconscious energies. I may begin to activate my reading of Hector or of Malvolio through shifts in posture, gesture, and so on with some conscious regard for the meaning of my movements and feelings, but my body in motion and in feelings is much too complex and multifaceted for action to be guided in all its aspects by intention. My body "takes over" and allows me to note, at least momentarily, what "it" proceeds to do and feel and judge through my behavior.

Even without intending specifically to enact a part, I may find while reading that my patterned behavior reveals response and personality. I may find myself characteristically tilting my head or torso forward or back or to the side when I read certain kinds of scenes, or I may shuffle my feet edgily, or I may sit up in a straight, balanced, coordinated posture when something in the action seems to arouse such behavior. Any of a thousand other movements could signal instincts for fight or flight or signal divergences among child, parent, and adult stances I either habitually or freshly adopt.[33] Reading is behavior, and reading Shakespeare is revealing behavior.

The more sensitive I become to kinetic patterns within the plays—to ways in which Samson may bite his thumb (*Romeo and Juliet*, 1.1.42–51), to ways Hamlet may have "acted" in Ophelia's closet, to what Hamlet and Horatio may have seen in Claudius's responses to dumb show and play in play, to Leontes observing Hermione and Polixenes, to Troilus observing Cressida and Diomed, and so forth—the more sensitive I may then become to my own responses in facial expression, posture, gesture, and internal signaling. In groups on stage, who faces whom, with what posture and eye contact, and how near or far away, can signal (in "proxemic" terms) a great deal about relative dominance and submission, and many other matters.

Even such seemingly trivial items as winking and blinking can suggest much: there is the wink of pretending not to see and the wink of sexual suggestion. Some winking apparently connotes covering and uncovering of genitals or the revealing suppression of sexual wishes.[34] At any given personal reading, then, one may ask how other, varied readers would respond to the following?

> *Burgundy.* Pardon the frankness of my mirth, if I
> answer you for that. If you would conjure in her, you
> must make a circle; if conjure up love in his true   295
> likeness, he must appear naked and blind. Can you
> blame her then, being a maid yet rosed over with the
> virgin crimson of modesty, if she deny the appearance
> of a naked blind boy in her naked seeing self? It were,
> my lord, a hard condition for a maid to consign to.   300
> *King Henry.* Yet they do wink and yield, as love is
> blind and enforces.
> *Burgundy.* They are then excused, my lord, when they
> see not what they do.
> *King Henry.* Then, good my lord, teach your cousin to   305
> consent winking.
> *Burgundy.* I will wink on her to consent, my lord, if
> you will teach her to know my meaning. . . .
>   (*Henry V*, 5.2.293–308)

Here, as in so much of Shakespeare's sexual language, the talk seems to reflect the speakers' conscious control of meanings through intentional puns and self-conscious imagery, yet, again as in so much of Shakespeare's sexual language, the puns and images slip into an array of phantasmagoric possibilities. Does Henry conjure "in" Katharine's "circle" with naked part? with an invoked blind Cupid? In how many fashions might "appearance" be taken? Is the "naked blind boy" physical? emotional? part of Henry? part of Katharine? an embryo? What is the "hard condition"? Is "winking" here mainly a chaste pretence that what's happening is unknown? Or a seductive stimulation? Or neither? both? In one of many possible readings, Henry and Burgundy could actually wink as they used the word "wink." Just how they would wink, each reader can enact, and in such enacting a good deal might be discovered about how the reader's *body* has been interpreting the passage. (Are all the winks, for instance, one-eyed blinks? Or is Katharine's imagined winking, female and two-eyed for modesty, and the male one-eyed in salaciousness? Which eye will you wink, invoking perhaps more of which brain hemisphere and with what significance? How fast a wink, invoking how much of the face and how much head motion, if any? What if you "can't" or hate to wink?)

No doubt, some would argue that the text is meant to be read more abstractly, with less physically close reading, yet from what sources would such abstractional intent be inferred? The text was created, after all, precisely for physical enactment. Its author was an actor. The rewards of enactive reading, furthermore, can hardly be fairly assessed by those eschewing the method without a fair trial, a trial that risks little and promises much in the way of extended freedom, and more conscious (and perhaps subconscious) life. No doubt, equally, it would be possible to overpractice or overintensify the sorts of whole-body responses here advocated. A balance must be reached between empathetic, through-line readings and analytic, micro-sensing. Sometimes, generic or stereotypical imagery may suit the passage and the reader's mood and interest better than autobiographical or extremely precise imagery, though there are studies indicating that, generally, more time-consuming, intensive imaging produces better comprehension.[35]

Practicing nonverbal response and kinetic analysis honors the point that "the great weight of emotional communication is handled by paralanguage and kinesics."[36] Emotion in Shakespeare rides upon timbre, pitch, pace, pause, loudness, stress, emphasis, interjections and outcries including nonlanguage sounds such as sighs, coughs, yells, or screams, laughter, and all the complex determinants of feeling tone. "The more one examines speech in its full interactional context (and not simply in its written representation), the more one finds examples of utterances in which the primary determinants of the speaker's identity and purpose and of the listener's response are paralinguistic ('Say it as if you mean

it,' 'You don't SOUND as if you're a clergyman,' and the unavoid-
able 'It wasn't what he said, but the way that he said it')."[37] It is
thus imperative that readers who hope to take Shakespeare at all
seriously enter into a performative relation with his texts by
practicing the range of simpler and more complex exercises suggested here and earlier. At the same time, an analytic perspective
suits some forms of exploration into characters' language, demeanor, movement, and touching. Long overdue in Shakespeare
study, for example, are systematic analyses of gender, class, age,
and power differentials in relative terms of address, names, you-
thou distinctions, patterns of interruption, phrases of hesitancy
and self-doubt, qualifying phrases, employment of subjunctives
and optatives, self-disparagement, disdain, hostile silences, self-
disclosure, tag-questions and requests, initiating humor, use of
storytelling and anecdotes, use of nonstandard and dialect
speech, and so on.[38] Who keeps to a dignified or tight demeanor
and who is lax or loose? Whose clothing is formal or informal?
Who touches whom and in what manner? Can one note restric-
tive or invitational postures and gestures, eye-contact and facial
expressions? How may the characters respect or violate each other's immediate "territory"? And so on.

Finally, the crucial element in all such exploration is a thirst or
appetite for closer, risk-taking connection to both verbal text and
nonverbal textures of response. The two feed each other. The
term "explore" seems to derive from the cry (*plorare*) of hunters,
and a hunting instinct helps one identify and explore textual moments where few words speak for huge concerns. Many readers
may react with awe, for instance, to Macbeth's image of "Pity,
like a naked newborn babe / Striding the blast" (1.7.21–22).
"Striding" is usually glossed as "bestriding" or "riding," but in
Shakespeare "bestride" may mean "stride" and "mount" as well
as "ride," so that the sense of the babe suddenly walking the
wind arises. Phonically, the sequence, "babe striding," sounds
like "ba-be-striding," as if "babe" is foreshortened or captured
by "bestriding." The babe no sooner begins its sonic existence
than it rises up to sit and walk (untimely from its mother's
womb). The shock of the passage inheres in the space, obliter-
ated, between "babe" and "striding," the space or instant in
which seemingly helpless, pitiful infancy quickly acquires vast
power and turns accusatory. Full proprioceptive engagement
with the image might honor such practice as holding the baby and

being the baby held with all the attendant sensations of each. Then the shift from feeling nurturant or naked to feeling a "striding" of the blast can open up a titanic conflict in the Macbeth who terrorizes his feelings of pity (for babes or "the seeds or time" or "the seeds of Banquo" or "nature's germens"), finding that new life turns immediately threatening, that a pitiful birth actually contains within it deathly forces far beyond what might ordinarily be sensed "of woman born."

8

Sense-Reading in the Classroom

Is Sense-Reading Too Emotional for Practical Classroom Use?

To be so desperately afraid of babies and cherubim, to identify them with fear itself (compare, "If trembling I inhabit then,
protest me / The baby of a girl" [3.4.106–7]), Macbeth must be
crazy. Crazy like a fox, or shadow. Macbeth inhabits shadowland;
he speaks for the shadow who knows that all new life threatens
our death. Knows it. Fears it. Hates it. But could never "explain"
it. So, if the play *Macbeth* is to occupy more than the thinnest
wafer of a reader's consciousness, that reader needs to go looking
for, lurking after, that shadow. And since much of the shadowy,
dreamy, comalike experience of Shakespeare whispers, birrlike,
in thickets antithetical to all our rational education, making
sense of Shakespeare, as outlined here, would seem banished
from the classroom, as also from academia generally, where
"most critics regard attempts to incorporate emotional response
in accounts of a play as woolly humanist empathizing."[1]

As teacher and critic, I want to speak up for the almost-lost
"crazy," emotive, somatic energy of Shakespeare and other art,
its chthonic power to touch unconscious, bodily fears and desires.
Shakespeare *is* shadow. Shakespeare *is* an altered state, one giving access to sickness and, hence, to health. "Only a few of the
problems people suffer from can be dealt with by remaining in
this reality. The solutions to most problems require wisdom and
experience of altered states. We need to learn how to switch realities fluently, how to be able to transport information back and
forth between an altered state and a normal primary process."[2]
Reading Shakespeare can itself be an intervention that helps us

withdraw projections and reabsorb shadow, but such reading has to take risks, dare deep play, and feel like the following recipe:

> It is proper to ask then, "How does one go about eating the shadow or retrieving a projection, practically?"
>
> In daily life one might suggest making the sense of smell, taste, touch, and hearing more acute, making holes in your habits, visiting primitive tribes, playing music, creating frightening figures in clay, playing the drum, being alone for a month, regarding yourself as a genial criminal. A woman might try being a patriarch at odd times of the day, to see how she likes it, but it has to be playful. A man might try being a witch at odd times of the day, and see how it feels, but it has to be done playfully. He might develop a witch laugh and tell fairy stories, as the woman might develop a giant laugh and tell fairy stories.[3]

I submit that reading Shakespeare enactively invokes most activities mentioned in the quoted passage, yet such enactive, sensory reading would wear a mask of anathema in the classroom, would it not? Or else it would be assimilated into watery, useless forms?

STUDENTS CAN SENSE-READ DIALOGUE AND STAGE MOVEMENT: EXAMPLES FROM *A MIDSUMMER NIGHT'S DREAM* AND *ROMEO AND JULIET*

If teachers would first model for students the teachers' own forms of "constructive cognitive and visceral activity"[4] with Shakespeare and then let students individually and in small groups work out unsupervised performances, then progress might be made. Students need to find how Shakespeare's language can teach them ways of making sense that cursory cerebral reading habits tend to discourage or foreclose. Typically, however, practical work with students rarely aims vigorously at poetically energized psychosomatic centers of the plays. Yet it might.

Consider teaching, for example, the opening to *A Midsummer's Night's Dream*:

> *Theseus.*
>   Now, fair Hippolyta, our nuptial hour
>   Draws on apace. Four happy days bring in
>   Another moon; but, O, methinks, how slow

> This old moon wanes! She lingers my desires,
> Like to a stepdame or a dowager   5
> Long withering out a young man's revenue.
> *Hippolyta.*
> Four days will quickly steep themselves in night;
> Four nights will quickly dream away the time;
> And then the moon, like to a silver bow
> New bent in heaven, shall behold the night   10
> Of our solemnities.

(1.1.1–11)

While recognizing that students may react to "those words" of the play by becoming "bored and defiant," teacher advocates of "Shakespeare set free" may too readily counsel a solution such as students posing in tableaux vivants versions of Theseus and Hippolyta "in poses suggesting romantic longing. For example, they might stand a bit apart and gaze at each other with arms outstretched."[5] I would hope the students who enacted such an arguably frozen, improbable, tableau rendering of the verse would be encouraged by teachers to question and revise it. To begin with, as another teacher has suggested (in connection with *A Midsummer Night's Dream*), "in all the practical work, the way in which it is followed up in discussion will depend to a large extent on the ages of the students with whom you are working. But any age group could and should be asked which words and/or images stand out from the rest. You might also get them to talk about dreams and dreaming."[6]

Considering merely the verbs employed by Theseus and Hippolyta, student readers might compare the kinesthetic, motor sense of Theseus' "draws on," "bring in," "lingers" (protracts, makes longer), and "withering" to the less motor-involved sense of Hippolyta's "steep," "dream away," and "behold." For Theseus, the days produce the new moon; for Hippolyta the nights do. For Theseus, the days bring in the new moon; for Hippolyta, the nights dream away the time before the new moon. Hippolyta restates the process whereby Theseus's "four days" run against the edge, the "but," the sonically/visually personified "O" of the "old moon" slowly waning and lingering and withering. In Hippolyta's imagination, the four days immerse and soak themselves, "steep" themselves, in a liquid, transformative medium of night converting time to a dream, "quickly" with suggestions of rapidity and also fresh, pregnant aliveness. Replacing the entropic and perhaps detumescent feel of Theseus's desires "withering out," Hippolyta summons the taut energy of the "new bent" bow that will "behold" the wedding night not only with regardful sight but also with suggestions of a more material beholding. Nothing in the method of such analysis would be difficult for students to emulate, for they are simply encouraged to observe, note, and feel in the same keen and energetic and memorable fashion they already employ for any experience that truly interests them.

Hippolyta's image of the new moon as silver bow suits, of course, associations of moon with Diana and Hippolyta as virginal, Amazonian huntress and warrior. Amazon myths explore many problems in gender relations, including the question of whether or how "the daughter must marry."[7] Theseus soon adverts to "the cold fruitless moon" and to "Diana's altar" (1.1.73, 89), reflecting another facet of his fearful links between moon and female (stepdame, dowager) withering. Still, while Hippolyta (and Hermia) may not openly challenge and defeat male fears and domination, Hippolyta's response to Theseus, her taking over and changing his moon-image, asserting the primacy of steeping, dreaming, feminine night over masculine desiring day, proves to be the response of other characters and of even the larger play. Lysander converts Theseus's anxiety of the dowager moon withering out revenue into his own "widow aunt, a dowager / Of great revenue" (1.1.157–58) who will help them marry. Lysander also extends Hippolyta's Diana/Phoebe moon when he speaks of its power to "behold" and to endue "with liquid pearl the bladed grass" (1.1.209–10).

"Feminine" submission steeps and changes male anxiety into a re-creative "story of the night," a transfiguring lunacy that grows both "strange and admirable" (4.2.23–27). The pattern of this submission characterizes relations of Theseus/Hippolyta, Oberon/Titania, the young lovers, and perhaps even Pyramus/ Thisbe. After the expressed moon-fears of Theseus, Egeus, and Oberon, the project of the play is to "find out moonshine" (3.1.50) in Bottom's affably human terms, "to disfigure, or to present, the person of Moonshine" (3.1.56–67) as man in the moon, double-gendered, with "sunny beams," a lunacy that mingles tragic and comic into a consecrative, hallowed frolic.

Thus the opening exchange between Theseus and Hippolyta might be "seen as a 'miniature' of Shakespeare at large and used to alert students to aspects of his inheritance and emerging habits."[8] Such alerting can hardly take place, however, when students are physically posed as Theseus and Hippolyta statically stretching arms toward each other with romantic longing. Instead, let students play Theseus as fretfully possessive or as assured of Hippolyta's mature love (as he appears in Shakespeare's later play, *The Two Noble Kinsmen)* or as self-consciously grinning at his own unromantic, economic metaphors for his desires (as revenue) or as shaking his fist at "this old moon." Let Hippolyta stand still as she speaks; or let her gesture and move (replacing Theseus's pique at the moon with an enactment of its beholding bow). In any event, let it be seen and felt that Hippolyta is responding to and answering Theseus, not merely providing a mimic to his stance.

However students may enact the scene through external expression, far more important, in my estimation, would be their inner embodiment that tries out the proprioceptive feel of the verbs (particularly "withering" and "steeps" in a drying, rewetting progression), the slowing drag in the ear of "but, O, methinks, how slow / This old moon wanes," and the almost certain mockery through which Hippolyta replaces Theseus's *"like to* a stepdame" with *"like to* a silver bow."

I do not believe there is anything arcane or oversophisticated in this somatic or performative approach. Any student can read portions of Shakespeare aloud. Any student can imitate stage actions and find, in the process, that "action is eloquence" (*Coriolanus,* 3.2.78). Any student can be taught rudiments of Shakespeare's metrical art. All I advocate, really, is one kind of teaching poetic drama, a kind that attends to the poetry in the drama. It seems obvious, furthermore, that "once we can get our pupils to see the point of poetry *in* drama, they are more likely to feel the need of poetry *out* of drama."[9] If Shakespeare teachers will help their students not only understand ideas in Shakespeare but also care a little for their living transactions with its poetry, then such teachers will more certainly enrich their students' imaginations, helping them to find where fancy is bred, "in the heart or in the head? / How begot, how nourished" (*Merchant of Venice,* 3.2.64–65).

Teachers of younger students tend, in my experience, to shy away from Shakespeare's language, assigning instead film-viewing or background work on biography and the Elizabethan age.

Experience in such classrooms leads me to encourage a wholly different approach. I choose moments in the plays of particularly strong and accessible emotion, and I work on ways to get students to read aloud. I read like a robot, with no emotion in my voice. This leads to interest in what emotion is being suppressed and how it might be intoned. Or we read aloud in chorus, several times, until the words are familiar, unthreatening. Or we sit in a circle, and I read the first word of the passage; the student next to me reads the second word, and so on. Then I read a phrase or a sentence; the next student reads the next phrase or sentence, and so on around. After a while, I or anyone may comment on anything noted about a word, phrase, or sentence. Continual encouragement is offered to "try it out," "see how it sounds," "see what gesture might go with that," "how might the speaker move when saying that?" I may "demonstrate," often with obvious incompetence, rousing others to do better.

If the class were studying *Macbeth*, the teacher might make the desk the cauldron and start to walk around it chanting "Double, double, toil and trouble." Any student willing to say the line can join the circling Witch. When more students arrive, more lines can be assigned in any of dozens of ways. Or the teacher may ask students: "In what tone of voice does Macbeth ask his wife, 'If we should fail?'?" (1.7.60). And in what tone does she answer him: "We fail?"? Actresses have delivered the line angrily or with surprise or matter-of-factly or with a shrug of their shoulders or with a whisper or a shout, and so on. Show the students that *they* can decide how the text works, and watch them go at it. It belongs to them, not to actors or teachers. They can make its meaning, to a large extent. When Sir Toby, in *Twelfth Night*, says to Malvolio (2.3.94), "Sneck up!," does Toby flip Malvolio off? or turn his back? or thumb his nose? or put his face in Malvolio's? Many guesses are good; none should be offered without personal experience, experiment, embodiment.

From such local work, a teacher may expand consideration to include more comprehensive tones and body-expression of unified scene-parts. How does Capulet as angry father hover over the kneeling Juliet (3.5.164) and rasp out, "My fingers itch"? Does Juliet cringe? Many students are authorities on such parent-child conflicts and are willing to interpret and even demonstrate here. What happens to Juliet physically in the rest of the scene? When does she rise from her knees? What comfort does she receive from her mother? from the Nurse? Where does she, literally, turn? In what sense does she turn inward from Capulet, Lady Capulet, Paris, Friar Laurence, all the older generation, to the confining comfort of her bed, the drug, the tomb? Let students feel Juliet's bodily experience, and they will not forget the play.

In many Shakespeare classrooms, I believe, some of the time likely to be devoted to watching films and videos of *Romeo and Juliet* may be better spent in helping the class find kinesthetic rhythms of the play, in walking its talk. How rhythmically the play alternates its fighting and loving as the thumb-biting, blade-flourishing quarrel of the first scene gives way to the palm- and lip-kissing of Romeo and Juliet at the Capulet's ball (1.5.101–11); the deathly swordplay of Tybalt, Mercutio, and Romeo yields to the lovers' kissing at Juliet's balcony/chamber (3.5.42); and finally Romeo's mortal fight with his rival, Paris, precedes the lover's dying kisses in the tomb (5.3.115, 166).

In addition to spending as much time as possible in explicating and discussing Shakespeare's language in *Romeo and Juliet*, teachers may usefully touch on pressure points of somatic engagement and memory. The opening prologue-sonnet, for example stresses that the lovers' overthrows "doth with their death bury their parent's strife" (1.0.8). The "doth"/"death" chime can remind us that "doing" here leads deathward (compare "Now old desire doth in his deathbed lie" 2.0.1); to do includes to die. Even (or especially) "love" is "death-marked" (1.0.9), and students can build actionally upon the lexical base of reminders that "doing" may include daring to love and die (as "do" and "die" throughout Shakespeare include lovemaking):

> O, then, dear saint, let lips do what hands do
>
> (1.5.104)

> And what love can do, that dares love attempt
>
> (2.2.68)

> Then love-devouring death do what he dare
>
> (2.6.7)

> Lovers can see to do their amorous rites
>
> (3.2.8)

Do as thou wilt, for I have done with thee

(3.5.205)

Romeo, too, is "done" (1.4.39) in love-sickness, which Mercutio, in punning on "done" and "dun," suggests (1.4.40–43) is a useless stillness and inactivity (like death).

To provide kinesthetic exercise corresponding to the three waves of doing and undoing we have identified, teachers may employ choral readings or silent miming in groups or rehearsed student performance or other methods aimed at enlivening such passages as the following:

> *Gregory.* I will frown as I pass by, and let them take it   40
>   as they list.
> *Samson.* Nay, as they dare. I will bite my thumb at
>   them, which is disgrace to them if they bear it.
>   [*Samson makes taunting gestures.*]
> *Abraham.* Do you bite your thumb at us, sir?
> *Samson.* I do bite my thumb, sir.   45
> *Abraham.* Do you bite your thumb at us, sir?
> *Samson.* [*aside to Gregory*] Is the law of our side if I
>   say ay?
> *Gregory.* [*aside to Samson*] No.
> *Samson* [*to Abraham*] No, sir, I do not bite my thumb   50
>   at you, sir, but I bite my thumb, sir.
> *Gregory.* Do you quarrel, sir?
> *Abraham.* Quarrel sir? No, sir.
> *Samson.* But if you do, sir, I am for you. I serve as good
>   a man as you.
>   (*Romeo and Juliet*, 1.1.40–55)

In context, students can improvise the "taunting gestures" and manner of thumb-biting to stress a sense of sexual energies in the feud's "doing" (compare, all in act 1, scene 1: "thrust to the wall," "maidenheads," "Draw thy tool," "my naked weapon is out," "long sword," "flourishes his blade," and so on) that underscore from the beginning the play's powerful amalgam of violent desire and violent death. Students who feel such power in their own voices, gestures, postures, and movements from the first scene may well appreciate the transmuted forms of such feeling in the exchanged "sins" when Romeo and Juliet physically meet (1.5.94–111) to do what hands and lips "do." I dare say students who opine that Shakespeare is "boring" may readily admit that the meeting of Romeo and Juliet is one they hesitate to enact, even in private, such is the power of the somatic engagement, yet to let the class approach, however mildly and safely, the kinesthetic reality of the meeting can pull even reluctant students into making genuine sense of Shakespeare.

When, in the context of full-play discussion, Romeo's killing of Tybalt in "fire-eyed fury" (2.1.123) is enacted next to his death-like parting from Juliet ("Come, death, and welcome" [3.5.124]) and Romeo's killing of Paris (who urged him, again, to "fury" [5.3.63]) is enacted before his last embrace of the sleeping Juliet ("Thus with a kiss I die" [5.3.120]), then students may conceive a corporeal rhythm of contrasts that can anchor the play in somatic, feelingful memory. Experience of *Romeo and Juliet* will not then slide away into forgotten verbal commentary, and the enacted physical contrasts of feuding families and fated lovers will help to energize Shakespeare's *many-sensed* or *cross-sensory* poetry of "sick health," "still-waking sleep," "choking gall," "preserving sweet," of withering summer, limping winter, earth-treading stars, wormwood on the nipple, love pricked for pricking, maids pressed on their backs, lovers ripening like medlars and pears and likened to gloves, birds, natural idiots, bestriders of gossamer, snow on a raven's back, or a seasick weary bark, while love itself comes on like lightning or a bud blown to flower or the boundless sea or fire and powder consumed with kissing or a poison that restores. Aroused to empathy by their kinesthetic and literally organic engagement, students may more easily exercise their imaginations to feel the taste, temperature, and touch of love so portrayed.

Such classroom exercises, furthermore, provide graphic contrasts among the sizes of groups on stage as the crowds in feuding clans (1.1) give way to the few youths dueling deadly (3.1) to the lone paired combat of Paris and Romeo (5.3). That dwindling of numbers on stage matches, of course, the increasing isolation and confinement of the lovers away from open street, dance, and orchard to close bedroom and tomb. Sense-making thus enhances perception of whole-play features as well as of microcosmic ones. In rousing within students enough sympathy for Romeo and Juliet to balance the obviously negative play-judgments of their impetuous, prideful, death-centered exclusivity, classroom sense-work allows, moreover, for keen appreciation of how the lovers' intimacy feeds perniciously on the families' feud, appreciation of how their love proves its light by seeking out contrasting darkness and cherishes its life by summoning death. To enhance their power and intensity, Romeo and Juliet accept ever greater confinement, leading finally to death itself, and students who find ways deeply, truly to feel as well as recognize this paradox may find something of worth to remember in Shakespeare, if not also in their own love-life.

Students Can Embody and Experience Shakespeare's Problematic Connections of Exhilaration, License, and Liberty

When students make sense of Shakespeare by registering the feel of "withering" or "steeps" or "itch," they find that imaginative fancy is bred not just in head but in heart and body. Shakespeare's language is material or physical, too, in more than bodily imagery. Take the matters of humor and abuse.

Students, along with general readers, require means to work from merely recognizing Shakespeare's humor and abusive language to embodying it. Like Falstaff, Lear's Fool, the Porter in *Macbeth*, Autolycus, Caliban, and many other carnivalized creatures in Shakespeare, Bottom in *A Midsummer Night's Dream* wins freedom out of grotesque conditions:

> The raging rocks
> And shivering shocks
> Shall break the locks
> Of prison gates;
> And Phibbus' car   30
> Shall shine from far
> And make and mar
> The foolish Fates.
>
> (1.2.26–33)

A function of such speech is to produce exhilaration in actor who speaks and audience who laughs. If this is a tyrant's vein (as Bottom seems to think), why is the "prison" opened? It sounds more like the harrowing of Hell or like divine creation: let there be light, and let dark fate now be overthrown. In context, the point is Bottom's blithe ego, unconscious of bad poetry, swept away by raw excess of rhyme, alliteration, volume, and stomping beats. Without the sort of sense-reading that induces smiling, laughing, and their manifold respiratory and neurophysiological responses,[10] the passage offers relatively little. Its physical sense outweighs all other sense.

Teachers can always read such passages aloud or, better yet, arrange choral reading in unison or antiphonal readings or student-prepared performances. Part of the goal is to approximate the particular feeling for exhilarating laughter and carnivalesque freedom in abuse that Shakespeare's language of the body often incites:

> Come, tears, confound,
> Out, sword, and wound
> The pap of Pyramus;
> Ay, that left pap
> Where heart doth hop.
> (*Midsummer Night's Dream*, 5.1.291–95)

Think how much of Shakespeare shades from the scurrilities of Pistol, Lavatch, Lucio, Thersites, Apemantus, Bolt, Stephano, and the like, who revel in the grotesque, anticlassical body, toward the pervasive abuse and argument of countless dialogues throughout the plays. Surely, the oft-copied lists of "Shakespearean Insults" and cross-matching terms of Shakespearean abuse that circulate so ubiquitously in Shakespeare classrooms recall one pole of Shakespeare's liberating attraction. "A vague memory of past carnival liberties and carnival truth still slumbers in these modern forms of abuse. The problem of their irrepressible linguistic vitality has as yet not been seriously posed."[11] Let Shakespeare students master their Insult Kits and Terms of Abuse and then turn to the passages and plays from which such exhilaration flows. Adding voice, gesture, posture, and movement changes the quality of energy involved and can lead directly, incisively, to root issues of social engagement. The exhilaration of Bottom may seem farcical buffoonery, an object of condescension. Or it may appear temperate and free, humane and self-authenticating beyond the reach of censorious or satirical authority. How is the craftsmen's play, in the final scene of *A Midsummer Night's Dream*, then, to be played? and received? Exploring the exhilaration of Bottom and his cohorts in this physical, material manner provides one classroom version of creative Carnival: "the comprehensive rethinking of the social world in terms of common, everyday material and physical experience . . . [bringing] all knowledge of social reality down to earth and [placing] the body, its needs and its capabilities, at the center of the social process."[12]

In such questioning, students move beyond conventional bounds of aesthetic education and the sort of insights that typify it (as follows):

> Reading aloud to children is enormously important at *all* levels of their education. It should now readily be seen how reading aloud with plenty of expression is an essential part of teaching them how to feel. Through intonation, pauses, changes of pace and volume, indeed through changes of facial expression and even posture, the reader brings the words on the page to life and helps children to feel the significance and meaning of human situations hitherto foreign to their experience, learns how the human race in general, or the people of the Western world, perhaps, have learnt to respond to important events, and so on.[13]

Beyond that, by bodily enacting the exhilaration of Bottom and Falstaff and Quickly and Tearsheet, Juliet's Nurse and Mistress Overdone and Pompey Bum and a host of others, students can seize the chance to reexamine part of the stance of Shakespeare and of "literature" itself in relation to culture. Freshly allied with, or problematically opposed to, both low and middle culture, Shakespeare makes new sense, and students can newly assess the new-old argument:

> Wherever men laugh and curse, particularly in a familiar environment, their speech is filled with bodily images. The body copulates, defecates, overeats, and men's' speech is flooded with genitals, bellies, defecations, urine, disease, noses, mouths, and dismembered parts. Even when the flood is contained by norms of speech, there is still an eruption of these images into literature, especially if the literature is gay or abusive in character. The common human fund of familiar and abusive gesticulations is also based on these sharply defined images.
>
> This boundless ocean of grotesque bodily imagery within time and space extends to all languages, all literatures, and the entire system of gesticulation; in the midst of it the canon of art, belles lettres, and political conversation of modern times is a tiny island. This limited canon never prevailed in antique literature. In the official literature

of European peoples it has existed only for the last four hundred years.[14]

Confronting such an argument through experience of their own Shakespearean exhilaration, a physical and emotional experience of complex organic vitality,[15] students become better-equipped to arbitrate authentically among the babble of voices constituting today's "culture wars." For them, Shakespeare comes to live in the vibrantly contested field between high-canonical and low-carnival judgments.

TEACHERS MUST WARD OFF REPRESSIVE ADAPTATIONS OF SENSE-READING

Despite the enthusiasm of the preceding section, a dark side to sense-reading in the classroom must be conceded. As much as I advocate combining corporal and conceptual senses of Shakespeare, I easily imagine how dreadful it might be if academics really began cottoning to the methods and exhortations outlined here. Can you envision the courses that would arise? "Physical Etymology: Practice in Feeling Originary Senses of Words Such as 'Understand,' 'Anguish,' and the Like." "Proprioceptive Reading 202." "Kinesthetic Imagination 304." "Psychosomatic Impact of the Epyllion 599." All might be coopted and transmogrified into the most useless and silly regime. We would say of such criticism what has been said of modernist criticism as a whole: "Criticism in its most important and its most vital sense had been gutted and turned into its very opposite: an ideology."[16]

What good does it do, on the other hand, pessimistically to assume that no liberative concern for sense-reading could survive, much less flourish, in schools? How easy it is to write off formal schooling in English or drama as merely a vehicle "of the established classes to impose their beliefs on society by imposing their norms of language use."[17] When cultural reproduction theories "dissolve human agency,"[18] they ignore, I believe, opportunities for resistance that crop up within the contradictory, practical settings where education actually takes place. I have been suggesting means by which the study of Shakespeare might alter perception and intervene in cultural practice, might "provide a creative base for active experiments with cultural production (verbal, visual, and aural) which enhance, improve, and diversify rather than narrow and homogenize our cultural life."[19] Despite the vexed history of aesthetic ideals, one who links the reading of Shakespeare to the mysterious, improvisatory life of our bodies may foster individual and group capacities to change personal experience and surrounding worlds.

I know that the sensuous and the concrete in art and in ourselves can never be observed or celebrated beyond political frames of reference:

> The discourse of Shakespeare is unabashedly perverse, bending constantly away from some "normative" referent, staggering and deferring the signified, luxuriating in its sumptuous transgression of strict semantic economy. It is this libidinal excess which humanism recuperates, gullibly, as "human richness" or "sensuous concretion," blind to the mastery, violence and manipulation implicit in any such idiom.[20]

My idiom (of the sensuously concrete) hopes, nonetheless, to invoke a cultural practice that radically alters perception,[21] that appropriates Shakespeare, unpredictably, for relatively private and free postures of ordinary persons. In this arena of debate over aesthetic education, extremes may strangely meet. As Gramsci wished to develop "in his proletarian readers a consciousness of their own aesthetic sensibilities and of their own skills and abilities as practical critics of the art produced in a society of their own making,"[22] so, too, relatively elite theorists may argue: "The study of the distinctive values of art, which is the proper subject for aesthetic education, may well produce those changed attitudes and values that social reformers want to achieve by more direct methods. It is reasonable to suppose that by honoring the autonomy of art, aesthetic education can contribute indirectly to an enhanced quality of life."[23]

However conceived and taught, neither theory nor Shakespeare will bake much bread or leave much taste until incorporated into practical and sensuous responses of readers, students, teachers, actors, playgoers. As students, many of us have been driven not out of our minds so much as out of our bodies. We now need to risk losing our minds (as overabstractly employed) to come to our senses. "I lay it down as an educational axiom that in teaching you will come to grief as soon as you forget that your pupils have bodies."[24] We may see, increasingly, ultraradical and perhaps unhelpful extensions of that opinion: "The educational goal of the traditional culture has been to learn to read the environment. The educational goal of the mutational culture is to learn to read oneself as soma."[25] Conceding the extremism of such views, I submit, nonetheless, that teachers who encourage their students to experience Shakespeare through their bodies offer at least one new chance for the students to reach toward a creative freedom (as long as our bodies remain sufficiently undomesticated): "In other words, the body represents the rawness of nature, the non-respectable, and the potentially uncontrollable. It stands in opposition to the Establishment."[26] So it stands now, but perhaps not in the future. We have little choice, however, except to explore this seemingly final frontier.

Like learning to speak or to enjoy any art, reading Shakespeare involves the acquisition of skills. It does not consist in knowing abstract concepts and rules. I have therefore avoided prescriptions of learning or teaching formulae. Many people believe that "beginners start with specific cases and, as they become more proficient, abstract and 'interiorize' more and more sophisticated rules. It might turn out that skill acquisition moves in just the opposite direction: from abstract rules to particular cases."[27] The important thing is not to think about Shakespeare but to think Shakespeare; students who are encouraged to consult and improvise upon their own body/mind responses to incidents of stance, gesture, movement, tone, and meaning can rapidly discover the conceptual blanks they need filled in to unify their work, to make it coherent. "The improvising hand thinks in units,"[28] and improvising students, who learn that Shakespeare is more about action than thought, can explore dimensions and limits of many sorts of coherent action. Tracking the beats of Hippolyta's replies to Theseus throughout *A Midsummer Night's Dream*, for example, students may wonder whether Theseus (or any other man in the play) signals appreciation for a woman's counter-wisdom. No matter how much lively and useful research such inquiry produced into generic expectations for static comic characters or into feminist and psychoanalytic critical readings, the students' concrete, actional, improvisatory testing of such a Theseus could tap a wider and deeper range of relationships than critical abstractions might hope to summarize. Such improvisatory testing could also enhance the students' own sense of authentic authority in relation to Shakespeare.[29] "Could," that is, if the students can be brought to function with as much spontaneity as they often exhibit outside of class. But then, "if it isn't possible to let students speak and act with the same freedom they have outside the school, then it might be better not to teach them drama at all." That "same freedom" outside school teems, of course, with social constraints, just as every classroom participates, inevitably, in tensions of social stratification, credentializing, group prejudices, and the like. Still, at least moments of improvisational exploration in Shakespearean speech and movement may encourage student interrogation not only of standard, set interpretations but also of purely verbal, or written, categories of response.

I submit that Shakespeare can become a prime educational means in our culture for regaining sensory imagination. His texts uniquely offer and demand it. Our lives thirst for it. Let us slake that thirst.

9

Conclusion: Walking Westward

IN RECENT HISTORY, TEACHERS AT ALL "LEVELS" HAVE TENDED TO use Shakespeare to teach something other than Shakespeare: vocabulary, elocution, rhetoric, theater craft, good taste, moral wisdom, cultural study, politics. Shakespeare obviously *connects* to all these things, but, still, it seems a bit sad to use such a mysterious and glorious instrument for such external and, in some respects, limited purposes. With this admonishment in mind, if you still think I want you to *use* Shakespeare to liberate your body, I hope you will consider the possibility that you are wrong. I do think one can write with a fair degree of persuasiveness on behalf of a liberating bodily education:

> An education that connects us with our body would teach us the difference between what we are experiencing and what we are thinking and fantasizing about. When we are connected with our body, the present moment comes more into focus and we can then begin to make decisions from there. The life that is streaming through our body, with its rich currents of temperatures, pulsations, vibrations, swellings, and congealings, becomes our reference point for choices and responses. When we wonder about a direction to take, or an alternative to assess, we can consult the intelligence that resides in our body. This type of education is revolutionary, in the sense that it gives power to the individual. It fosters a way of being that supports and trusts the energy that moves through all living things.[1]

To me, however, the reason to make bodily sense of Shakespeare is to know Shakespeare better, not to use Shakespeare as a self-help agency. If one finds, in the process, a promising "anatomy of change," so much the better, but, just as one cannot participate meaningfully in a ritual by attending mainly to one's organs or to hoped-for feelings of catharsis, one cannot meaningfully read or see Shakespeare in the same way. One must go to the play. The question is how to take the whole person on the trip. The "whole person" cannot, admittedly, be approached with any great success until we understand much better needs of persons and culture to "reconvene our senses,"[2] but individual persons are at least partly free to take limited, tentative, improvisatory steps.

At the risk of being reductive, let me sum up what I have been advocating: 1) a sustained habit of scrupulously close reading and unusually energetic imagining, 2) cross-referenced by sharp memory of other passages and perhaps some occasional etymological work, and accompanied by 3) sensitive attention to somatic response so as to work toward conceptualizing *and feeling* an entire-body reaction to a given passage, character, relationship, or work; 4) successful completion of step 3 requires prior work at recovering ways to recognize and gauge the body's reactions; 5) successful completion of the entire task requires, at times, a suspension of judgment, especially judgment emanating from the cerebral cortex. That is, one must be willing to postpone or reconfigure purely intellectual reactions.

Though it really "only" promotes an active, physical, sensory reading that allows for unusually accurate, intense perception and expression of literary emotion *and* cognition, such a program demands a great deal. Unless introduced gradually through initially simple exercises, it can demand too much from students who are struggling just to figure out the story line. Still, encouragement to sense-read can aid students to find a great deal more in Shakespeare than mere story lines, quick judgments of characters, and tidy summaries of themes. One can always begin with the enlivening connection between careful reading and learned somatic imagination. Why *is* anger "red-looked"? In what *sense* can a day "steep" itself in night? What else but sensory memory can vivify experience of a text? Have not Shakespeare and all true poets urged us to return to sense, to save appearances, to suit words to actions, to let language gesture and dance inside our bodies?

Much more could be done, of course, to describe or exemplify styles of reading Shakespeare so as to "make sense" of his texts through concrete responses to imagery, sound-play, word patterns, and the counter-eloquence of action. How, for example, does Shakespeare's nearly obsessive concern with issues of succession, primogeniture, patrilinearity, and familial gratitude play itself out around deeply felt but never quite expressible fears of mortality in characters and spectators? We could examine further Shakespeare's language of the body, including bawdy language, and ways in which all of our human senses are surprisingly promoted and demoted through Shakespeare's texts. We could inspect varied behaviors open to spectators and actors of Shakespeare in relation to each other and perhaps find out why so many performers and audiences struggle unsuccessfully to move beyond a pallid, superficial meeting of minds and bodies. We could test ways in which contemporary theory and criticism may dampen down or fire up lively sense-reading. And we could explore much further the hedonic and adaptive dimension of sense-reading, ways in which freshly accessing the pleasures of rhythm, somatic imagery, synaesthesia, and kinesthetic and proprioceptive engagement with Shakespeare may enhance our understanding of his significance as well as enhance our biologically adaptive memory, perceptiveness, and grasp of order, organicity, and wholeness.[3]

Those are all matters, however, for a different book. The purpose of this one has been served if you find yourself even provisionally piqued to try out your personal versions of a more strenuous and joyful sense-reading than you have explored before. I believe that the hallmarks of the sense-reading method are simply courage and care: courage to resist one's natural, normal defenses against disturbing, even pleasurably disturbing, thoughts and feelings, and care for the way words work and for our manifold responses.

Returning to the beginning:

> Shall I compare thee to a summer's day?
> Thou art more lovely and more temperate.

Only you can make those abstractions truly live, and, in making them live, you can find how a summer's day, a sonnet, and a friend may be lovely and temperate in literal sight, sound, smell, taste, touch, and inward feeling. You can find more. You can find where *you* live, *you* in your mind and body, also as lovely and temperate as any summer day, poem, or friend. This finding will provide not only the profoundest play; it will prepare you for the work of world, and time. For, in the last analysis, making sense of Shakespeare, or any art, can bring more life only by admitting life's opposites.

In this little book, I may have employed some conflicting arguments, unexamined assumptions, fallacious interpretations, overreliance on secondary sources, abrasive or murky writing, and other features open to criticism. For all such faults, I wish to convey my regrets. Academic readers in particular may consider my practice undertheorized, but I beg them to consider that, as a distinguished Renaissance scholar puts it: "intelligent and even reflective performance of a praxis is not the same as having the ability to give an abstract and systematic account of the principles that actually or supposedly underlie that praxis."[4] Thirty years ago, in graduate school, I took a year-long course in Theory of Poetry by the then dean of literary theorists, William K. Wimsatt, Jr. (co-author of the famous antisubjectivist essay, "The Affective Fallacy," mentioned in my preface). I had the temerity to begin one of my papers with a sentence I have used in this book: "Imagination means as it moves." I wish you could have seen the look of utter horror on Mr. Wimsatt's face as he began to perceive where I was coming from. I knew then how an improper academic was supposed to feel, like a leopard in the temple. And I soon saw that Mr. Wimsatt's Shakespeare and mine served rather different (though not totally different) aims. After three decades, I found a modicum of support for some of my views, as suggested in the foregoing chapters.

I have desired here in part to show you that a diverse and courageous band of body-reverencers have been working through disparate fields to bring human beings (including those who study Shakespeare), again, to their senses and, in so doing, to help bring their senses to Shakespeare. I know I am but a servant and conduit for better wisdoms. Still, I hope these pages may assist some persons to make better sense of Shakespeare, if not also themselves, and to make that better sense in many relevant ways. That has been the principal goal.

Notes

PREFACE

1. Geoffrey H. Hartman, *Minor Prophecies: The Literary Essay in the Culture Wars* (Cambridge and London: Harvard University Press, 1991), 195.

2. Philip Sidney, "An Apology for Poetry," in *Elizabethan Critical Essays*, ed. G. Gregory Smith (Oxford: Clarendon Press, 1904), 154, 160.

3. Leonard B. Meyer, *Emotion and Meaning in Music* (Chicago and London: University of Chicago Press, 1956), 268.

4. See Paul Crowther, *Critical Aesthetics and Postmodernism* (Oxford: Clarendon Press, 1993), 36.

5. William K. Wimsatt, Jr., and Monroe C. Beardsley, "The Affective Fallacy," in Wimsatt's *The Verbal Icon* (Lexington: University of Kentucky Press, 1954), 21–39. See Fabian Gudas, "Affective Fallacy," in *The New Princeton Encyclopedia of Poetry and Poetics*, ed. Alex Preminger and T. V. F. Brogan (Princeton: Princeton University Press, 1993), 12; Deborah Bowen, "Wimsatt, William Kurtz, Jr.," in *Encyclopedia of Contemporary Literary Theory*, ed. Irena R. Makaryk (Toronto: University of Toronto Press, 1995), 491–94.

6. Garrett Stewart, *Reading Voices: Literature and the Phonotext* (Berkeley and Los Angeles: University of California Press, 1990), 2; concerning Stanley Fish, Norman Holland, and other reader-response critics, see note 15, below; on the psychobiology of aesthetic experience, see, Victor Turner, "Are There Universals of Performance in Myth, Ritual, and Drama?" in *By Means of Performance: Intercultural Studies of Theatre and Ritual*, ed. Richard Schechner and Willa Appel (Cambridge and New York: Cambridge University Press, 1990), 8–18; Eugene G. d'Aquili and Charles D. Laughlin, Jr., "The Neurobiology of Myth and Ritual," in *The Spectrum of Ritual: A Biogenetic Structural Analysis*, ed. by Eugene G. d'Aquili, Charles D. Laughlin, Jr., and John McManus (New York: Columbia University Press, 1979), 152–82; Richard Schechner, "Magnitudes of Performance," in *By Means of Performance*, ed. by Schechner and Appel, 19–49; D. E. Berlyne, *Aesthetics and Psychobiology* (New York: Appelton-Century-Crofts, 1971); Ellen Dissanayake, *Homo Aestheticus: Where Art Comes From and Why* (New York: Free Press—Macmillan, 1992).

7. To review major criticism of Shakespeare from the seventeenth and eighteenth centuries, see D. Nichol Smith, ed., *Shakespeare Criticism: A Selection* (London: Oxford University Press, 1946); D. Nichol Smith, ed., *Eighteenth-Century Essays on Shakespeare*, 2nd ed. (Oxford: Clarendon Press, 1963); see also Brian Vickers, *Shakespeare: The Critical Heritage* (London and Boston: Routledge and K. Paul, 1974–78); the nineteenth-century critics mentioned are Edward Dowden, *Shakspere: A Critical Study of his Mind and Art*, 1881, 3rd.

ed. (London, Routledge, 1962); Edward Dowden, *Introduction to Shakespeare*, 1907 (reprint, Freeport, N.Y.: Books for Libraries Press, 1970); A. C. Bradley, *Shakespearean Tragedy*, (1904; reprint, New York: St. Martin's Press, 1985).

8. G. Wilson Knight, *The Wheel of Fire: Essays in Interpretation of Shakespeare's Sombre Tragedies* (London: Oxford University Press, 1930); G. Wilson Knight, *The Imperial Theme: Further Interpretations of Shakespeare's Tragedies Including the Roman Plays* (London and New York: Oxford University Press, 1931); G. Wilson Knight, *The Crown of Life: Essays in Interpretation of Shakespeare's Final Plays*, 2nd ed. (1947, London: Methuen, 1948); Caroline F. E. Spurgeon, *Shakespeare's Imagery and What It Tells Us* (1935; reprint, Boston: Beacon Hill, 1958); Wolfgang Clemen, *The Development of Shakespeare's Imagery*, 1936 (revised ed., New York: Hill and Wang, 1962); Edward A. Armstrong, *Shakespeare's Imagination: A Study of the Psychology of Association and Inspiration* (London: L. Drummond, 1946).

9. Harley Granville-Barker, *Prefaces to Shakespeare*, 4 vols. (Princeton: Princeton University Press, 1963); Elmer Edgar Stoll, *Shakespeare Studies: Historical and Comparative in Method*, 1927 (reprint, New York: Ungar, 1960; Elmer Edgar Stoll, *Art and Artifice in Shakespeare*, 1933 (reprint, London: Methuen, 1963); Alfred Harbage, *Shakespeare's Audience* (New York: Columbia University Press, 1941); Alfred Harbage, *Conceptions of Shakespeare* (Cambridge, Mass.: Harvard University Press, 1966); Bernard Beckerman, *Shakespeare at the Globe, 1599–1609* (New York: Macmillan, 1962); C. L. Barber, *Shakespeare's Festive Comedy: A Study of Dramatic Form and Its Relation to Social Custom* (Princeton: Princeton University Press, 1959); John Holloway, *The Story of the Night: Studies in Shakespeare's Major Tragedies* (London: Routledge and Kegan Paul, 1961); Michael Goldman, *Shakespeare and the Energies of Drama* (Princeton: Princeton University Press, 1972); Michael Goldman, *Acting and Action in Shakespearean Tragedy* (Princeton: Princeton University Press, 1985); Stephen Booth, *King Lear, Macbeth, Indefinition, and Tragedy* (New Haven and London: Yale University Press, 1983).

10. Tommy Ruth Waldo, "Beyond Words: Shakespeare's Tongue-Tied Muse," in *Shakespeare's More Than Words Can Witness: Essays on Visual and Nonverbal Enactment in the Plays*, ed. Sidney Homan (Lewisburg: Bucknell University Press, 1980), 170; Philip C. McGuire, *Speechless Dialect: Shakespeare's Open Silences* (Berkeley and Los Angeles: University of California Press, 1985), xv; Alexander Leggatt, "Shakespeare and the Actor's Body," *Renaissance and Reformation* 10, no. 1 (1986): 106; Terence Hawkes, *That Shakespeherian Rag: Essays on a Critical Process* (London and New York: Methuen, 1986), 90.

11. David Richman, *Laughter, Pain, and Wonder: Shakespeare's Comedies and the Audience in the Theater* (Newark: University of Delaware Press, 1990), 12.

12. See, for example, Kent Cartwright, *Shakespearean Tragedy and Its Double: The Rhythms of Audience Response* (University Park: Pennsylvania State University Press, 1991), 37, 98, 106.

13. Jean E. Howard, *Shakespeare's Art of Orchestration: Stage Technique and Audience Response* (Urbana and Chicago: University of Illinois Press, 1984), 6.

14. David Bevington, *Action Is Eloquence: Shakespeare's Language of Gesture* (Cambridge and London: Harvard University Press, 1984), 24.

15. Well-known theorists and practitioners of reader-response criticism include: Louise M. Rosenblatt, *Literature as Exploration*, 1937, 4th ed. (New York: The Modern Language Association of America, 1983); Louise M. Rosenblatt, *The Reader, the Text, the Poem: The Transactional Theory of the Literary Work* (Carbondale: Southern Illinois University Press, 1978); Walter J. Slatoff, *With Respect to Readers: Dimensions of Literary Response* (Ithaca and London: Cornell University Press, 1970); Wolfgang Iser, *The Implied Reader: Patterns of Communication in Prose Fiction from Bunyan to Beckett* (Baltimore: Johns Hopkins University Press, 1974); Wolfgang Iser, *The Act of Reading: A Theory of Aesthetic Response* (Baltimore: Johns Hopkins University Press, 1978); Wolfgang Iser, *Prospecting: From Reader Response to Literary Anthropology* (Baltimore: Johns Hopkins University Press, 1989); Hans Robert Jauss, *Toward An Aesthetics of Reception*, trans. by Timothy Bahti (Minneapolis: University of Minnesota Press, 1982); Norman N. Holland, *The Dynamics of Literary Response* (New York: Oxford University Press, 1968); Norman N. Holland, *5 Readers Reading* (New Haven: Yale University Press, 1975); Norman N. Holland, *Poems in Persons: An Introduction to the Psychoanalysis of Literature* (New York: Norton, 1973); Stanley Eugene Fish, *Is There a Text in this Class?: The Authority of Interpretive Communities* (Cambridge, Mass.: Harvard University Press, 1980); Alan C. Purves, "The Aesthetic Mind of Louise Rosenblatt," in *The Experience of Reading: Louise Rosenblatt and Reader-Response Theory*, ed. by John Clifford (Portsmouth, N.H.: Boynton/Cook Publishers, 1991), 209–17; Alan C. Purves and Richard Beach, *Literature and the Reader: Research in Response to Literature, Reading Interests, and the Teaching of Literature* (Urbana, Ill.: National Council of Teachers of English, 1972); David Bleich, "Epistemological Assumptions in the Study of Response," in *Reader-Response Criticism: From Formalism to Post-Structuralism*, ed. by Jane P. Tompkins (Baltimore and London: Johns Hopkins University Press, 1986).

16. George T. Wright, *Shakespeare's Metrical Art* (Berkeley and Los Angeles: University of California Press, 1988), 107, 182.

17. Charles H. Frey, "Interpreting *The Winter's Tale*," *Studies in English Literature: 1500–1900* 18 (1978): 207–29.

18. Frey, "*The Tempest* and the New World," *Shakespeare Quarterly* 30 (1979): 29–41.

19. Frey, *Experiencing Shakespeare: Essays on Text, Classroom, and Performance* (Columbia, Mo.: University of Missouri Press, 1988).

20. Frey, "Embodying the Play," in *The Tempest: Theory in Practice*, ed. Nigel Wood (Buckingham: Open University Press, 1993), 67–96; "Goals and Limits in Student Performance of Shakespeare," in *Teaching Shakespeare Today: Practical Approaches and Productive Strategies*, ed. James E. Davis and Ronald E. Salomone (Urbana, Ill.: National Council of Teachers of English, 1993), 72–78; "The Bias of Nature," *The Upstart Crow* 13 (1993): 2–15; "Making Sense of Shakespeare: A Reader-Based Response," in *Teaching Shakespeare into the Twenty-First Century*, ed. Ronald E. Salomone and James E. Davis (Athens: Ohio University Press, 1997), 96–103.

Introduction. Abstract and Concrete Senses in Shakespeare

1. John A. Schumacher, *Human Posture: The Nature of Inquiry* (Albany: State University of New York Press, 1989), 210.

2. Ellen Dissanayake, *Homo Aestheticus: Where Art Comes From and Why* (New York: Free Press—Macmillan, 1992), 185.

3. Barbara A. Mowat and Paul Werstine, eds., *Romeo and Juliet* (New York: Washington Square Press, 1992), 70.

4. *Shakespeare's Plays in Quarto*, ed. Michael J. B. Allen and Kenneth Muir (Berkeley and Los Angeles: University of California Press, 1981), 170.

5. E. K. Chambers, *Shakespeare: A Survey* (1925; reprint, New York: Hill and Wang, 1963), 116; John Russell Brown, ed., *The Merchant of Venice*, The Arden Shakespeare (1955; reprint, London and New York: Methuen, 1984), xlv–xlvi; Isaac Asimov, *Asimov's Guide to Shakespeare* (Garden City, N.Y.: Doubleday, 1970), 1.501.

6. In order to correct editors' dubious changes of their copy-text, I quote in this section from *William Shakespeare: The Complete Works*. Original Spelling Edition, ed. Stanley Wells and Gary Taylor (Oxford: Clarendon Press, 1986), lines 186–87.

7. Compare Michael Steig, *Stories of Reading: Subjectivity and Literary Understanding* (Baltimore and London: Johns Hopkins University Press, 1989), 12: "It is also my experience, and that of my students, that attention to one's own or reports of another's reading experiences and associations *does* frequently lead to 'dramatic encounters,' 'surprises,' and a sense of 'discovery' of something that seems to be *in* the text."

8. See Charles Frey, *Experiencing Shakespeare: Essays on Text, Classroom, and Performance* (Columbia, Mo.: University of Missouri Press, 1988), 29–47.

9. Brian Vickers, *Appropriating Shakespeare: Contemporary Critical Quarrels* (New Haven: Yale University Press, 1993), 430.

Chapter 1. Sense-Reading Shakespeare's Sounds

1. Stephen Greenblatt, et al., eds. *The Norton Shakespeare: Based on the Oxford Edition* (New York: Norton, 1997), xi.

2. Hans Kreitler and Shulamith Kreitler, *Psychology of the Arts* (Durham, N.C.: Duke University Press, 1972), 151.

3. On metrically induced arousal and de-arousal, see D. E. Berlyne, *Aesthetics and Psychobiology* (New York: Appleton-Century-Crofts, 1971), 237–39; on metrically induced neurological entrainment, see Joseph Glickson, Reuven Tsur, and Chanita Goodblatt, "Absorption and Trance-Inductive Poetry," *Empirical Studies of the Arts* 9, no. 2 (1992): 115–22, quotation from 117. Edward O. Snyder and Ronald E. Shor, "Trance-Inductive Poetry: A Brief Communication," *International Journal of Clinical and Experimental Hypnosis* 31, no. 1 (1983): 1–7, discuss the trance-inducing properties of certain poetic rhythms; A. D. Diment, Wendy Louise Walker, and A. G. Hammer, "Response to Poetry

in Hypnosis and the Waking State: A Study of Non-Suggested Aspects of the Hypnotic State," *Australian Journal of Clinical and Experimental Hypnosis* 9, no. 1 (1981): 19–40, discuss effects of hypnotic poetry upon thought processes.

4. Concerning special attention given to stressed syllables by listeners, see Mark A. Pitt and Samuel G. Arthur, "The Use of Rhythm in Attending to Speech," *Journal of Experimental Psychology, Human Perception, and Performance* 16, no. 3 (1990): 564–73; on emotions stimulated by prosodic features, see Robert J. Duffy et al., "The Effects of Time/Frequency Distortion on the Prosodic Features of Speech," *United States Naval Submarine Medical Center Report* No. 680 (1971): 1–10; Alessandra Sansavini, Josiane Bertoncini, and Giuliana Giovanelli, "Newborns Discriminate the Rhythm of Multisyllabic Stressed Words," *Developmental Psychology* 33, no. 1 (1997): 3–11.

5. Zachary F. Mainen and Terrence J. Sejenowski, "Reliability of Spike Timing in Neocortical Neurons," *Science* 268 (1995): 1503–07; and see Terrence J. Sejenowski, "Time for a New Neural Code," *Nature* 376 (1995): 21–22; John Hogan, "It's All in the Timing: Neurons May Be More Punctual Than Had Been Supposed," *Scientific American* 273, no. 2 (1995): 16–17. Compare, on neuronal responses to poetic rhythms, Frederick Turner, *Natural Classicism: Essays on Literature and Science* (1985; reprint, Charlottesville: University of Virginia Press, 1992), 95.

6. Anthony Storr, *Music and the Mind* (New York: Free Press, 1992), 39; Macdonald Critchley and R. A. Henson, eds., *Music and the Brain* (London: Wm. Heinemann Medical Books, 1977), 209–16; Don G. Campbell, "Imagery and the Physiology of Music," in *Music: Physician for Times to Come*, ed. Don Campbell (Wheaton, Ill.: Quest Books, 1991), 244; John A. Sloboda, "Music Structure and Emotional Response: Some Empirical Findings," *Psychology of Music* 19, no. 2 (1991): 110–20; Sherman O. VanderArk and Daniel Ely, "Biochemical and Galvanic Skin Responses to Music Stimuli by College Students in Biology and Music," *Perceptual and Motor Skills* 74, no. 3 (1992): 1079–90.

7. On arts fostering species evolution, see Richard L. Gregory, "Aesthetics," *The Oxford Companion to the Mind* (Oxford: Oxford University Press, 1987), 8–10; the two quoted phrases are from Ellen Dissanayake's *Homo Aestheticus: Where Art Comes From and Why* (New York: Free Press—Macmillan, 1991), 60, 147.

8. Eugene G. d'Aquili and Charles D. Laughlin, Jr., "The Neurobiology of Myth and Ritual," in *The Spectrum of Ritual: A Biogenetic Structural Analysis*, ed. Eugene G. d'Aquili, Charles D. Laughlin, Jr., and John McManus (New York: Columbia University Press, 1979), 157.

9. Barbara W. Lex, "The Neurobiology of Ritual Trance," in d'Aquili, *Spectrum of Ritual*, 136; Richard Schechner, "Magnitudes of Performance," in *By Means of Performance: Intercultural Studies of Theatre and Ritual*, ed. Richard Schechner and Willa Appel (Cambridge and New York: Cambridge University Press, 1990), 39–40. And see, Berlyne, *Aesthetics and Psychobiology*, 64–69.

10. D'Aquili and Laughlin, "Neurobiology of Myth and Ritual," 177; compare Victor Turner, "Are There Universals of Performance in Myth, Ritual, and Drama?," in Schechner and Appel, *By Means of Performance*, 13.

11. See Frederick Turner, "The Neural Lyre," in his *Natural Classicism*, 61–105.

12. Derek Attridge, *The Rhythms of English Poetry* (London and New York: Longman, 1982), 298.

13. Raymond A. Anselment, *The Realms of Apollo: Literature and Healing in Seventeenth-Century England* (Newark: University of Delaware Press, 1995), 45.

14. Edward O. Snyder, *Hypnotic Poetry: A Study of Trance-Inducing Technique in Certain Poems and Its Literary Significance* (Philadelphia: University of Pennsylvania Press, 1930), x.

15. Quotations in this paragraph are from, respectively, Derek Attridge, *Poetic Rhythm: An Introduction* (Cambridge: Cambridge University Press, 1995), 9; Richard Cureton, "Helen Vendler and the Music of Poetry," *Versification: An Interdisciplinary Journal of Literary Prosody* 1, no. 1 (10 March 1997): 4; at http://sizcoll.u-shizuoka-ken.ac.jp/versif/Docs/VersRev_397_Cureton.html. 4; and Amittai Aviram, *Telling Rhythm: Body and Meaning in Poetry* (Ann Arbor: University of Michigan Press, 1994), 121.

16. Kreitler and Kreitler, *Psychology of the Arts*, 154.

Chapter 2. Sense-Reading Shakespeare's Nonvisual Imagery

1. See, for example, X. J. Kennedy and Dana Gioia, *An Introduction to Poetry*, 9th ed. (New York: Longman, 1998), 91.

2. For a representative article, see Frank C. Bakker, Marc W. J. Boschker, and Tjuling Chung, "Changes in Muscular Activity While Imagining Weight Lifting in Using Stimulus or Response Propositions," *Journal of Sport and Exercise Psychology* 18 (1996): 313–24.

3. Jerome Beaty and J. Paul Hunter, *The Norton Introduction to Literature*, 7th ed. (New York: W.W. Norton, 1998), 937. Caroline F. E. Spurgeon, *Shakespeare's Imagery and What It Tells Us* (1935; reprint, Boston: Beacon, 1958), 82–83.

Chapter 3. Resistance to Shakespearean Sense-Reading

1. Cheshire Calhoun, "Cognitive Emotions?" in *What Is an Emotion?: Classical Readings in Philosophical Psychology*, ed. Cheshire Calhoun and Robert C. Solomon (New York and Oxford: Oxford University Press, 1984), 330.

2. On determination and construction of emotion, see, for example, David R. Heise and John O'Brien, "Emotion Expression in Groups," in *Handbook of Emotions*, ed. Michael Lewis and Jeannette M. Haviland (New York and London: Guilford Press, 1993), 493. The quotation is from Carroll E. Izard, "Organizational and Motivational Functions of Discrete Emotions," ibid., 634.

3. Caroline Walker Bynum, *Holy Feast and Holy Fast: The Religious Significance of Food to Medieval Women* (Berkeley and Los Angeles: University of California Press, 1987), 299.

4. Jane Gallop, *Thinking Through the Body* (New York: Columbia University Press, 1988), 7.

5. Ibid., 18; see also, Seymour Fisher, *Body Consciousness* (New York: Jason Aronson, 1974), 18, 45; Madeleine R. Grumet, "Bodyreading," *Teachers College Record* 87, no. 2 (1985): 183.

6. George Dennison, *The Lives of Children: The Story of the First Street School* (New York: Random House, 1969), 252.

7. Oliver Sacks, *The Man Who Mistook His Wife for a Hat—and Other Clinical Tales* (New York: Harper and Row, 1987), 20 (quotations before indented quotation), 174–75 (indented quotation).

8. Dennison, *Lives of Children*, 169.

9. Kristin Linklater, *Freeing Shakespeare's Voice: The Actor's Guide to Talking the Text* (New York: Theatre Communications Group, 1992), 195.

10. Fisher, *Body Consciousness*, 139–40.

11. Elaine Scarry, "Introduction," in *Literature and the Body: Essays on Populations and Persons*, Selected Papers from the English Institute, 1986 (Baltimore and London: Johns Hopkins University Press, 1986), vii.

12. Dissociation of self from body is treated by Jose A. Yaryura-Tobias, *The Integral Being* (New York: H. Holt, 1987), 77–78; the quotation about images being taken into the body is from Robert Bly's *Iron John: A Book about Men* (Reading, Mass.: Addison-Wesley, 1990), ix.

13. Grumet, "Bodyreading," 185.

14. See Ellen J. Esrock, *The Reader's Eye: Visual Imaging as Reader Response* (Baltimore and London: Johns Hopkins University Press, 1994), 61, 118.

15. Elaine Batcher, *Emotion in the Classroom: A Study of Children's Experience* (New York: Praeger, 1981), 146.

16. David Howes, "Introduction," in *The Varieties of Sensory Experience: A Sourcebook in the Anthropology of the Senses*, ed. David Howes (Toronto: University of Toronto Press, 1991), 9.

17. Joan M. Erikson, *Wisdom and the Senses: The Way of Creativity* (New York and London: W. W. Norton, 1989), 25; and see, Robert Masters and Jean Houston, *Listening to the Body* (New York: Dell, 1978), 218.

18. Robert Rivlin, *Deciphering the Senses: The Expanding World of Human Perception* (New York: Simon and Schuster, 1984), 16; but see, on evolving literary treatments of the senses, Louise Vinge, *The Five Senses: Studies in a Literary Tradition* (Lund: LiberLäromedel, 1975).

19. On the gendered senses, see Constance Classen, *Worlds of Sense: Exploring the Senses in History and Across Cultures* (London and New York: Routledge, 1993), 9; on conscious interoception, see D. Vaitl, "Interoception," *Biological Psychology* 42, no. 1–2 (1996): 1–27.

20. John Downing and Che Kan Leong, *Psychology of Reading* (New York: Macmillan, 1982), 161; and see, F. J. McGuigan, "Electrical Measurement of Covert Processes as an Explication of 'Higher Mental Events'," in *The Psychophysiology of Thinking: Studies of Covert Processes*, ed. F. J. McGuigan and R. A. Schoonover (New York: Academic Press, 1973), 343–85, on measurable differences in cerebral blood flow when sentences are silently articulated in the reader's own voice and then in an imagined other person's voice.

21. See, Jefferson A. Singer and Peter Salovey, *The Remembered Self: Emo-

tion and Memory in Personality (New York: Free Press, 1993), 130–31; Sabine Kroeze, et al., "Symptom Reporting and Interoceptive Attention in Panic Patients," *Perceptual and Motor Skills* 82, no. 3 (1996): 1019–26.

22. McGuigan, "Electrical Measurement," 359.

23. See Esrock, *Reader's Eye*, 35.

24. Gregory A. Miller, et al., "Individual Differences in Imagery and the Psychophysiology of Emotion," *Cognition and Emotion* 1, no. 4 (1987): 386.

25. Peter J. Lang, "Cognition in Emotion: Concept and Action," in *Emotions, Cognition, and Behavior*, ed. Carroll E. Izard, Jerome Kagan, and Robert B. Zajonc (Cambridge: Cambridge University Press, 1984), 203–7.

26. Ibid., 212.

27. Meyer R. deJong, et al., "Bodily Sensations, Facial EMG, and Autonomic Changes in the Course of Prolonged Emotional Imagery," *Journal of Psychophysiology* 7, no. 1 (1993): 34–45; Evelyn R. Fiorito and Robert F. Simons, "Emotional Imagery and Physical Anhedonia," *Psychophysiology* 31, no. 5 (1994): 513–21.

28. Victor M. Rentel, Christine Pappas, and Barbara Pettegrew, "The Utility of Psychophysiological Measures for Reading Research," in *Psychophysiological Aspects of Reading and Learning*, ed. Victor M. Rentel, Samuel A. Corson, and Bruce R. Dunn (New York: Gordon and Breach, 1985), 145.

29. Lawrence E. Marks, *Sensory Processes: The New Psychophysics* (New York and London: Academic Press, 1974), 233.

30. Pasi Falk, *The Consuming Body* (London: Sage, 1994), 11.

31. Robert R. Hoffman and Richard P. Honeck, "Proverbs, Pragamatics, and the Ecology of Abstract Categories," in *Cognition and Symbolic Structures: The Psychology of Metaphoric Transformation*, ed. Robert E. Haskell (Norwood, N.J.: Ablex Publishing, 1987), 128.

32. Harry J. Jerison, "Vigilance, Discrimination, and Attention," in *Attention: Contemporary Theory and Analysis*, ed. David I. Mostofsky (New York: Appleton-Century-Crofts, 1970), 143.

33. Stephen Michael Kosslyn, *Ghosts in the Mind's Machine: Creating and Using Images in the Brain* (New York and London: W.W. Norton, 1983), 173, 174.

34. See Allan Paivio, *Imagery and Verbal Processes* (New York: Holt, Rinehart and Winston, 1971).

35. Walter B. Weimer, "A Conceptual Framework for Cognitive Psychology: Motor Theories of the Mind," in *Perceiving, Acting, and Knowing: Toward an Ecological Psychology*, ed. Robert Shaw and John Bransford (Hillsdale, N.J.: L. Erlbaum Associates, 1977), 280.

36. Esrock, *Reader's Eye*, 180–81, 204.

37. Ibid., 124.

38. Fisher, *Body Consciousness*, 15.

39. Ibid.

40. Frederick Perls, Ralph Hefferline, and Paul Goodman, *Gestalt Therapy: Excitement and Growth in the Human Personality* (New York: Dell, 1954), 85, 245.

41. See H. J. Chaytor, *From Script to Print: An Introduction to Medieval Literature* (Cambridge: Cambridge University Press, 1950), 6–10; Roger Chartier,

"The Practical Impact of Writing," in *Passions of the Renaissance*, trans. Arthur Goldhammer, ed. Roger Chartier (Cambridge: Harvard University Press, 1989), 124–27. Vol. 3 of *A History of Private Life*, ed. Phillipe Aries and Georges Duby. 5 vols., 1987–90.

42. Eric A. Havelock, *The Muse Learns to Write: An Introduction to the Anthropology of Art* (Lanham, Md.: University Press of America, 1985), 78, 28.

43. Walter J. Ong, *Orality and Literacy: The Technologizing of the Word* (London and New York, Methuen, 1982), 115, 67, 72.

CHAPTER 4: FURTHER CONTEXTS OF RESISTANCE TO SHAKESPEAREAN SENSE-READING

1. Thomas O. Sloan, "Introduction," in *The Oral Study of Literature*, ed. Robert Beloof, et al. (New York: Random House, 1966), 8.

2. Wallace A. Bacon and Robert S. Breen, *Literature as Experience* (New York: McGraw-Hill, 1959), 4–6.

3. Ibid., 10, 20.

4. Ibid., 26; and see Wallace A. Bacon, *Oral Interpretation and the Teaching of Literature in Secondary Schools* (New York: Speech Communications Association, 1974), 38, 51; Bacon, *The Art of Interpretation* (New York: Holt, Rinehart and Winston, 1966), 6, 13, 36.

5. Victoria Kahn, *Rhetoric, Prudence, and Skepticism in the Renaissance* (Ithaca and London: Cornell University Press, 1985), 19.

6. See, for example, Richard Beach's overview with its restriction of imagery to vision and its notion that emotional responses are subjectively "reader-based," not based in widespread, common perceptions of concrete experience. Richard Beach, *A Teacher's Introduction to Reader-Response Theories* (Urbana, Ill.: National Council of Teachers of English, 1993), 57, 69.

7. Walter J. Slatoff, *With Respect to Readers: Dimension of Literary Response* (Ithaca and London: Cornell University Press, 1970), 6, and see 32; see also, Alan Purves and Richard Beach, *Literature and the Reader: Research in Response to Literature, Reading Interests, and the Teaching of Literature* (Urbana, Ill.: National Council of Teachers of English, 1972), (disappointingly) on "physical determinants of response," 22–23.

8. See, for example, Norman N. Holland, *The Dynamics of Literary Response* (New York: Oxford University Press, 1968); *5 Readers Reading* (New Haven: Yale University Press, 1975); *Poems in Persons: An Introduction to the Psychoanalysis of Literature* (New York: Norton, 1973).

9. David Bleich, "Epistemological Assumptions in the Study of Response," in *Reader-Response Criticism: From Formalism to Post-Structuralism*, ed. Jane P. Tompkins (Baltimore and London: Johns Hopkins Univerrsity Press, 1986), 137.

10. Eugene Kintgen, *The Perception of Poetry* (Bloomington: Indiana University Press, 1983), 1.

11. David Bleich, *Readings and Feelings: An Introduction to Subjective Criticism* (Urbana, Ill.: National Council of Teachers of English, 1975), 148.

12. Carolyn Allen, "Louise Rosenblatt and Theories of Reader Response," in

The Experience of Reading: Louise Rosenblatt and Reader-Response Theory, ed. John Clifford (Portsmouth, N.H.: Boynton/Cook Publishers, 1991), 20.

13. Alan Purves, "The Aesthetic Mind of Louise Rosenblatt," in *The Experience of Reading*, ed. John Clifford, 213.

14. Philip M. Anderson and Gregory Rubano, *Enhancing Aesthetic Reading and Response* (Urbana, Ill.: National Council of Teachers of English, 1991), 18, 19; for their bipolar scaling, see 14–23.

15. Beach, *Teacher's Introduction*, 69.

16. Elizabeth Freund, *The Return of the Reader: Reader-Response Criticism* (London and New York: Methuen, 1987), 10.

17. Deborah Brandt, *Literacy as Involvement: The Acts of Writers, Readers, and Texts* (Carbondale: Southern Illinois University Press, 1990), 67.

18. Marjorie Godlin Roemer, "Which Reader's Response?" *College English* 49, 8 (1987): 920.

19. Philip K. Bock, "Elizabethan Ethnosemantics," *Deutsche Shakespeare Gesellschaft West Jahrbuch* (1990): 163.

20. On Elizabethan conceptions of the heart, see F. David Hoeniger, *Medicine and Shakespeare in the English Renaissance* (Newark: University of Delaware Press, 1992), 89, 169.

21. Bleich, *Readings and Feelings*, 11.

22. Sloan, "Introduction," in *the Oral Study of Literature*, 8; Bleich, *Readings and Feelings*, 11.

23. Frederick Turner, "The Neural Lyre," in *Natural Classicism: Essays on Science and Literature* (1985; reprint, Charlottesville: University of Virginia Press, 1992), 103–4.

24. See Bobby C. Alexander, *Victor Turner Revisited: Ritual as Social Change* (Atlanta, Ga.: Scholars Press, 1991), 1–66.

25. Timothy J. Lukes, *The Flight Into Inwardness: An Exposition and Critique of Herbert Marcuse's Theory of Liberative Aesthetics* (Selinsgrove, Pa.: Susquehanna University Press, 1985), 162.

26. Evelyn Payne Hatcher, *Art as Culture: An Introduction to the Anthropology of Art* (Lanham, Md.: University Press of America, 1985), 87.

27. On Western attitudes toward human bodies, see, for example, Frank Bottomley, *Attitudes to the Body in Western Christendom* (London: Lepus Books, 1979); James B. Nelson, *Between Two Gardens: Reflections on Sexuality and Religious Experience* (New York: Pilgrim Press, 1983); Francis Barker, *The Tremulous Private Body: Essays on Subjection* (London and New York: Methuen, 1984); Morris Berman, *Coming to Our Senses: Body and Spirit in the Hidden History of the West* (New York: Simon and Schuster, 1989).

28. Nadia Tazi, "Celestial Bodies: A Few Stops on the Way to Heaven," in *Fragments for a History of the Human Body*, ed. Michael Feher, part 2 (New York: Zone, 1989), 540.

29. Elizabeth Cook, *Seeing Through Words: The Scope of Late Renaissance Poetry* (New Haven and London: Yale University Press, 1986), 143.

30. Marie-Helene Davies, *Reflections of Renaissance England: Life, Thought, and Religion Mirrored in Illustrated Pamphlets: 1535–1640*, Princeton Theological Monograph Series No. 1 (Allison Park, Pa.: Pickwick Publications, 1986), 64, 22.

31. Devon L. Hodges, *Renaissance Fictions of Anatomy* (Amherst: University of Massachusetts Press, 1985), 15; but see Luke Wilson, "William Harvey's *Prelectiones*: The Performance of the Body in the Renaissance Theater of Anatomy," *Representations* 17 (1987): 89. On Vesalius, see Glenn Harcourt, "Andreas Vesalius and the Anatomy of Antique Sculpture, *Representations* 17 (1987): 28–61.

32. James R. Siemon, *Shakespearean Iconoclasm* (Berkeley and Los Angeles: University of California Press, 1985), 40.

33. David Freedberg, *The Power of Images: Studies in the History and Theory of Response* (Chicago and London: University of Chicago Press, 1989), 430.

34. Paul Crowther, *Art and Embodiment: From Aesthetics to Self-Consciousness* (Oxford: Clarendon Press, 1993), 7.

35. Freedberg, *The Power of Images*, 439.

36. Barker, *The Tremulous Private Body*, 12.

37. Norbert Elias, *The Civilizing Process*, trans. Edmund Jephcott (New York: Pantheon Books, 1982), 257; compare Mikhail Bakhtin, *Rabelais and His World*, 1965, trans. Helene Iswolsky (Bloomington: Indiana University Press, 1984), 322n.8.

38. But see Juliet Dusinberre, "The Taming of the Shrew: Women, Acting, and Power," *Studies in the Literary Imagination* 26, no. 1 (1993): 80–81, arguing for a triumphant silencing of Petruchio/Burbage by an apprentice acting Kate.

39. Crowther, *Critical Aesthetics and Postmodernism*, 205–6; but see Andrew J. Strathern, *Body Thoughts* (Ann Arbor: University of Michigan Press, 1996), 198, on "embodiment" as an antitheoretical, antiabstractive, "muted universalism," a "new humanism . . . intended to bring us back to ourselves" and likely to meet with only mixed success.

40. Geoffrey Hartman, *Saving the Text: Literature/Derrida/Philosophy* (Baltimore and London: Johns Hopkins University Press), 149–50.

41. Mark Johnson, *The Body in the Mind: The Bodily Basis of Meaning, Imagination, and Reason* (Chicago and London: University of Chicago Press, 1987), xv.

42. George Lakoff, *Women, Fire, and Dangerous Things: What Categories Reveal About the Mind* (Chicago and London: University of Chicago Press, 1987), 380–408; and see Carol E. McMahon, "Psychosomatic Concepts in the Works of Shakespeare," *Journal of the History of the Behavioral Sciences* 12 (1976): 227; and compare, Thomas Steele Hall, *Ideas of Life and Matter: Studies in the History of General Physiology, 600* B.C.–1900 A.D. (Chicago: University of Chicago Press, 1969), 243–46.

43. Lakoff, *Women, Fire, and Dangerous Things*, 407; but see Strathern, *Body Thoughts*, 190–91.

44. Compare Bakhtin, *Rabelais and His World*; Peter Stallybrass and Allon White, *The Politics and Poetics of Transgression* (Ithaca, N.Y.: Cornell University Press, 1986), 1–26.

45. Catherine Belsey, *Critical Practice* (London and New York: Methuen, 1980), 139.

46. Terence Hawkes, *Meaning by Shakespeare* (London and New York: Routledge, 1992), 147.

47. John Blacking, "Towards an Anthropology of the Body," in *The Anthropology of the Body*, ed. John Blacking (London and New York: Academic Press, 1977), 1–8; and see Drew Leder, *The Absent Body* (Chicago and London: University of Chicago Press, 1990), 29.

48. David Howes, "Introduction," in *The Varieties of Sensory Experience: A Sourcebook in the Anthropology of the Senses*, ed. David Howes (Toronto: University of Toronto Press, 1991), 17.

49. Crowther, *Critical Aesthetics*, 49.

50. Bryan S. Turner, preface to *The Consuming Body*, by Pasi Falk (London: Sage, 1994), xiii, and see Falk, ibid., 6.

51. Constance Classen, *Worlds of Sense: Exploring the Senses in History and Across Cultures* (London and New York: Routledge, 1993), 6–7; and see Howes, "Introduction," in *The Varieties of Sensory Experience*, 1–19.

52. Compare A. Nicolopoulou and J. Weintraub, "On Liberty, Cultural Relativism, and Development," *Culture and Psychology* 2, no. 3 (1996): 273–84.

53. Hatcher, *Art as Culture*, 110–11, 203.

54. Crowther, *Art and Embodiment*, 6, 117.

55. Lorna McDougall, "Symbols and Somatic Structures," in *The Anthropology of the Body*, ed. John Blacking (London and New York: Academic Press, 1977), 402.

56. Ellen Dissanayake, *Homo Aestheticus: Where Art Comes from and Why* (New York: Free Press—Macmillan, 1992), 219.

57. Jonathan Benthall, "Introduction," in *The Body as a Medium of Expression: Essays Based on a Course of Lectures Given at the Institute of Contemporary Arts, London*, ed. Jonathan Benthall and Ted Polhemus (New York: Dutton, 1975), 6–7.

58. Seymour Fisher, *Body Consciousness* (New York: Jason Aronson, 1974), 6.

59. Richard Seltzer, "How Proudly It Heals: In Praise of the Body Republic," *Lear's* 2, no. 4. (June 1989): 43.

60. Stephen Greenblatt, *Shakespearean Negotiations: The Circulation of Social Energy in Renaissance England* (Berkeley and Los Angeles: University of California Press, 1988), 86.

61. Gail Kern Paster, *The Body Embarrassed: Drama and the Disciplines of Shame in Early Modern England* (Ithaca, N.Y.: Cornell University Press, 1993), 4.

62. Linda Woodbridge, *The Scythe of Saturn: Shakespeare and Magical Thinking* (Urbana and Chicago: University of Illinois Press, 1994), 46–47, citing Mark Johnson's *The Body in the Mind*.

63. See n. 60, above.

CHAPTER 5. WORKING BEYOND RESISTANCE

1. Deane Juhan, *Job's Body: A Handbook for Bodywork* (Barrytown: Station Hill Press, 1987), 162.

2. Antonin Artaud, *The Theater and Its Double*, trans. Mary Caroline Richards (1938, New York: Grove, 1958), 80.

3. Alexander Leggatt, "Shakespeare and the Actor's Body," *Renaissance and Reformation* 10, no. 1 (1986): 106.

4. D. E. Berlyne, *Aesthetics and Psychobiology* (New York: Appleton-Century-Crofts, 1971), 110.

5. Hans Kreitler and Shulamith Kreitler, *Psychology of the Arts* (Durham, N.C.: Duke University Press, 1972), 28, and see 257–84 arguing that literary reading involves kinesthetic imitation.

6. R. P. Blackmur, *Language as Gesture: Essays in Poetry* (New York: Harcourt, Brace, 1952), 19–20.

7. For background on these figures, see, for example, Robert Marrone, *Body of Knowledge: An Introduction to Body/Mind Psychology* (Albany: State University of New York Press, 1990).

8. Stanley Keleman, *Somatic Reality* (Berkeley: Center Press, 1979), 47.

9. Arnold Mindell, *River's Way: The Process Science of the Dreambody* (London: Routledge and Kegan Paul, 1985), 24.

10. See, Joseph H. Goodbread, *The Dreambody Toolkit* (New York and London: Routledge and Kegan Paul, 1987), 26.

11. Arnold Mindell, *Dreambody: The Body's Role in Revealing the Self* (Boston: Sigo Press, 1982), 29, 5.

12. Paul Rozin, Jonathan Haidt, and Clark R. McCauley, "Disgust," in *Handbook of Emotions*, ed. Michael Lewis and Jeannette M. Haviland (New York and London: Guilford Press, 1993), 585, 584.

13. Joseph Heller and William A. Henkin, *Bodywise* (New York: St. Martin's Press, 1986), 169.

14. Arnold Mindell, *Working With the Dreaming Body* (Boston: Routledge and Kegan Paul, 1985) 37–47; Goodbread, *The Dreambody Toolkit*, 111.

15. Mindell, *Working With the Dreaming Body*, 38.

16. Artaud, *The Theater and Its Double*, 119.

17. Stanley Keleman, *Your Body Speaks Its Mind* (Berkeley: Center Press, 1978),93.

18. Juhan, *Job's Body*, 223; and compare Herbert Weiner, "Contemporary Research and the Mind-Body Problem," in *Body and Mind: Past, Present, Future*, ed. R. W. Rieber (New York: Academic Press, 1980), 237, arguing that one's consciousness of an event is only one of several neural processes caused by the event.

19. Keleman, *Somatic Reality*, 52.

20. Recent reviews of the research on facial feedback hypotheses include Daniel N. McIntosh, "Facial Feedback Hypotheses: Evidence, Implications, and Directions," *Motivation and Emotion* 20, no. 2 (1996): 121–47; Paul Ekman, "Facial Expression and Emotion," *American Psychologist* 48, 4 (1993): 384–92. See also, Jack George Thompson, *The Psychobiology of Emotions* (New York and London: Plenum Press, 1988), 332–43.

21. Linda A. Camras, Elizabeth A. Holland, and Mary Jill Patterson, "Facial Expression," in *Handbook of Emotions*, ed. Lewis, 204.

22. Jens Forster and Fritz Strack, "Influence of Overt Head Movements on Memory for Valenced Words: A Case of Conceptual-Motor Compatibility," *Journal of Personality and Social Psychology* 71, no. 3 (1996): 421–30.

23. Paul Ekman, "Expression and the Nature of Emotion," in *Approaches to*

Emotion, ed. Klaus R. Scherer and Paul Ekman (Hillsdale, N.J.: L. Erlbaum Associates, 1984), 332.

24. On muted forms of basic or primary emotions, see Robert Plutchik, "Emotion: A General Psychoevolutionary Theory," in ibid., 203.

25. On intensifying heat and pressure of rage and anger, see Thompson, *The Psychobiology of Emotions*, 77; on attempted domination among hostile animals through expressions of anger, see Plutchik, "Emotion," in *Approaches to Emotion*, ed. Scherer, 210 (speculative extension of the principle to attempted domination of nonanimal threats is my own).

26. R. B. Zajonc, Sheila T. Murphy, and Marita Inglehart, "Feeling and Facial Efference: Implications of the Vascular Theory of Emotion," *Psychological Review* 96, no. 3 (1989): 395–416; Marrone, *Body of Knowledge*, 77–78; R. B. Zajonc, Sheila T. Murphy, and Daniel N. McIntosh, "Brain Temperature and Subjective Emotional Experience," in *Handbook of Emotions*, ed. Lewis, 209–20.

27. A. C. Bradley, *Shakespearean Tragedy* (1904; reprint, New York: St. Martin's Press, 1985), 28.

28. See Michael Myrtek and Georg Brugner, "Perception of Emotions in Everyday Life: Studies with Patients and Normals," *Biological Physiology* 42 (1996): 147–64.

29. Melissa L. Ferguson and Edward S. Katkin, "Visceral Perception, Anhedonia, and Emotion," *Biological Psychology* 42 (1996): 141.

CHAPTER 6. UNDERMIND SHAKESPEARE

1. Arnold Mindell, *River's Way: The Process Science of the Dreambody* (London: Routledge and Kegan Paul, 1985), 22.

2. Deane Juhan, *Job's Body: A Handbook for Bodywork* (Barrytown: Station Hill Press, 1987), 257–59.

3. See T. J. Scheff, *Catharsis in Healing, Ritual, and Drama* (Berkeley: University of California Press, 1979), 86.

4. Arnold Mindell, *Coma: Key to Awakening* (Boston: Shambhala, 1989), 39.

5. This is the form of the story analyzed by Arnold Mindell, *Dreambody: The Body's Role in Revealing the Self* (Boston: Sigo Press, 1982), 55–117; and see Arnold Mindell, *Working With the Dreaming Body* (Boston: Routledge and Kegan Paul, 1985), 48–59.

6. Arthur Lessac, *Body Wisdom: The Use and Training of the Human Body* (New York: Drama Book Publishers, 1978), 18.

7. Joseph Goodbread, *The Dreambody Toolkit* (New York and London: Routledge and Kegan Paul, 1987), 162.

8. Mindell, *Dreambody,* 77.

9. Compare the description of this body/character type in Alexander Lowen, *The Language of the Body* (New York: Collier Macmillan, 1958), 161–93.

10. Michael Goldman, *Shakespeare and the Energies of Drama* (Princeton: Princeton University Press, 1985), 167.

11. Lessac, *Body Wisdom*, 28.

12. Alfred Ziegler, *Archetypal Medicine*, trans. Gary V. Hartman (Dallas, Tex.: Spring Publications, 1983), 106.

13. Arthur Kirsch, "Hamlet's Grief," in *Hamlet*, ed. Harold Bloom (New York and Philadelphia: Chelsea House, 1990), 137.

14. On sense of mortality in *Hamlet*, see Maynard Mack, "The World of *Hamlet*," in *Everybody's Shakespeare: Reflections Chiefly on the Tragedies* (Lincoln: University of Nebraska Press, 1993), 107–27.

15. Mindell, *Working With the Dreaming Body*, 32.

16. Adnan K. Abdulla, *Catharsis in Literature* (Bloomington: Indiana University Press, 1985), 119.

17. Therese Bertherat and Carol Bernstein, *The Body Has Its Reasons* (Rochester, Vt.: Healing Arts Press, 1989), 133.

18. On the separateness of image memory and verbal memory, see Allan Paivio and Kalman Csapo, "Picture Superiority in Free Recall: Imagery or Dual Coding?" *Cognitive Psychology* 5, no. 2 (1973): 176–206; on the long-term, indelible character of nonverbal, emotional memories that bypass the neocortex, see J. E. LeDoux, "Emotional Memory: In Search of Systems and Synapses," *Annals of the New York Academy of Sciences* (1993): 149–57; and see Robert P. Hart and Gregory J. O'Shanick, "Forgetting Rates for Verbal, Pictorial, and Figural Stimuli," *Journal of Clinical and Experimental Neuropsychology* 15, no. 2 (1993): 245–65, suggesting that nonverbal memory storage is more stable than verbal memory storage.

19. Bill Moyers, *Healing and the Mind* (New York: Doubleday, 1993), 76, 209, 347.

20. Ziegler, *Archetypal Medicine*, 34–35.

CHAPTER 7. PRACTICE

1. Lawrence E. Marks, Robin J. Hammeal, and Marc H. Bornstein, *Perceiving Similarity and Comprehending Metaphor*, Monographs of the Society for Research in Child Development, Serial No. 215, 52, no. 1 (1987): 2.

2. Compare George Lakoff and Mark Turner, *More Than Cool Reason: A Field Guide to Poetic Metaphor* (Chicago and London: University of Chicago Press, 1989), 33.

3. See Janet Adelman, *Suffocating Mothers; Fantasies of Maternal Origin in Shakespeare's Plays, Hamlet to The Tempest* (New York and London: Routledge, 1992), 147–61.

4. See Ralph B. Hupka, et al., "The Colors of Anger, Envy, Fear, and Jealousy: A Cross-Cultural Study," *Journal of Cross-Cultural Psychology* 28, no. 2 (1997): 156–71.

5. Jeffrey Pittam and Klaus R. Scherer, "Vocal Expression and Communication of Emotion," in *Handbook of Emotions*, ed. Michael Lewis and Jeannette M. Haviland (New York and London: Guilford Press, 1993), 195.

6. John Mordechai Gottman, "Studying Emotion in Social Interaction," in Lewis and Haviland, eds., *Handbook of Emotions*, 482.

7. George T. Wright, *Shakespeare's Metrical Art* (Berkeley and Los Angeles: University of California Press, 1988), 16.

8. Donald Wesling, *The Scissors of Meter: Grammetrics and Reading* (Ann Arbor: University of Michigan Press, 1996), 44.

9. Richard Strozzi Heckler, *The Anatomy of Change: East/West Approaches to Body/Mind Therapy* (Boston and London: Shambhala, 1985), 19–53.

10. Frederick Turner, *Natural Classicism: Essays on Literature and Science* (Charlottesville: University of Virginia Press, 1992), 95.

11. Frederick Bracher, "The Silent Foot in Pentameter Verse," *PMLA* 62 (1947): 1105.

12. Ernst Terhardt, "Music Perception in the Auditory Hierarchy," *Music and the Mind Machine: The Psychophysiology and Psychopathology of the Sense of Music*, ed. R. Steinberg (Berlin: Springer-Verlag, 1995), 83–84.

13. John Barton, *Playing Shakespeare* (London and New York: Methuen, 1984), 53.

14. Isaac Asimov, *Asimov's Guide to Shakespeare*, (Garden City, N.Y.: Doubleday, 1970), 1:xii.

15. David Bevington, ed., *The Complete Works of Shakespeare*, 4th ed. (New York: HarperCollins, 1991), lxxx; compare, John Michael Vinopal, "English Renaissance Pronunciation," available at website, http://www.resort.com/~banshee/Faire/Language/pronunciation.html.

16. Fausto Cercignani, *Shakespeare's Works and Elizabethan Pronunciation* (Oxford: Clarendon Press, 1981), 5, 8–9, 21, 131–32.

17. And see, Wilhelm Viëtor, *A Shakespeare Reader: In the Old Spelling and with a Phonetic Transcription* (New York: Frederick Ungar, 1963), 19–21, illustrating by phonetic transcription this precise phenomenon.

18. Stephen Booth, *An Essay on Shakespeare's Sonnets* (New Haven and London: Yale University Press, 1969), 131.

19. Gillian Beer, "Rhyming as Comedy: Body, Ghost, and Banquet," in *English Comedy*, ed. Michael Cordner, Peter Holland, and John Kerrigan (Cambridge and New York: Cambridge University Press, 1994), 194.

20. Graham Bradshaw, *Shakespeare's Scepticism* (Brighton: Harvester, 1987), 256.

21. Ron Kurtz, *Body-Centered Psychotherapy* (Mendocino, Calif.: LifeRhythm, 1990); Richard Strozzi Heckler, *Anatomy of Change*; Stanley Keleman, *Somatic Reality* (Berkeley: Center Press, 1979); Alexander Lowen, *The Language of the Body* (New York: Collier Macmillan, 1958).

22. Heckler, *Anatomy of Change*, 117.

23. Susan Sontag, *Against Interpretation and Other Essays* (New York: Farrar, Straus and Giroux, 1966), 13.

24. Wallace A. Bacon and Robert S. Breen, *Literature as Experience* (New York: McGraw-Hill, 1959), 4.

25. Seymour Fisher, *Body Consciousness* (New York: Jason Aronson, 1974), 17–18.

26. Bacon and Breen, *Literature as Experience*, 35.

27. See David A. Steere, *Bodily Expressions in Psychotherapy* (New York: Brunner/Mazel, 1982), 9, 73; and see Brian Bates, *The Way of the Actor: A Path to Knowledge and Power* (Boston: Shambhala, 1988), 111.

28. Gottman, "Studying Emotion," in *Handbook of Emotions*, Lewis and Haviland, eds., 483.

29. Compare, James J. Gross, Barbara L. Fredrickson, and Robert W. Levenson, "The Psychophysiology of Crying," *Psychophysiology* 31, no. 5 (1994): 460–68.

30. See Dolf Zillmann, Karla J. Schweitzer, and Norbert Mundorf, "Menstrual Cycle Variation of Women's Interest in Erotica," *Archives of Sexual Behavior* 23, no. 5 (1994): 579–97.

31. On patterns of spectator engagement while viewing Shakespearean drama, see Maynard Mack, "Engagement and Detachment in Shakespeare's Plays," in *Essays on Shakespeare and Elizabethan Drama in Honor of Hardin Craig*, ed. Richard Hosley (Columbia: University of Missouri Press, 1962), 275–96.

32. Norman N. Holland, *Poems in Persons: An Introduction to the Psychoanalysis of Literature* (New York: Norton, 1973), 133.

33. On the signals of posture and gesture, compare Steere, *Bodily Expressions in Psychotherapy*; Mary Ritchie Key, *Paralanguage and Kinesics* (Metuchen, N.J.: Scarecrow Press, 1975); Ralph A Smith, *The Sense of Art: A Study in Aesthetic Education* (New York and London: Routledge, 1989).

34. See John Paul Spiegel and Pavel Machotka, *Messages of the Body* (New York: Free Press, 1974), 66.

35. Ellen J. Esrock, *The Reader's Eye: Visual Imaging as Reader Response* (Baltimore and London: Johns Hopkins University Press, 1994), 120.

36. Key, *Paralanguage and Kinesics*, 21; compare Edward T. Hall, *The Dance of Life: The Other Dimension of Time* (New York: Doubleday, 1983), 4: "the nonverbal, behavioral part of communication is the provenance of the common man and the core culture that guides his life."

37. David Crystal, "Paralinguistic Behavior as Continuity Between Animal and Human Communication," in *Language and Man: Anthropological Issues*, ed. William C. McCormack and Stephen A. Wurm. International Congress of Anthropological and Ethological Sciences, 9th, 1973, Chicago (The Hague and Paris: Mouton, 1976), 19–20; compare Terence Hawkes, *That Shakespeherian Rag: Essays on a Critical Process* (London and New York: Methuen, 1986), 78–80; and see, Steere *Bodily Expressions in Psychotherapy*, 252–57.

38. See Nancy M. Henley. *Body Politics: Power, Sex, and Nonverbal Communication* (Englewood Cliffs, N.J.: Prentice Hall, 1977), 67–81.

CHAPTER 8. SENSE-READING IN THE CLASSROOM

1. Howard Mills, *Working with Shakespeare* (Lanham, Md.: Barnes and Noble Books, 1993), 223.

2. Arnold Mindell, *City Shadows: Psychological Interventions in Psychiatry* (London and New York: Routledge, 1988), 165.

3. Robert Bly, *A Little Book on the Human Shadow* (San Francisco: Harper and Row, 1988), 42.

4. Edward L. Rocklin, " 'An Incarnational Art': Teaching Shakespeare," *Shakespeare Quarterly* 41, no. 2 (1990): 151.

5. Judith Elstein, "A Midsummer Night's Dream," in *Shakespeare Set Free:*

Teaching Romeo and Juliet, Macbeth, A Midsummer Night's Dream, ed. Peggy O'Brien, et al. (New York: Washington Square Press, 1993), 37, 49.

6. Peter Reynolds, *Practical Approaches to Teaching Shakespeare* (Oxford: Oxford University Press, 1991), 49.

7. William Blake Tyrell, *Amazons: A Study in Athenian Mythmaking* (Baltimore and London: Johns Hopkins University Press, 1984), 127.

8. Mills, *Working with Shakespeare*, 25.

9. A. K. Hudson, *Shakespeare and the Classroom*, 2nd ed. (London: Heinemann, 1960), 16.

10. See Willibald Ruch, "Exhilaration and Humor," in *Handbook of Emotions*, ed. Michael Lewis and Jeannette M. Haviland (New York and London: Guilford Press, 1993), 605–16.

11. Mikhail Bakhtin, *Rabelais and His World*, trans. Helene Iswolsky (Bloomington: Indiana University Press, 1984), 27.

12. Michael D. Bristol, *Carnival and Theater: Plebeian Culture and the Structure of Authority in Renaissance England* (New York and London: Methuen, 1985), 67.

13. Francis Dunlop, *The Education of Feeling and Emotion* (London: George Allen and Unwin, 1984), 91–92.

14. Bakhtin, *Rabelais and His World*, 319.

15. On the physical components of exhilaration, see Ruch, "Exhilaration and Humor," in *Handbook of Emotions*, Lewis and Haviland, eds., 605–16.

16. Chris Baldick, *The Social Mission of English Criticism: 1848–1932* (Oxford: Clarendon Press, 1982), 234.

17. Robert Pattison, *On Literacy: the Politics of the Word from Homer to the Age of Rock* (New York: Oxford University Press, 1982), ix.

18. Stanley Aronowitz and Henry Giroux, *Education Under Siege: The Conservative, Liberal, and Radical Debate Over Schooling* (South Hadley, Mass.: Bergin and Garvey, 1985), 70.

19. Brian Doyle, *English and Englishness* (London and New York: Routledge, 1989), 142.

20. Terry Eagleton, "Afterword," in *The Shakespeare Myth*, ed. Graham Holderness (Manchester: Manchester University Press, 1988), 204.

21. See Eagleton, "The Ideology of the Aesthetic," in *Politics of Pleasure: Aesthetics and Cultural theory*, ed. Stephen Regan (Buckingham and Philadelphia: Open University Press, 1992), 14.

22. Robert S. Dombroski, *Antonio Gramsci* (Boston: G. K. Hall, 1989), 50.

23. Ralph A. Smith, *The Sense of Art: A Study in Aesthetic Education* (New York and London: Routledge, 1989), 169.

24. Alfred North Whitehead, as quoted by Wallace A. Bacon and Robert Breen, *Literature as Experience* (New York: McGraw-Hill, 1959), 276; for same quotation, see also, Roger Shattuck, "How to Rescue Literature," *The New York Review of Books* 27, no. 6 (17 April 1980): 33.

25. Thomas Hanna, *Bodies in Revolt: A Primer in Somatic Thinking* (New York: Holt, Rinehart and Winston, 1970), 295.

26. Seymour Fisher, *Body Consciousness* (New York: Jason Aronson, 1974), 139.

27. Hubert L. Dreyfus, "What Computers Still Can't Do," *The Key Reporter* 59, no. 2 (winter 1993/94): 6.

28. David Sudnow, *Talk's Body: A Meditation Between Two Keyboards* (New York: Knopf, 1979), 14; see also, his *Ways of the Hand: The Organization of Improvised Conduct* (Cambridge: Harvard University Press, 1978).

29. Compare, Bristol, *Carnival and Theater*, 212: "After the festive agon is concluded, the energy of a resourceful improvisatory competence is the only authority that remains."

30. Keith Johnstone, *Impro: Improvisation and the Theatre* (New York: Theatre Arts Books, 1979), 87; see also, Milton E. Polsky, *Let's Improvise* (Englewood Cliffs, N.J.: Prentice Hall, 1980), 232.

CHAPTER 9. CONCLUSION: WALKING WESTWARD

1. Richard Strozzi Heckler, *The Anatomy of Change: East/West Approaches to Body/Mind Therapy* (Boston and London: Shambhala, 1985), 12.

2. David Howes, "Introduction," in *The Varieties of Sensory Experience: A Sourcebook in the Anthropology of the Senses*, ed. David Howes (Toronto: University of Toronto Press, 1991), 8.

3. Compare Maura C. Flannery, "The Biology of Aesthetics," *The American Biology Teacher* 55, no. 8 (1993): 498–500.

4. Richard Strier, *Resistant Structures: Particularity, Radicalism, and Renaissance Texts* (Berkeley and Los Angeles: University of California Press, 1995), 68.

Works Cited

Abdulla, Adnan K. *Catharsis in Literature*. Bloomington: Indiana University Press, 1985.

Adelman, Janet. *Suffocating Mothers: Fantasies of Maternal Origin in Shakespeare's Plays, Hamlet to The Tempest*. New York and London: Routledge, 1992.

Alexander, Bobby C. *Victor Turner Revisited: Ritual as Social Change*. Atlanta, Ga.: Scholars Press, 1991.

Allen, Carolyn. "Louise Rosenblatt and Theories of Reader Response." In *The Experience of Reading: Louise Rosenblatt and Reader-Response Theory*, edited by John Clifford, 15–22. Portsmouth, N.H.: Boynton/Cook Publishers, 1991.

Anderson, Philip M., and Gregory Rubano. *Enhancing Aesthetic Reading and Response*. Urbana, Ill.: National Council of Teachers of English, 1991.

Anselment, Raymond A. *The Realms of Apollo: Literature and Healing in Seventeenth-Century England*. Newark: University of Delaware Press, 1995.

Armstrong, Edward. *Shakespeare's Imagination: A Study of the Psychology of Association and Inspiration*. London: L. Drummond, 1946.

Aronowitz, Stanley, and Henry Giroux. *Education Under Siege: The Conservative, Liberal, and Radical Debate Over Schooling*. South Hadley, Mass.: Bergin and Garvey, 1985.

Artaud, Antonin. *The Theater and Its Double*. 1938. Translated by Mary Caroline Richards. Reprint, New York: Grove Press, 1958.

Asimov, Isaac. *Asimov's Guide to Shakespeare*. 2 vols. Garden City, N.Y.: Doubleday, 1970.

Attridge, Derek. *Poetic Rhythm: An Introduction*. Cambridge: Cambridge University Press, 1995.

———. *The Rhythms of English Poetry*. London and New York: Longman, 1982.

Aviram, Amittai F. *Telling Rhythm: Body and Meaning in Poetry*. Ann Arbor: University of Michigan Press, 1994.

Bacon, Wallace A. *The Art of Interpretation*. New York: Holt, Rinehart and Winston, 1966.

———. *Oral Interpretation and the Teaching of Literature in Secondary Schools*. New York: Speech Communications Association, 1974.

———, and Robert S. Breen. *Literature as Experience*. New York: McGraw-Hill, 1959.

Bakhtin, Mikhail. *Rabelais and His World*. 1965. Translated by Helene Iswolsky. Bloomington: Indiana University Press, 1984.

Bakker, Frank C., Marc W. J. Boschker, and Tjuling Chung. "Changes in Muscular Activity While Imagining Weight Lifting in Using Stimulus or Response Propositions." *Journal of Sport and Exercise Psychology* 18 (1996): 313–24.

Baldick, Chris. *The Social Mission of English Criticism: 1848–1932*. Oxford: Clarendon Press, 1983.

Barber, C. L. *Shakespeare's Festive Comedy: A Study of Dramatic Form and Its Relation to Social Custom*. Princeton: Princeton University Press, 1959.

Barker, Francis. *The Tremulous Private Body: Essays on Subjection*. London and New York: Methuen, 1984.

Barton, John. *Playing Shakespeare*. London and New York: Methuen, 1984.

Batcher, Elaine. *Emotion in the Classroom: A Study of Children's Experience*. New York: Praeger, 1981.

Bates, Brian. *The Way of the Actor: A Path to Knowledge and Power*. Boston: Shambhala, 1988.

Beach, Richard. *A Teacher's Introduction to Reader-Response Theories*. Urbana, Ill.: National Council of Teachers of English, 1993.

Beaty, Jerome, and J. Paul Hunter, eds. *The Norton Introduction to Literature*. 7th ed. New York: W. W. Norton, 1998.

Beckerman, Bernard. *Shakespeare at the Globe, 1599–1609*. New York: Macmillan, 1962.

Beer, Gillian. "Rhyming as Comedy: Body, Ghost, and Banquet." In *English Comedy*. Edited by Michael Cordner, Peter Holland, and John Kerrigan. 180–96. Cambridge and New York: Cambridge University Press, 1994.

Belsey, Catherine. *Critical Practice*. London and New York: Methuen, 1980.

Benthall, Jonathan. "Prospectus." In *The Body as a Medium of Expression: Essays Based on a Course of Lectures Given at the Institute of Contemporary Arts, London*. Edited by Jonathan Benthall and Ted Polhemus, 5–12. New York: Dutton, 1975.

Bertherat, Therese, and Carol Bernstein. *The Body Has Its Reasons*. Rochester, Vt.: Healing Arts Press, 1989.

Berlyne, D. E. *Aesthetics and Psychobiology*. New York: Appleton-Century-Crofts, 1971.

Berman, Morris. *Coming to Our Senses: Body and Spirit in the Hidden History of the West*. New York: Simon and Schuster, 1989.

Bevington, David, ed. *The Complete Works of Shakespeare*. 4th ed. New York: HarperCollins, 1991.

———. *Action Is Eloquence: Shakespeare's Language of Gesture*. Cambridge and London: Harvard University Press, 1984.

Blacking, John. "Towards an Anthropology of the Body." In *The Anthropology of the Body*. Edited by John Blacking, 1–28. London and New York: Academic Press, 1977.

Blackmur, R. P. *Language as Gesture: Essays in Poetry*. New York: Harcourt, Brace, 1952.

Bleich, David. "Epistemological Assumptions in the Study of Response." In *Reader-Response Criticism: From Formalism to Post-Structuralism*. Edited by Jane P. Tompkins, 134–63. Baltimore and London: Johns Hopkins University Press, 1986.

———. *Readings and Feelings: An Introduction to Subjective Criticism*. Urbana, Ill.: National Council of Teachers of English, 1975.

Bly, Robert. *Iron John: A Book about Men*. Reading, Mass.: Addison-Wesley, 1990.

———. *A Little Book on the Human Shadow*. San Francisco: Harper and Row, 1988.

Bock, Philip K. "Elizabethan Ethnosemantics." *Deutsche Shakespeare Gesellschaft West Jahrbuck*, Bochum, Germany, (1990): 157–66.

Booth, Stephen. *An Essay on Shakespeare's Sonnets*. New Haven and London: Yale University Press, 1969.

———. *King Lear, Macbeth, Indefinition, and Tragedy*. New Haven and London: Yale University Press, 1983.

Bottomley, Frank. *Attitudes to the Body in Western Christendom*. London: Lepus Books, 1979.

Bowen, Deborah. "Wimsatt, William Kurtz, Jr." In *Encyclopedia of Contemporary Literary Theory*. Edited by Irena R. Makaryk, 481–94. Toronto: University of Toronto Press, 1995.

Bracher, Frederick. "The Silent Foot in Pentameter Verse." *PMLA* 62 (1947): 1100–7.

Bradley, A. C. *Shakespearean Tragedy*. 1904. Reprint, New York: St. Martin's Press, 1985.

Bradshaw, Graham. *Shakespeare's Scepticism*. Brighton: Harvester, 1987.

Brandt, Deborah. *Literacy as Involvement: The Acts of Writers, Readers, and Texts*. Carbondale: Southern Illinois University Press, 1990.

Bristol, Michael D. *Carnival and Theater: Plebeian Culture and the Structure of Authority in Renaissance England*. New York and London: Methuen, 1985.

Brown, John Russell, ed. *The Merchant of Venice*. The Arden Shakespeare. 1955. Reprint, London and New York: Methuen, 1984.

Bynum, Caroline Walker. *Holy Feast and Holy Fast: The Religious Significance of Food to Medieval Women*. Berkeley and Los Angeles: University of California Press, 1987.

Calhoun, Cheshire. "Cognitive Emotions?" In *What Is an Emotion?: Classic Readings in Philosophical Psychology*. Edited by Cheshire Calhoun and Robert C. Solomon, 327–42. New York and Oxford: Oxford University Press, 1984.

Campbell, Don G. "Imagery and the Physiology of Music." In *Music: Physician for Times to Come*. Edited by Don Campbell, 243–54. Wheaton, Ill.: Quest Books, 1991.

Camras, Linda A., Elizabeth A. Holland, and Mary Jill Patterson. "Facial Expression." In *Handbook of Emotions*. Edited by Michael Lewis and Jeannette M. Haviland, 199–205. New York and London: Guilford Press, 1993.

Cartwright, Kent. *Shakespearean Tragedy and Its Double: The Rhythms of Audience Response*. University Park: Pennsylvania State University Press, 1991.

Cercignani, Fausto. *Shakespeare's Works and Elizabethan Pronunciation*. Oxford: Clarendon Press, 1981.

Chambers, E. K. *Shakespeare: A Survey*. 1925. Reprint, New York: Hill and Wang, 1963.

Chartier, Roger. "The Practical Impact of Writing." *In Passions of the Renaissance*. Translated by Arthur Goldhammer. Edited by Roger Chartier, 111–59. Cambridge: Harvard University Press, 1989. Vol. 3 of *A History of Private Life*. Edited by Philippe Aries and Georges Duby. 5 vols. 1987–90.

Chaytor, H. J. *From Script to Print: An Introduction to Medieval Literature*. Cambridge: Cambridge University Press, 1950.

Classen, Constance. *Worlds of Sense: Exploring the Senses in History and Across Cultures*. London and New York: Routledge, 1993.

Clemen, Wolfgang. *The Development of Shakespeare's Imagery*. 1936. Revised edition. New York: Hill and Wang, 1962.

Cook, Elizabeth. *Seeing Through Words: The Scope of Late Renaissance Poetry*. New Haven and London: Yale University Press, 1986.

Critchley, Macdonald, and R. A. Henson, eds. *Music and the Brain*. London: Wm Heinemann Medical Books, 1977.

Crowther, Paul. *Art and Embodiment: From Aesthetics to Self-Consciousness*. Oxford: Clarendon Press, 1993.

———. *Critical Aesthetics and Postmodernism*. Oxford: Clarendon Press, 1993.

Crystal, David. "Paralinguistic Behavior as Continuity Between Animal and Human Communication." In *Language and Man: Anthropological Issues*. Edited by William C. McCormack and Stephen A. Wurm, 13–27. International Congress of Anthropological and Ethological Sciences (9th, 1973; Chicago). The Hague and Paris: Mouton, 1976.

Cureton, Richard D. "Helen Vendler and the Music of Poetry." *Versification: An Interdisciplinary Journal of Literary Prosody*. 1, no. 1 (10 March 1997): 1–4. At website:http://sizcoll.u-shizuoka-ken.ac.jp/versif/Docs/VersRev_397_Cureton.html.

Davies, Marie-Helene. *Reflections of Renaissance England: Life, Thought, and Religion Mirrored in Illustrated Pamphlets: 1535–1640*. Princeton Theological Monograph Series, no. 1. Allison Park, Pa.: Pickwick Publications, 1986.

D'Aquili, Eugene G., and Charles D. Laughlin, Jr. "The Neurobiology of Myth and Ritual." In *The Spectrum of Ritual: A Biogenetic Structural Analysis*. Edited by Eugene G. d'Aquili, Charles D. Laughlin, Jr., and John McManus, 152–82. New York: Columbia University Press, 1979.

DeJong, Meyer R., et al. "Bodily Sensations, Facial EMG, and Autonomic Changes in the Course of Prolonged Emotional Imagery." *Journal of Psychophysiology* 7, no. 1 (1993): 34–45.

Dennison, George. *The Lives of Children: The Story of the First Street School*. New York: Random House: 1969.

Diment, A. D., Wendy Louise Walker, and A. G. Hammer. "Response to Poetry in Hypnosis and the Waking State: A Study of Non-Suggested Aspects of the Hypnotic State." *Australian Journal of Clinical and Experimental Hypnosis* 9, 1 (1981): 19–40.

Dissanayake, Ellen. *Homo Aestheticus: Where Art Comes From and Why*. New York: Free Press—Macmillan, 1992.

Dombroski, Robert S. *Antonio Gramsci*. Boston: G. K. Hall, 1989.

Dowden, Edward. *Shakspere: A Critical Study of His Mind and Art*. 1881. 3rd ed. London, Routledge, 1962.

———. *Introduction to Shakespeare*. 1907. Reprint, Freeport, N.Y.: Books for Libraries Press, 1970.

Downing, John, and Che Kan Leong. *Psychology of Reading*. New York: Macmillan, 1982.

Doyle, Brian. *English and Englishness*. London and New York: Routledge, 1989.

Dreyfus, Hubert L. "What Computers Still Can't Do." *The Key Reporter* 59, no. 2 (winter 1993/94): 4–9.

Duffy, Robert J., et al. "The Effects of Time/Frequency Distortion on the Prosodic Features of Speech." *U.S. Naval Submarine Medical Center Report* 680 (1971): 1–10.

Dunlop, Francis. *The Education of Feeling and Emotion*. London: George Allen and Unwin, 1984.

Dusinberre, Juliet. "*The Taming of the Shrew*: Women, Acting, and Power." *Studies in the Literary Imagination* 26, no. 1 (1993): 67–84.

Eagleton, Terry. Afterword. In *The Shakespeare Myth*. Edited by Graham Holderness, 203–08. Manchester: Manchester University Press, 1988.

———. "The Ideology of the Aesthetic." In *Politics of Pleasure: Aesthetics and Cultural Theory*. Edited by Stephen Regan, 17–31. Buckingham and Philadelphia: Open University Press, 1992.

Ekman, Paul. "Expression and the Nature of Emotion." In *Approaches to Emotion*. Edited by Klaus R. Scherer and Paul Ekman, 319–43. Hillsdale, N.J.: L. Erlbaum Associates, 1984.

Ekman, Paul. "Facial Expression and Emotion." *American Psychologist* 48, 4 (1993): 384–92.

Elias, Norbert. *The Civilizing Process*. Translated by Edmund Jephcott. New York: Pantheon Books, 1982

Elstein, Judith. "*A Midsummer Night's Dream*." In *Shakespeare Set Free: Teaching Romeo and Juliet, Macbeth, A Midsummer Night's Dream*. Edited by Peggy O'Brien, et al. 37–115. New York: Washington Square Press, 1993.

Erikson, Joan M. *Wisdom and the Senses: The Way of Creativity*. New York and London: Norton, 1988.

Esrock, Ellen J. *The Reader's Eye: Visual Imaging as Reader Response*. Baltimore and London: Johns Hopkins University Press, 1994.

Falk, Pasi. *The Consuming Body*. London: Sage, 1994.

Ferguson, Melissa L., and Edward S. Katkin. "Visceral Perception, Anhedonia, and Emotion." *Biological Psychology* 42 (1996): 131–45.

Fiorito, Evelyn R., and Robert F. Simons. "Emotional Imagery and Physical Anhedonia." *Psychophysiology* 31, no. 5 (1994): 513–21.

Fish, Stanley Eugene. *Is There a Text in This Class?: The Authority of Interpretive Communities.* Cambridge, Mass.: Harvard University Press, 1980.

Fisher, Seymour. *Body Consciousness.* New York: Jason Aronson, 1974.

Flannery, Maura C. "The Biology of Aesthetics." *The American Biology Teacher* 55, no. 8 (1993): 497–500.

Forster, Jens, and Fritz Strack. "Influence of Overt Head Movements on Memory for Valenced Words: A Case of Conceptual-Motor Compatibility." *Journal of Personality and Social Psychology* 71, no. 3 (1996): 421–30.

Freedberg, David. *The Power of Images: Studies in the History and Theory of Response.* Chicago and London: University of Chicago Press, 1989.

Freund, Elizabeth. *The Return of the Reader: Reader-Response Criticism.* London and New York: Methuen, 1987.

Frey, Charles H. "Interpreting *The Winter's Tale.*" *Studies in English Literature: 1500–1900* 18 (1978): 207–29.

———. "*The Tempest* and the New World." *Shakespeare Quarterly* 30 (1979): 29–41.

———. *Experiencing Shakespeare: Essays on Text, Classroom, and Performance.* Columbia, Mo.: University Missouri Press, 1988.

———. "Embodying the Play." In *The Tempest: Theory in Practice.* Edited by Nigel Wood, 67–96. Buckingham: Open University Press, 1993.

———. "Goals and Limits in Student Performance of Shakespeare." In *Teaching Shakespeare Today: Practical Approaches and Productive Strategies.* Edited by James E. Davis and Ronald E. Salomone, 72–78. Urbana, Ill.: National Council of Teachers of English, 1993.

———. "The Bias of Nature." *The Upstart Crow* 13 (1993): 2–15.

———. "Making Sense of Shakespeare: A Reader-Based Response." In *Teaching Shakespeare Into the 21st Century.* Edited by Ronald E. Salomone and James E. Davis, 96–103. Athens: Ohio University Press, 1997.

Gallop, Jane. *Thinking Through the Body.* New York: Columbia University Press, 1988.

Glickson, Joseph, Reuven Tsur, and Chanita Goodblatt. "Absorption and Trance-Inductive Poetry." *Empirical Studies of the Arts* 9, no. 2 (1992): 115–22.

Goldman, Michael. *Shakespeare and the Energies of Drama.* Princeton: Princeton University Press, 1972.

———. *Acting and Action in Shakespearean Tragedy.* Princeton: Princeton University Press, 1985.

Goodbread, Joseph. H. *The Dreambody Toolkit.* New York and London: Routledge and Kegan Paul, 1987.

Gottman, John Mordechai. "Studying Emotion in Social Interaction." In *Handbook of Emotions.* Edited by Michael Lewis and Jeannette M. Haviland, 475–87. New York and London: Guilford Press, 1993.

Granville-Barker, Harley. *Prefaces to Shakespeare*. 4 vols. Princeton: Princeton University Press, 1963.

Greenblatt, Stephen. *Shakespearean Negotiations: The Circulation of Social Energy in Renaissance England*. Berkeley and Los Angeles: University of California Press, 1988.

Gregory, Richard L. "Aesthetics." In *The Oxford Companion to the Mind*, 8–10. Oxford: Oxford University Press, 1987.

Gross, James J., Barbara L. Fredrickson, and Robert W. Levenson. "The Psychophysiology of Crying." *Psychophysiology* 31, no. 5 (1994): 460–68.

Grumet, Madeleine R. "Bodyreading." *Teachers College Record* 87, no. 2 (1985): 175–93.

Gudas, Fabian. "Affective Fallacy." In *The New Princeton Encyclopedia of Poetry and Poetics*. Edited by Alex Preminger and T. V. F. Brogan, 12. Princeton: Princeton University Press, 1993.

Hall, Edward T. *The Dance of Life: The Other Dimension of Time*. New York: Doubleday, 1983.

Hall, Thomas Steele. *Ideas of Life and Matter: Studies in the History of General Physiology, 600* B.C.–1900 A.D. Chicago: University of Chicago Press, 1969.

Hanna, Thomas. *Bodies in Revolt: A Primer in Somatic Thinking*. New York: Holt, Rinehart and Winston, 1970.

Harbage, Alfred. *Conceptions of Shakespeare*. Cambridge: Harvard University Press, 1966.

———. *Shakespeare's Audience*. New York: Columbia University Press, 1941.

Harcourt, Glenn. "Andreas Vesalius and the Anatomy of Antique Sculpture." *Representations* 17 (1987): 28–61.

Hart, Robert P., and Gregory J. O'Shanick. "Forgetting Rates for Verbal, Pictorial, and Figural Stimuli." *Journal of Clinical and Experimental Neuropsychology* 15, no. 2 (1993): 245–65.

Hartman, Geoffrey H. *Minor Prophecies: The Literary Essay in the Culture Wars*. Cambridge and London: Harvard University Press, 1991.

———. *Saving the Text: Literature/Derrida/Philosophy*. Baltimore and London: Johns Hopkins University Press, 1981.

Hatcher, Evelyn Payne. *Art as Culture: An Introduction to the Anthropology of Art*. Lanham, Md.: University Press of America, 1985.

Havelock, Eric. A. *The Muse Learns to Write: Reflections on Orality and Literacy*. New Haven: Yale University Press, 1986.

Hawkes, Terence. *Meaning by Shakespeare*. London and New York: Routledge, 1992.

———. *That Shakespeherian Rag: Essays on a Critical Process*. London and New York: Methuen, 1986.

Heckler, Richard Strozzi. *The Anatomy of Change: East/West Approaches to Body/Mind Therapy*. Boston and London: Shambhala, 1985.

Heise, David R., and John O'Brien. "Emotion Expression in Groups." In *Handbook of Emotions*. Edited by Michael Lewis and Jeannette M. Haviland, 489–97. New York and London: Guilford Press, 1993.

Heller, Joseph, and William A. Henkin. *Bodywise*. New York: St. Martin's Press, 1986.

Henley, Nancy M. *Body Politics: Power, Sex, and Nonverbal Communication*. Englewood Cliffs, N.J.: Prentice Hall, 1977.

Hodges, Devon L. *Renaissance Fictions of Anatomy*. Amherst: University of Massachusetts Press, 1985.

Hoeniger, F. David. *Medicine and Shakespeare in the English Renaissance*. Newark: University of Delaware Press, 1992.

Hoffman, Robert R., and Richard P. Honeck. "Proverbs, Pragmatics, and the Ecology of Abstract Categories." In *Cognition and Symbolic Structures: The Psychology of Metaphoric Transformation*. Edited by Robert E. Haskell, 121–40. Norwood, N.J.: Ablex Publishing, 1987.

Hogan, John. "It's All in the Timing: Neurons May Be More Punctual Than Had Been Supposed." *Scientific American* 273, no. 2 (1995): 16–17.

Holland, Norman N. *The Dynamics of Literary Response*. New York: Oxford University Press, 1968.

———. *5 Readers Reading*. New Haven: Yale University Press, 1975.

———. *Poems in Persons: An Introduction to the Psychoanalysis of Literature*. New York: Norton, 1973.

Holloway, John. *The Story of the Night: Studies in Shakespeare's Major Tragedies*. London: Routledge and Kegan Paul, 1961.

Howard, Jean E. *Shakespeare's Art of Orchestration: Stage Technique and Audience Response*. Urbana and Chicago: University of Illinois Press, 1984.

Howes, David. Introduction. In *The Varieties of Sensory Experience: A Sourcebook in the Anthropology of the Senses*. Edited by David Howes, 3–21. Toronto: University of Toronto Press, 1991.

Hudson, A. K. *Shakespeare and the Classroom*. 2nd ed. London: Heinemann, 1960.

Hupka, Ralph B., et al. "The Colors of Anger, Envy, Fear, and Jealousy: A Cross-Cultural Study." *Journal of Cross-Cultural Psychology* 28, no. 2 (1997): 156–71.

Iser, Wolfgang. *The Act of Reading: A Theory of Aesthetic Response*. Baltimore: Johns Hopkins University Press, 1978.

———. *The Implied Reader: Patterns of Communication in Prose Fiction from Bunyan to Beckett*. Baltimore: Johns Hopkins University Press, 1974.

———. *Prospecting: From Reader Response to Literary Anthropology*. Baltimore: Johns Hopkins University Press, 1989.

Izard, Carroll E. "Organizational and Motivational Functions of Discrete Emotions." In *Handbook of Emotions*. Edited by Michael Lewis and Jeannette M. Haviland, 631–41. New York and London: Guilford Press, 1993.

Jauss, Hans Robert. *Toward an Aesthetics of Reception*. Translated by Timothy Bahti. Minneapolis: University of Minnesota Press, 1982.

Jerison, Harry J. "Vigilance, Discrimination, and Attention." In *Attention: Contemporary Theory and Analysis*. Edited by David I. Mostofsky, 127–48. New York: Appleton-Century-Crofts, 1970.

Johnson, Mark. *The Body in the Mind: The Bodily Basis of Meaning, Imagination, and Reason*. Chicago and London: University of Chicago Press, 1987.

Johnson, Samuel. *Samuel Johnson on Shakespeare*. Edited by W. K. Wimsatt, Jr. New York: Hill and Wang, 1960.

———. *Selections from Johnson on Shakespeare*. Edited by Bertrand H. Bronson and Jean M. O'Meara. New Haven: Yale University Press, 1986.

Johnstone, Keith. *Impro: Improvisation and the Theatre*. New York: Theatre Arts Books, 1979.

Joseph, R. *The Naked Neuron: Evolution and the Language of the Body and Brain*. New York and London: Plenum Press, 1993.

Juhan, Deane. *Job's Body: A Handbook for Bodywork*. Barrytown: Station Hill Press, 1987.

Kahn, Victoria. *Rhetoric, Prudence, and Skepticism in the Renaissance*. Ithaca and London: Cornell University Press, 1985.

Keleman, Stanley. *Somatic Reality*. Berkeley: Center Press, 1979.

———. *Your Body Speaks Its Mind*. Berkeley: Center Press, 1975.

Kennedy, X. J., and Dana Gioia. *An Introduction to Poetry*. 9th ed. New York: Longman, 1998.

Key, Mary Ritchie. *Paralanguage and Kinesics*. Metuchen, N.J.: Scarecrow Press, 1975.

Kintgen, Eugene R. *The Perception of Poetry*. Bloomington: Indiana University Press, 1983.

Kirsch, Arthur. "Hamlet's Grief." In *Hamlet*. Edited by Harold Bloom, 122–38. New York and Philadelphia: Chelsea House, 1990. Originally published in *ELH: English Literary History* 48, no. 1 (spring 1981): 17–36.

G. Wilson Knight. *The Crown of Life: Essays in Interpretation of Shakespeare's Final Plays*. 1947. 2nd ed. London: Methuen, 1948.

———. *The Imperial Theme: Further Interpretations of Shakespeare's Tragedies Including the Roman plays*. London and New York: Oxford University Press, 1931.

———. *The Wheel of Fire; Essays in Interpretation of Shakespeare's Sombre Tragedies*. London: Oxford University Press, 1930.

Kosslyn, Stephen Michael. *Ghosts in the Mind's Machine: Creating and Using Images in the Brain*. New York and London: Norton, 1983.

Kreitler, Hans, and Shulamith Kreitler. *Psychology of the Arts*. Durham, N.C.: Duke University Press, 1972.

Kroeze, Sabine, et al. "Symptom Reporting and Interoceptive Attention in Panic Patients." *Perceptual and Motor Skills* 82, no. 3 (1996): 1019–26.

Kurtz, Ron. *Body-Centered Psychotherapy*. Mendocino, Calif.: LifeRhythm, 1990.

Lakoff, George. *Women, Fire, and Dangerous Things: What Categories Reveal About the Mind*. Chicago and London: University of Chicago Press, 1987.

———, and Mark Turner. *More than Cool Reason: A Field Guide to Poetic Metaphor*. Chicago and London: University of Chicago Press, 1989.

Lang, Peter. J. "Cognition in Emotion: Concept and Action." In *Emotions, Cog-*

nition, and Behavior. Edited by Carroll E. Izard, Jerome Kagan, and Robert B. Zajonc, 193–226. Cambridge: Cambridge University Press, 1984.

Langer, Susanne. *Mind: An Essay on Human Feeling.* Baltimore: Johns Hopkins University Press, 1967.

Leder, Drew. *The Absent Body.* Chicago: University of Chicago Press, 1990.

LeDoux, J. E. "Emotional Memory: In Search of Systems and Synapses." *Annals of the New York Academy of Sciences* (1993): 149–57.

Leggatt, Alexander. "Shakespeare and the Actor's Body." *Renaissance and Reformation* 10, no. 1 (1986): 95–107.

Lessac, Arthur. *Body Wisdom: The Use and Training of the Human Body.* New York: Drama Book Publishers, 1978.

Lex, Barbara W. "The Neurobiology of Ritual Trance." In *The Spectrum of Ritual: A Biogenetic Structural Analysis.* Edited by Eugene G. d'Aquili, Charles D. Laughlin, Jr., and John McManus, 117–51. New York: Columbia University Press, 1979.

Linklater, Kristin. *Freeing Shakespeare's Voice: The Actor's Guide to Talking the Text.* New York: Theatre Communications Group, 1992.

Lowen, Alexander. *The Language of the Body.* New York: Collier Macmillan, 1958.

Lukes, Timothy. J. *The Flight Into Inwardness: An Exposition and Critique of Herbert Marcuse's Theory of Liberative Aesthetics.* Selinsgrove, Pa.: Susquehanna University Press, 1985.

Mack, Maynard. "Engagement and Detachment in Shakespeare's Plays." In *Essays on Shakespeare and Elizabethan Drama in Honor of Hardin Craig.* Edited by Richard Hosley, 275–96. Columbia, Mo.: University of Missouri Press, 1962.

———. "The World of *Hamlet.*" In *Everybody's Shakespeare: Reflections Chiefly on the Tragedies,* 107–27. Lincoln: University of Nebraska Press, 1993. Originally published in *The Yale Review* 41 (1952): 502–23.

Mainen, Zachary F., and Terrence J. Sejenowski. "Reliability of Spike Timing in Neocortical Neurons." *Science* 268 (1995): 1503–7.

Marks, Lawrence E. *Sensory Processes: The New Psychophysics.* New York and London: Academic Press, 1974.

———, Robin J. Hammeal, and Marc H. Bornstein. *Perceiving Similarity and Comprehending Metaphor.* Monographs of the Society for Research in Child Development. Serial No. 215. 52, no. 1 (1987).

Marrone, Robert. *Body of Knowledge: An Introduction to Body/Mind Psychology.* Albany: State University of New York Press, 1990.

Masters, Robert, and Jean Houston. *Listening to the Body.* New York: Dell, 1978.

McDougall, Lorna. "Symbols and Somatic Structures." In *The Anthropology of the Body.* Edited by John Blacking, 390–406. London and New York: Academic Press, 1977.

McGuigan, F. J. "Electrical Measurement of Covert Processes as an Explication of 'Higher Mental Events.'" In *The Psychophysiology of Thinking: Studies of*

Covert Processes. Edited by F. J. McGuigan and R. A. Schoonover, 343–85. New York: Academic Press, 1973.

McGuire, Philip C. *Speechless Dialect: Shakespeare's Open Silences.* Berkeley and Los Angeles: University of California Press, 1985.

McIntosh, Daniel N. "Facial Feedback Hypotheses: Evidence, Implications, and Directions." *Motivation and Emotion* 20, no. 2 (1996): 121–47.

McMahon, Carol E. "Psychosomatic Concepts in the Works of Shakespeare." *Journal of the History of the Behavioral Sciences* 12 (1976): 275–82.

Meyer, Leonard B. *Emotion and Meaning in Music.* Chicago and London: University of Chicago Press, 1956.

Miller, Gregory A., et al. "Individual Differences in Imagery and the Psychophysiology of Emotion." *Cognition and Emotion* 1, no. 4 (1987): 367–90.

Mills, Howard. *Working with Shakespeare.* Lanham, Md.: Barnes and Noble Books, 1993.

Mindell, Arnold. *City Shadows: Psychological Interventions in Psychiatry.* London and New York: Routledge, 1988.

———. *Coma: Key to Awakening.* Boston: Shambhala, 1989.

———. *Dreambody: The Body's Role in Revealing the Self.* Boston: Sigo Press 1982.

———. *River's Way: The Process Science of the Dreambody.* London: Routledge and Kegan Paul, 1985.

———. *Working with the Dreaming Body.* Boston: Routledge and Kegan Paul, 1985.

Moyers, Bill. *Healing and the Mind.* New York: Doubleday, 1993.

Myrtek, Michael, and Georg Brugner. "Perception of Emotions in Everyday Life: Studies with Patients and Normals." *Biological Physiology* 42 (1996): 147–64.

Nell, Victor. *Lost in a Book: The Psychology of Reading for Pleasure.* New Haven: Yale University Press, 1988.

Nelson, James B. *Between Two Gardens: Reflections on Sexuality and Religious Experience.* New York: Pilgrim Press, 1983.

Nicolopoulou, A., and J. Weintraub. "On Liberty, Cultural Relativism, and Development." *Culture and Psychology* 2, no. 3 (1996): 273–83.

Ong, Walter J. *Orality and Literacy: The Technologizing of the Word.* London and New York: Methuen, 1982.

Paivio, Allan. *Imagery and Verbal Processes.* New York: Holt, Rinehart and Winston, 1971.

———, and Kalman Csapo. "Picture Superiority in Free Recall: Imagery or Dual Coding?" *Cognitive Psychology* 5, no. 2 (1973): 176–206.

Paster, Gail Kern. *The Body Embarrassed: Drama and the Disciplines of Shame in Early Modern England.* Ithaca: Cornell University Press, 1993.

Pattison, Robert. *On Literacy: The Politics of the Word from Homer to the Age of Rock.* New York: Oxford University Press, 1982.

Perls, Frederick, Ralph Hefferline, and Paul Goodman. *Gestalt Therapy: Excitement and Growth in the Human Personality.* New York: Dell, 1954.

Pitt, Mark A., and Samuel G. Arthur. "The Use of Rhythm in Attending to Speech." *Journal of Experimental Psychology, Human Perception, and Performance* 16, no. 3 (1990): 564–73.

Pittam, Jeffrey, and Klaus R. Scherer. "Vocal Expression and Communication of Emotion." In *Handbook of Emotions*. Edited by Michael Lewis and Jeannette M. Haviland, 185–97. New York and London: Guilford Press, 1993.

Plutchik, Robert. "Emotions: A General Psychoevolutionary Theory." In *Approaches to Emotion*. Edited by Klaus R. Scherer and Paul Ekman, 197–219. Hillsdale, N.J.: L. Erlbaum Associates, 1984.

Polsky, Milton E. *Let's Improvise*. Englewood Cliffs, N.J.: Prentice Hall, 1980.

Pope, Alexander, ed. *The Works of Mr. William Shakespear*. London: J. and J. Knapton, 1728.

Purves, Alan C. "The Aesthetic Mind of Louise Rosenblatt." In *The Experience of Reading: Louise Rosenblatt and Reader-Response Theory*. Edited by John Clifford, 209–17. Portsmouth, N.H.: Boynton/Cook Publishers, 1991.

———, and Richard Beach. *Literature and the Reader: Research in Response to Literature, Reading Interests, and the Teaching of Literature*. Urbana, Ill.: National Council of Teachers of English, 1972.

Rentel, Victor M., Christine Pappas, and Barbara Pettegrew, "The Utility of Psychophysiological Measures for Reading Research." In *Psychophysiological Aspects of Reading and Learning*. Edited by Victor M. Rentel, Samuel A. Corson, and Bruce R. Dunn, 123–55. New York: Gordon and Breach, 1985.

Reynolds, Peter. *Practical Approaches to Teaching Shakespeare*. Oxford: Oxford University Press, 1991.

Richman, David. *Laughter, Pain, and Wonder: Shakespeare's Comedies and the Audience in the Theater*. Newark: University of Delaware Press, 1990.

Rivlin, Robert. *Deciphering the Senses: The Expanding World of Human Perception*. New York: Simon and Schuster, 1984.

Rocklin, Edward L. " 'An Incarnational Art': Teaching Shakespeare." *Shakespeare Quarterly* 41, no. 2 (1990): 147–59.

Roemer, Marjorie Godlin. "Which Reader's Response?" *College English* 49, no. 8 (1987): 911–21.

Rosenblatt, Louise M. *Literature as Exploration*. 1937. 4th ed. New York: The Modern Language Association of America, 1983.

———. *The Reader, the Text, the Poem: The Transactional Theory of the Literary Work*. Carbondale: Southern Illinois University Press, 1978.

Rozin, Paul, Jonathan Haidt, and Clark R. McCauley. "Disgust." In *Handbook of Emotions*. Edited by Michael Lewis and Jeannette M. Haviland, 575–94. New York and London: Guilford Press, 1993.

Ruch, Willibald. "Exhilaration and Humor." In *Handbook of Emotions*. Edited by Michael Lewis and Jeannette M. Haviland, 605–16. New York and London: Guilford Press, 1993.

Sacks, Oliver. *The Man Who Mistook His Wife for a Hat—and Other Clinical Tales*. New York: Harper and Row, 1987.

Sansavini, Alessandra, Josiane Bertoncini, and Giuliana Giovanelli, "Newborns

Discriminate the Rhythm of Multisyllabic Stressed Words." *Developmental Psychology* 33, no. 1 (1997): 3–11.

Scarry, Elaine. Introduction. In *Literature and the Body: Essays on Populations and Persons*. Edited by Elaine Scarry, vii–xxvii. Selected Papers from the English Institute, 1986. Baltimore and London: Johns Hopkins University Press, 1986.

Schechner, Richard. "Magnitudes of Performance." In *By Means of Performance: Intercultural Studies of Theatre and Ritual*. Edited by Richard Schechner and Willa Appel, 19–49. Cambridge and New York: Cambridge University Press, 1990.

Scheff, T. J. *Catharsis in Healing, Ritual, and Drama*. Berkeley: University of California Press, 1979.

Schumacher, John A. *Human Posture: The Nature of Inquiry*. Albany: State University of New York Press, 1989.

Sejenowski, Terrence J. "Time for a New Neural Code." *Nature* 376 (1995): 21–22.

Seltzer, Richard. "How Proudly It Heals: In Praise of the Body Republic." *Lear's* 2, no. 4 (June 1989): 42–43.

Shakespeare, William. *The Complete Works*. Original-Spelling Edition. Edited by Stanley Wells and Gary Taylor. Oxford: Clarendon Press, 1986.

———. *The Complete Works of Shakespeare*. 4th ed. Edited by David Bevington. New York: HarperCollins, 1992.

———. *The Norton Shakespeare: Based on the Oxford Edition*. Edited by Stephen Greenblatt, et al. New York and London: Norton, 1997.

———. *Romeo and Juliet*. The New Folger Library Shakespeare. Edited by Barbara A. Mowat and Paul Werstine. New York: Washington Square Press, 1992.

———. *Shakespeare's Plays in Quarto*. Edited by Michael J. B. Allen and Kenneth Muir. Berkeley and Los Angeles: University of California Press, 1981.

Shattuck, Roger. "How to Rescue Literature." *The New York Review of Books* 27, no. 6 (17 April 1980): 29–35.

Sidney, Philip. "An Apology for Poetry." In *Elizabethan Critical Essays*. Edited by G. Gregory Smith, 1: 148–207. Oxford: Clarendon Press, 1904.

Siemon, James R. *Shakespearean Iconoclasm*. Berkeley and Los Angeles: University of California Press, 1985.

Singer, Jefferson A., and Peter Salovey. *The Remembered Self: Emotion and Memory in Personality*. New York: Free Press, 1993.

Slatoff, Walter J. *With Respect to Readers: Dimensions of Literary Response*. Ithaca and London: Cornell University Press, 1970.

Sloan, Thomas O. Introduction. In *The Oral Study of Literature*. Edited by Robert Beloof, et al., 3–13. New York: Random House, 1966.

Sloboda, John A. "Music Structure and Emotional Response: Some Empirical Findings." *Psychology of Music* 19, no. 2 (1991): 110–20.

Smith, D. Nichol. *Eighteenth-Century Essays on Shakespeare*. 2nd ed. Oxford: Clarendon Press, 1963.

——, ed. *Shakespeare Criticism: A Selection*. London: Oxford University Press, 1946.

Smith, Ralph A. *The Sense of Art: A Study in Aesthetic Education*. New York and London: Routledge, 1989.

Snyder, Edward O. *Hypnotic Poetry: A Study of Trance-Inducing Technique in Certain Poems and Its Literary Significance*. Philadelphia: University of Pennsylvania Press, 1930.

——, and Ronald E. Shor. "Trance-Inductive Poetry: A Brief Communication." *International Journal of Clinical and Experimental Hypnosis* 31, no. 1 1983): 1–7.

Sontag, Susan. *Against Interpretation and Other Essays*. New York: Farrar, Straus and Giroux, 1966.

Spiegel, John Paul, and Pavel Machotka. *Messages of the Body*. New York: Free Press, 1974.

Spurgeon, Caroline F. E. *Shakespeare's Imagery and What It Tells Us*. 1935. Reprint, Boston: Beacon Hill, 1958.

Stallybrass, Peter, and Allon White. *The Politics and Poetics of Transgression*. Ithaca: Cornell University Press, 1986.

Steere, David A. *Bodily Expressions in Psychotherapy*. New York: Brunner/Mazel, 1982.

Steig, Michael. *Stories of Reading: Subjectivity and Literary Understanding*. Baltimore and London: Johns Hopkins University Press, 1989.

Stewart, Garrett. *Reading Voices: Literature and the Phonotext*. Berkeley and Los Angeles: University California Press, 1990.

Stoll, Elmer Edgar. *Art and Artifice in Shakespeare*. 1933. Reprint, London: Methuen, 1963.

——. *Shakespeare Studies: Historical and Comparative in Method*. 1927. Reprint, New York: Ungar, 1960.

Storr, Anthony. *Music and the Mind*. New York: Free Press, 1992.

Strathern, Andrew J. *Body Thoughts*. Ann Arbor: University of Michigan Press, 1996.

Strier, Richard. *Resistant Structures: Particularity, Radicalism, and Renaissance Texts*. Berkeley and Los Angeles: University of California Press, 1995.

Sudnow, David. *Talk's Body: A Meditation Between Two Keyboards*. New York: Knopf, 1979.

——. *Ways of the Hand: The Organization of Improvised Conduct*. Cambridge: Harvard University Press, 1978.

Tazi, Nadia. "Celestial Bodies: A Few Stops on the Way to Heaven." In *Fragments for a History of the Human Body*. Edited by Michel Feher, 518–52. Part 2. New York: Zone, 1989.

Terhardt, Ernst. "Music Perception in the Auditory Hierarchy." *Music and the Mind Machine: The Psychophysiology and Psychopathology of the Sense of Music*. Edited by R. Steinberg, 81–87. Berlin: Springer-Verlag, 1995.

Thompson, Jack George. *The Psychobiology of Emotions*. New York and London: Plenum Press, 1988.

Turner, Bryan S. Preface. In *The Consuming Body*, by Pasi Falk, vii–xvii. London: Sage, 1994.

Turner, Frederick. *Beauty: The Value of Values*. Charlottesville: University of Virginia Press, 1991.

———. *Natural Classicism: Essays on Literature and Science*. 1985. Reprint, Charlottesville: University of Virginia Press, 1992.

Turner, Victor. "Are There Universals of Performance in Myth, Ritual, and Drama?" In *By Means of Performance: Intercultural Studies of Theatre and Ritual*. Edited by Richard Schechner and Willa Appel, 8–18. Cambridge and New York: Cambridge University Press, 1990.

Tyrell, William Blake. *Amazons: A Study in Athenian Mythmaking*. Baltimore and London: Johns Hopkins University Press, 1984.

Vaitl, D. "Interoception." *Biological Psychology* 42, no. 1–2 (1996): 1–27.

VanderArk, Sherman O., and Daniel Ely. "Biochemical and Galvanic Skin Responses to Music Stimuli by College Students in Biology and Music." *Perceptual and Motor Skills* 74, no. 3 (1992): 1079–90.

Vickers, Brian. *Appropriating Shakespeare: Contemporary Critical Quarrels*. New Haven: Yale University Press, 1993.

———. *Shakespeare: The Critical Heritage*. 6 vols. London and Boston: Routledge and Kegan Paul, 1974–78.

Viëtor, Wilhelm. *A Shakespeare Reader: In the Old Spelling and with a Phonetic Transcription*. 1906. Reprint, New York: Frederick Ungar Publishing, 1963.

Vinge, Louise. *The Five Senses: Studies in a Literary Tradition*. Lund: Liber-Laromedel: 1975.

Vinopal, John Michael. "English Renaissance Pronunciation." http://www.resort.com/~banshee/Faire/Language/pronunciation.html.

Waldo, Tommy Ruth. "Beyond Words: Shakespeare's Tongue-Tied Muse." In *Shakespeare's More Than Words Can Witness: Essays on Visual and Nonverbal Enactment in the Plays*. Edited by Sidney Homan, 160–76. Lewisburg, Pa.: Bucknell University Press, 1980.

Weimer, Walter B. "A Conceptual Framework for Cognitive Psychology: Motor Theories of the Mind." In *Perceiving, Acting, and Knowing: Toward an Ecological Psychology*. Edited by Robert Shaw and John Bransford, 267–311. Hillsdale, N.J.: L. Erlbaum Associates, 1977.

Weiner, Herbert. "Contemporary Research and the Mind-Body Problem." In *Body and Mind: Past, Present, Future*. Edited by R. W. Rieber, 223–40. New York: Academic Press, 1980.

Wesling, Donald. *The Scissors of Meter: Grammetrics and Reading*. Ann Arbor: University of Michigan Press, 1996.

Wilson, Luke. "William Harvey's *Prelectiones*: The Performance of the Body in the Renaissance Theater of Anatomy." *Representations* 17 (1987): 62–95.

Wimsatt, William K., Jr., and Monroe C. Beardsley, "The Affective Fallacy." In *The Verbal Icon*, by W. K. Wimsatt, Jr., 21–39. Lexington: University of Kentucky Press, 1954. First published in *Sewanee Review* 57 (1949): 31–55.

Woodbridge, Linda. *The Scythe of Saturn: Shakespeare and Magical Thinking*. Urbana and Chicago: University of Illinois Press, 1994.

Wright, George T. *Shakespeare's Metrical Art*. Berkeley and Los Angeles: University of California Press, 1988.

Yaryura-Tobias, Jose A. *The Integral Being*. New York: Henry Holt, 1987.

Zajonc, Ralph B., Sheila T. Murphy, and Marita Inglehart. "Feeling and Facial Efference: Implications of the Vascular Theory of Emotion." *Psychological Review* 96, no. 3 (1989): 395–416.

———, Sheila T. Murphy, and Daniel N. McIntosh. "Brain Temperature and Subjective Emotional Experience." In *Handbook of Emotions*. Edited by Michael Lewis and Jeannette M. Haviland, 209–20. New York and London: Guilford Press, 1993.

Ziegler, Alfred. *Archetypal Medicine*. Translated by Gary V. Hartman. Dallas: Spring Publications, 1983.

Zillmann, Dolf, Karla J. Schweitzer, and Norbert Mundorf. "Menstrual Cycle Variation of Women's Interest in Erotica." *Archives of Sexual Behavior* 23, no. 5 (1994): 579–97.

Index